New Zealand

Grant Bourne & Sabine Körner-Bourne

Published by
Landmark Publishing Ltd
Waterloo House, 12 Compton, Ashbourne
Derbyshire, England DE6 1DA

Published in the USA by
Hunter Publishing Inc
130 Campus Drive, Edison NJ 08818

Grant Bourne and his wife Sabine met on a Kibbutz way back in 1982. Their shared passion for travel has since taken them through much of Europe, Asia, Africa and the Near East.
Born and brought up in New Zealand and now living in Germany's lovely Rhine Valley, Grant frequently returns home for lengthy visits. He and his wife have toured the two main islands from north to south and have notched up many hundreds of kilometres on foot through the country's magnificent national parks.
Grant and Sabine have written travel guides and articles in both English and German. They have also written a walking guide to the Bavarian Alps. On their new website, reader's can inform themselves about the latest developments affecting travel in New Zealand and much else besides:
http://home.t-online.de/home/Koerner-Bourne/kiwipage.htm

Acknowledgments

The authors are most grateful to the various tourist information centres for their generous help. We would also like to extend special thanks to Bernard and Jane, Steve and Cas, and Tim Whittaker; and very special thanks to Murray Bourne.

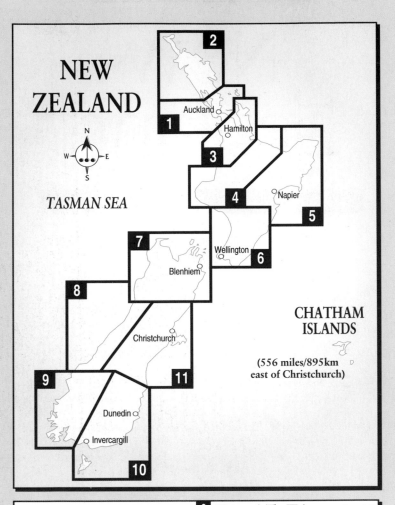

NEW ZEALAND

NEW ZEALAND
Regional Maps

LANDMARK VISITORS GUIDE

New Zealand

Grant Bourne & Sabine Körner-Bourne

Contents

Previous page: *View of Mt Egmont from Lake Mangamahoe Domain*

INTRODUCTION

Luxuriant rainforests, spectacular fiords, volcanoes, snow-capped mountains and long empty beaches of golden sand are just some of the ingredients that go to make New Zealand one of the most breathtakingly beautiful places in the world. No other country can boast such a variety of landscapes within such easy reach of one another. In some places the ski slopes and the seaside may be separated by no more than an hour's drive.

New Zealand is a land that offers lovers of the great outdoors all they could wish for. Activities include jet boating, white water rafting, kayaking, tramping and skiing. You can watch whales and swim with dolphins at Kaikoura or fish for a trout dinner at Taupo.

Apart from the enjoyment of sea, sun and sand, another attraction for many visitors is the fascinating culture of the country's first inhabitants, the Maori. Strongholds of Maori culture are the East Cape and Northland but it is probably Rotorua that provides the best introduction to the traditional Maori way of life. Excellent museums in places like Wanganui, Auckland and Wellington offer further insight into the history of this Polynesian people. But what, perhaps, makes a holiday in New Zealand something really special is simply the friendliness and hospitality of the Kiwis (colloquial name for all New Zealanders) themselves.

Above: Picton waterfront

History

Arrival of the Maori

Around 800 AD, centuries before Columbus discovered America, Polynesian adventurers boarded large double-hulled canoes and sailed across the vastness of the Pacific Ocean to find a group of isolated islands now known as New Zealand. These ancestors of the modern Maori called their new home *Aotearoa* and their epic migrations have been romanticised in the legend of the 'Great Fleet', a colonising expedition that set out from Hawaiki. Here, in the most remote corner of Polynesia, they evolved a flourishing culture, where the art of carving reached heights of accomplishment hitherto unknown anywhere in the Pacific.

The seeds of human history on New Zealand's virgin soil were sown; the next great phase of settlement was not to have its beginnings until centuries later when, in the wake of European colonial expansion, the **Dutch East India Company** sent Abel Janszoon Tasman off in search of new markets and new lands.

European Explorers

Tasman sighted the west coast of the South Island in 1642 but was prevented from landing by hostile Maoris who attacked one of the ship's boats and killed several of the crew. No doubt discouraged by this bloody encounter, Tasman did not make another attempt to go ashore and soon left the islands, believing that they might be part of an unknown continent that stretched as far as South America. However, the Dutch showed little interest in his discovery as this wild land did not promise any great treasures, and over a hundred years were to pass before Europeans were again to visit these distant shores.

Captain James Cook's first voyage into the South Pacific was a scientific expedition that had, among other things, the task of finding out whether or not the Terra Australis Incognita (Southern Continent) really existed.

In 1769 Cook's ship the *Endeavour* sailed within sight of the east coast of New Zealand, which was at that time still known by the Dutch name of Nieuw Zeeland. During the next six months he circumnavigated both main islands and charted the coastline.

Cook was, after a few initial skirmishes, able to establish friendly relations with the Maori and apart from gathering valuable information on the geography, as well as the flora and fauna of the islands, his voyage proved beyond doubt that New Zealand was not the fabled Southern Continent.

Cook's voyages (he visited New Zealand again in 1772 and 1776), along with those of later explorers like the Frenchmen Jean de Surville (1769, two months after Cook) and Marion du Fresne (1772), stimulated a great deal of interest in the South Pacific. For New Zealand, centuries of isolation from the rest of the world were at an end; the phase of European colonisation was no longer far away.

British Colonisation

The first arrivals were sealers who were followed by whalers, traders and adventurers. In 1814 the Reverend Samuel Marsden arrived in the **Bay of Islands** to establish the country's first mission. Other missionaries soon followed but, in the beginning, the Maoris saw Christianity less as a means of salvation than as a way to acquire European skills and goods. The most valued item of trade among the Maori was the gun and it was not long before it was put to devastating effect in inter-tribal conflicts.

Up until 1840 the settlement of New Zealand had been sporadic and mainly limited to the Bay of Islands but that was to change, when in 1837, Edward Gibbon Wakefield formed the **New Zealand Association** (it later became the New Zealand Company) in England. This company was the main driving force behind the organised colonisation of New Zealand in the first half of the nineteenth century.

A condition of lawlessness prevailed in the Bay of Island's settlement prior to 1840. Demands grew louder, both in New Zealand and at home, that Britain should annex the country and thus make it subject to British law. With enough problems in the colonies it already had, Britain was initially reluctant to take the step of making New Zealand officially a part of the British Empire. However growing pressure and fears that France might have its own plans for colonisation made Britain finally act. Captain William Hobson was sent to New Zealand as the Governor-designate and the **Treaty of Waitangi**, under which the

The Treaty of Waitangi

The first boatload of immigrants organised by Wakefield's company arrived shortly after the signing of the treaty and with them came a growing European hunger for land. Already by 1858 there were more Europeans in the country than there were Maori. In the Treaty of Waitangi it was stated that only the government could buy Maori land. This was meant to protect the Maori from being swindled by speculators. However speculation took place just the same and even the government was guilty of paying ridiculously low prices for land which was then sometimes resold to settlers for twenty times the original purchase price. On top of all this, the Maori considered that, even if they had sold the land, they had not sold the resources that grew upon it. Armed conflict between the races was quickly becoming inevitable.

In 1860 a shady land deal in Taranaki caused the outbreak of fighting between government troops and local Maori. This was the beginning of the **New Zealand Land Wars**, a series of localised conflicts which flared up in various parts of the North Island over the next twelve years. But in the end the Maori, who were often divided among themselves, could not hope to prevail against the vast resources of the British Empire. Those tribes that fought against the Crown lost not only the war, but also much of their land which was confiscated by the government.

Maori accepted British sovereignty over the country, was signed at the Bay of Islands on February 6, 1840.

An Agricultural Nation

In the South Island the problems between Maori and Pakeha (Maori name for white settlers) never developed to the point of serious warfare. By the middle of the nineteenth century, sheep farming was already established here as an important part of the economy. The discovery of gold in **Otago** and **Westland** in the 1860's, gave an added boost to the South Island's prosperity.

In the 1870's the colonial government's policy of overseas borrowing to finance the building of roads and railways, sparked off an economic boom which also brought a measure of prosperity to the war-torn North Island. Unfortunately the good times soon came to an end.

In 1878 the prices for wool and grain fell and the government was left wondering how it was going to pay its massive overseas debts. Before long the country was in the depths of recession, and thousands of unemployed workers left the colony to seek new opportunities in America and Australia.

Social welfare

The colony's first long depression had, however, its positive side: it provided the impetus for a series of wide, reaching social reforms that

Above: *Southern Alps*

made New Zealand one of the pioneers of the welfare state. They included the introduction of free, compulsory education in 1877 and a small pension for the aged poor in 1898. In 1893 New Zealand became the first country in the world to grant women the vote.

In 1882 a possible end to the depression was signalled by the first successful shipment of frozen meat to England. Though it took a few years, this trade eventually developed into a bonanza for New Zealand's farming industry. During the early years of the twentieth century, markets for dairy products also expanded and dairy farming soon became as important for the New Zealand economy as the raising of sheep for wool and meat. For the moment the country's problems seemed solved — the time of the prosperous and influential farmer had arrived.

The Twentieth Century

The Great Depression of the Thirties brought hardship once again, but prosperity returned with the world-wide economic recovery in 1935. In the same year the newly formed Labour Party was swept into power; the earlier reforms were extended and New Zealand now had one of the most comprehensive social welfare systems in the world. From the 1950's onwards, however, it was to be the conservative National Party, which had been formed during World War II, that dominated the political stage.

In 1947 New Zealand was granted full independence from Great Britain. Again the nation went through a period of economic boom which was to end with Britain's joining of the EC in 1973. The loss of the country's main overseas market (the trade barriers erected against non-EC countries made it difficult for New Zealand to be competitive) dealt a severe blow to the strongly export-oriented economy. Now many politicians began to perceive the welfare state as a luxury the land could ill afford. Even the liberally-minded Labour Party, who were in power between 1985 and 1990, began to cut back on social legislation and introduced a scheme of privatisation whereby formerly state-owned enterprises were sold to the private sector. After taking over from Labour, the conservative National Party continued with the radical economic reforms. At present a dramatic improvement of the economy suggests they are working.

One of the most important trends in modern New Zealand is the

Above: Milford Sound trip

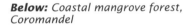

Below: Coastal mangrove forest, Coromandel

renaissance of Maori language and culture. The country is becoming increasingly aware of itself as a bi-cultural society which has its cultural roots both in Polynesia and Europe. There is also a growing awareness of the country's role as a Pacific nation and New Zealand is slowly but surely loosening its ties to 'Mother England'.

Arts, Culture & Entertainment

At least in the cities, New Zealand can boast a lively entertainment and arts scene with regular exhibitions of national and international art in the galleries, theatre, performances of classical music and so on. **Auckland** and **Wellington** are probably

11

the most interesting places as far as cultural activities are concerned, but other main cities like **Christchurch** and **Dunedin** also have much to offer. Dunedin, for instance, has a reputation for producing some of the country's best rock bands, though good live music, including jazz, can be heard in pubs and discos all around the country. For details of cultural events, consult one of the free city guides published by the city tourist information offices.

The arts and crafts scene also flourishes; potters, carvers, weavers and trinket-makers can be found offering their wares all over the country, from north to south. The work is often of a very high quality and can range from a simple bowl carved from beautiful native wood, to an original piece of pottery that is more an *objet d'art* than a practical utensil. Good places to go shopping for handicrafts include **Nelson** and **Kerikeri.**

Literature

New Zealand's most famous author internationally is probably still Katherine Mansfield (1888-1923). Her short stories *The Doll's House* and *The Garden Party and other Stories* are based on her childhood experiences. The house where she was born can be visited in Wellington.

In the period following World War II, it was the writer Frank Sargeson who dominated the literary scene. His many short stories and novels often concerned themselves

Film

The history of New Zealand cinema began in the 1890's with the production of short documentary films. In 1914 the first feature movie with a New Zealand background was presented to a local audience. However, it was not until the 1970's when the New Zealand Film Commission was established to encourage and support local productions, that the industry really got off the ground.

Over the last few decades New Zealand films have earned themselves an excellent reputation with overseas audiences. The best known directors in the 1970's and '80's were Roger Donaldson *Sleeping Dogs*, (1977) and *Smash Palace*, (1981) and Geoff Murphy *Goodbye Pork Pie*, (1980). Two directors who have earned international recognition for their more serious art-house films are Vincent Ward *Vigil*, (1984) and *The Navigator*, (1988) and Jane Campion. Campion, who was born in New Zealand but now lives and works in Australia, won an Academy Award for her film *The Piano*, (1993). Also much acclaimed was the film *Once Were Warriors* (1994), based on a novel by controversial Maori author Alan Duff. Another film that received international praise was Peter Jackson's *Heavenly Creatures* (1994). This movie tells the true story of a murder committed by two schoolgirls in the 1950's. Perhaps one of the most original films to come from New Zealand in recent years is the comedy *Topless Women Talk About Their Lives* (1997), directed by Harry Sinclair.

with the hardships of the Great Depression and were written in a style that captured the vernacular perfectly. Among the writers he influenced was Janet Frame, one of the country's most important contemporary novelists. Her autobiography *An Angel at my Table* was filmed by Jane Campion.

Very popular in the 1960's were the back-country novels of Barry Crump (1935-1996). Especially worth reading for its humorous description of the experiences of a professional deer culler is *A Good Keen Man* (1960). Also worthwhile are *Hang on a minute mate* (1961) and *Scrapwaggon* (1965). Another very popular New Zealand born author was Dame Ngaio Marsh (1899-1982). Her detective novels had an international public though, unlike the works of Crump, only a very few had New Zealand settings.

Maurice Shadbolt has built a good reputation with his historical novels on New Zealand themes. Among his more recent works are *Season of the Jew* (1986), *Monday's Warriors* (1990) and *The House of Strife* (1993). Other writers of note include novelists Ronald Hugh Morrieson and Maurice Gee and the poets James K Baxter and Denis Glover. (Some of the more important Maori writers are mentioned under Maoritanga below).

Maoritanga

Though the literature and art forms of European culture are still dominant in New Zealand, the last few decades have nevertheless shown a growing awareness for the achievements of *Maoritanga* (Maori culture). However the activities of Maori artists are by no means limited to such traditional crafts as wood carving or weaving, but extend into all fields of modern artistic endeavour.

Dame Kiri Te Kanawa is a world famous opera singer and, in the pictorial arts, painters like Gordon Walters and Robyn Kahukiwa have drawn on Maori rather than European sources for their inspiration. The influence of Maoritanga on subject, imagery and meaning is especially notable in the field of literature where Maori or part-Maori writers, like Booker Prize winner Keri Hulme (*Bone People*), Patricia Grace (*Potiki*), Witi Ihimaera (*The Matriarch*), and poet Hone Tuwhare, have earned themselves recognition both at home but and abroad.

Meeting houses

Those with an interest in traditional Maori culture will find **Rotorua**, as commercialised as it may be, the best and easiest place to study it. Meeting houses are found in many places in the country but are especially common in areas with large Maori communities such as **Northland**, **East Cape** and the **Auckland** area. Visitors should bear in mind however that the *marae* (strictly speaking, the place in front of a meeting house but the term is often used more loosely to refer to all the buildings around it) is sacred to the Maori and permission must be obtained before entering. In some tourist areas, tours are offered to local marae, thus allowing visitors a unique insight into contemporary Maori culture. Inquire at the tourist offices for details of such visits.

#

According to one long-accepted interpretation of Maori oral histories, New Zealand was discovered in AD 950 by Kupe, who set out from his island home of Hawaiki. Kupe eventually returned with precise sailing instructions which enabled the navigator Toi to find New Zealand again a few hundred years later.

Around 1350 a fleet of eight canoes that has come to be known as the Great Fleet, set out on a final wave of migration. On arriving in New Zealand the migrants separated to settle different parts of their new land. Even to this day the majority of Maori trace their origins to one of the canoes (waka) that came from Hawaiki.

Though the above scenario appeared to provide a very neat explanation of Maori origins, the exact dates and other details it offered have since been discredited as a misinterpretation of original sources by European scholars in the nineteenth and early twentieth centuries. More recent research has revealed that there probably never was a 'Great Fleet' as described in the European rendition of the legend. In actual fact, none of the Maori canoe traditions ever referred to an organised fleet of canoes, nor did they claim that they arrived in New Zealand at the same time.

Current opinion is that it was probably from somewhere in East Polynesia that the ancestors of the Maori began their epic voyages over the Pacific to New Zealand. Referred to in the oral traditions as Hawaiki (the word 'Hawaiki' means simply 'homeland' and does not refer to a specific island) their point of origin was possibly Tahiti or the Marquesas. More than a 1000 years ago the first small groups arrived on New Zealand's shores. Why they left their homeland and whether these voyages were by accident or design are still subjects of much debate.

Whatever the truth may be, the fact remains that these early Polynesians were remarkable navigators. Many centuries before the great European voyages of exploration, they had already colonised vast areas of Oceania. Finally, in large ocean-going canoes that may have carried up to 100 people, they found their way to New Zealand, the last of the island groups to be settled by this Pacific people.

The Moa-hunters

Early Polynesian settlers found New Zealand's climate significantly colder than that of their former island homes. The tropical plants they brought with them were difficult to grow, especially in the winter months, therefore agriculture was practiced only on a small scale. In order to supplement their diet they had to resort to fishing and hunting. Though the only animals they brought with them were the dog and rat, the forests abounded with bird-life which provided an important additional source of protein. Of particular importance were the **moa**, a large flightless bird of which there were several species. This is why the first phase of settlement is often referred to as the moa-hunter period, though the early settlers are also referred to as Archaic Maori.

What little is known about the moa-hunters is based mainly on archaeological evidence. They lived in small unfortified

villages, usually with coastal locations as it was here that they were able to find the greatest variety of food: fish and water-fowl were taken from the river mouths, while fern roots and birds could be found in the coastal forests. Though they were hunters, there is little evidence to suggest that warfare played a role in their society.

Moas were a principle source of food for about 200 years. Though they were found on both main islands, the largest species inhabited the open grasslands of the South Island. This is also where the majority of moa-hunter camp-sites have been discovered. The moa that was most commonly hunted in the South Island was *Euryapteryx gravis*, a massive, heavily-fleshed bird as tall as a man. In some places they also hunted *Dinornis maximus*, a moa that could grow to a height of over 9.8 feet (3m). However excessive hunting led to the extinction of the moa, and with the demise of these giant birds came the gradual change from Archaic Maori culture to the culture of the Classic period.

The Classic period

The decreasing number of moa and the growing importance of horticulture in the twelfth century, marked a turning point in Maori history. New methods of storing and cultivating crops, of which the kumara (sweet potato) was the most important, meant that the temporary campsites that had characterised moa-hunter culture could be exchanged for more permanent settlements. Housing became more substantial and villages were moved to locations that favoured gardening.

By the fourteenth century, cultivable land was a valuable asset that had to be protected. The *pa* or fortified village heralded a new age of tribal warfare that came to typify Classic Maori society as encountered by Europeans in the eighteenth century.

Improved horticultural methods and the permanent settlements this enabled, led to increased prosperity; especially in the north of the North Island where growing conditions were most favourable. This in turn allowed for the further development of art, architecture and religion. In response to changes in the way of life, Maori social organisation also evolved.

The largest unit in Classic Maori society was the tribe (*iwi*) which was made up of sub-tribes (*hapu*) consisting of several extended family groups (*whanau*). Life was to a large extent of a communal nature, with land being the most important form of property. The members of a hapu were bound together by oral genealogies (*whakapapa*) that enabled them to trace their descent from a common ancestor.

Within the hapu and iwi there were also divisions according to social rank. At the top of the ladder were the numerous *rangatira* (chiefs) who were presided over by the *ariki* (paramount chief), the head of the tribe. The next class were the *tuatua* or commoners, and occupying the lowest rung were the *taurekareka* or slaves who had been caught in battle.

Maori history

Religion

The tohunga were the priests of Maori religion. However there were various grades of tohunga, many of whom were specialists in some art or craft rather than in spiritual matters. The higher grades of tohunga were the scholars of their people; they could communicate with the gods and were trained in healing, magic, astronomy, genealogy and much else besides.

Maori religion knew many gods and, like the Greeks, they had a god of war (*Tu*) and a god of the sea (*Tangaroa*). Though it was believed for a time that the Maori worshipped a supreme god named *Io,* most scholars believe this to have been a later development under the influence of Christianity.

A key concept in religious and daily life was (and still is, to an extent) *tapu*. Tapu was a spiritual force that emanated from the gods and it exercised a regulating influence on Maori society. Its full meaning is complex but, like our concept of taboo (the anglicized form of tapu), it could mean 'sacred' or 'forbidden'.

Chiefs were considered tapu as was their personal property. To steal such property was therefore a breach of tapu. It was believed that any person foolish enough to do this, or to break any other of the laws of tapu, would eventually become sick and even die if the offence was serious enough. Tapu was also used to protect various natural resources. A forest, for example, was placed under tapu in order to allow bird-life to recover.

Warfare

Other important factors in Maori life were *mana* (spiritual power, prestige) and *utu* (revenge). One of the best ways to attain mana was in battle, and utu (along with quarrels over land) was one of the most common reasons for going to war. Utu might be sought for past defeats or anything else which diminished the tribe's mana. As a result, warfare played a major role in Maori society. It had its own rituals, songs and dances and from early childhood men were trained in the art of hand-to-hand combat. Though enemies were taken as slaves, some were also eaten. Eating a foe was not only the ultimate insult but also a way of acquiring their mana.

When attacked the Maori were able to retire behind the wooden palisades of the pa. These fortified hill-top villages were the Maori equivalent of the medieval fortress or walled town. Pas varied in size, but sites have been found that covered an area of 100 acres (40.5 hectares) and held up to 5000 people.

Though tribal wars were endemic for some 500 years prior to the arrival of Europeans, the Maori were by no means fighting constantly among themselves. War had its seasons (no fighting occurred when the kumara gardens needed attention), and there were often long periods of peace. In the intervals between fighting the Maori were able to tend their fields and indulge in trade. Being a stone-age culture they especially favoured obsidian and above all greenstone (jade) as items of exchange. Found only on the west coast of the South Island, greenstone was coveted for its beauty and hardness. Any tool, weapon or ornament made from this stone was a highly-valued possession.

Isolated as they were and working only with tools made of stone or bone, the Maori were nevertheless able to develop one of the most impressive of all Polynesian cultures. Their works of art belong to the outstanding achievements of Oceania in the pre-European period.

Maori Art

Though not proved beyond all doubt, it is now generally accepted that the ancestors of the Maori and other Polynesian peoples came from the coastal fringes of Southeast Asia. In a series of migrations over a period of many centuries, these Southeast Asian peoples eventually reached the Pacific region and brought with them cultures which had been influenced by the Chinese. Therefore some experts postulate that the origins of important elements in classical Maori art are to be found in China. This theory is supported by the similarity of the spiral motifs found in Maori art with curvilinear motifs in the art of the late Chou and Han dynasties. Among the oldest known examples of early Maori art are the fifteenth century rock drawings which are mostly found in the South Island.

Spiral motifs occur just about everywhere in Maori art but can be seen at their most complicated in the intricate wood carvings at which the Maori excel. Some of the most elaborate of these wood carvings are those decorating the facades of *pataka* (storehouse) and *whare hui* (meeting house). Spirals or curvilinear patterns are also prominent in in Maori tattoos. Today the *moko* (tattoo) is painted on and is usually only seen during official ceremonies or during Maori folklore concerts.

Along with the spiral, the most important element of traditional Maori carving is the human form, which can be portrayed in either a highly stylized or fairly realistic fashion. Characteristic of these carved figures or *tiki* are the large heads, the three-fingered hand and the out-thrust tongue which was an expression of defiance and warded against evil.

Perhaps the best known of all Maori ornaments is the *hei-tiki*. This neck pendant (*hei* 'hanging', *tiki*, the human form) portrays an embryo-like figure with prominent eyes, tongue and a head that is turned to one side. In Maori tradition, tiki figures symbolise an ancestor or series of ancestors and are still considered by many Maori as sacred. They were, and still are, carved from wood, stone, bone and, most prized of all, greenstone (jade). Cheap plastic tikis are sold in just about every souvenir shop.

Left: *Rewa's village, Kerikeri*

Below: *Northland children doing the Haka*

Opposite page: *Greenstone Hei Tiki*

Previous pages: *detail from the carved entrance gate, Whakarewarewa village, Rotorua*

Whare Whakairo

The crowning achievement of traditional Maori culture was the *whare whakairo* (carved meeting house). No other Polynesian culture has ever produced such a magnificently decorated building; intricate carvings covered almost all the wooden surfaces of the facade and interior, the gaps between the carved interior wall posts were filled with woven reed panels known as *kotukutuku* and painted *kowhaiwhai* patterns decorated the rafters. But the purpose behind all this was by no means purely decorative; the carvings, and indeed the building as a whole, symbolised the tribal ancestors and were a way of preserving tribal history and legends. A particularly fine example of a whare whakairo is the meeting house at Waitangi, in the Bay of Islands.

Song and dance also form an essential part of Maori culture. The action songs that are commonly staged for tourists in places like Rotorua combine, as the name suggests, elements of both. The rhythmic actions in these songs help to convey the meaning of the words.

During the famous *poi* dance, the musical rhythms are complimented by the graceful swinging of a ball attached to a length of string, the poi. In contrast to the poi dance, the *haka taparahi* is only performed by men. The dance consists of vigorous movements accompanied by a shouted chant and this is the famous haka that is performed by the All Black rugby team before a match. It is not a war dance as many people assume. The true war dance is the *peruperu* and, though similar to the haka taparahi, it is always performed with weapons — something that would no doubt have given the All Blacks an unfair advantage at the start of a game.

Flora and fauna

Flora

New Zealand's unique flora and fauna evolved in the course of millions of years of isolation. When the first Polynesians arrived they found a land almost entirely covered by evergreen rainforests. The far north of the North Island was dominated by impressive forests of giant kauri, whereas much of the rest of the island was covered by equally impressive podocarp forests. Podocarps like rimu, totara and miro belong to an extremely ancient family of conifers that first appeared around 190 million years ago, when dinosaurs still roamed the earth. In the South Island the southern beech forests dominated, but large areas were also covered by tussock grasslands.

Today, native forests cover only around 20 per cent of the total land area. Characteristic of the New Zealand forest or 'bush', as the locals prefer to call it, are the many varieties of fern. There are, in fact, around 180 different species of fern to be found here; one of the prettiest is the ponga or silver fern, a large tree fern that is found in most New Zealand rainforests.

The prettiest of New Zealand's flowering trees are the kowhai, with its delicate yellow flowers and the pohutukawa, which flowers bright red around Christmas time. New Zealand's only native palm tree is the nikau. It is mainly found in the North Island but there a also significant stands on the South Island's west coast.

Environmental

It took European settlers little more than a hundred years to cut down and burn vast tracts of native forest in order to win land for settlement and farming. Where green pastures dotted with fluffy white sheep (60 million of them!) now extend as far as the eye can see there were once dense forests filled with the sound of birds.

Some of these birds are now either extinct or extremely rare, as they could neither cope with the rapid loss of habitat nor with the introduction of predatory animals (cats, weasels). Today seven species of native bird are listed as endangered.

Deer, wild pigs, rabbits and opossums (plant-eating marsupial native to Australia) were also introduced by the early settlers and, in the absence of their natural enemies, they have multiplied to the point where they are pests. The large populations of red deer and opossums, for instance, have had a particularly devastating effect on the native forests. It is estimated that around 70 million opossums chew their way through 21,000 tons of leaves per day! Hunting of these, and other introduced animals, is therefore encouraged.

Fauna

New Zealand was originally a land that was virtually devoid of mammals. Except for two species of native bats, the tree tops and forest floors were dominated by birds. In the absence of ground-dwelling predators, flightless birds such as the now extinct giant moa were able to flourish, but the advent of man and the animals he introduced were to prove to be the nemesis of many. Of the flightless birds that still survive, it is New Zealand's national bird, the kiwi, that is most well-known. However the kea, the world's only mountain parrot, comes a close second. It can fly and its clownish behavior has made it very popular with all those who get a chance to see it in the wild.

Some of the more common birds that visitors are likely to see when walking through the native bush are the flightless weka, the insect eating fantail and the colourful native pigeon. Among New Zealand's rarest birds are the flightless takahe, a flightless parrot known as the kakapo and the kokako, a member of the wattle-bird family which can fly, but only just. Several species of penguins are found along the coasts of both main islands.

There are no snakes in New Zealand but the reptiles are represented by about 30 species of lizard and the remarkable Tuatara (*Sphenodon punctatus*). Though it looks like a lizard, the tuatara is in fact the last survivor of an ancient family of reptiles that reached its peak during the age of the dinosaurs, some 200 million years ago. Once found on the mainland it now only survives on a few scattered off-shore islands.

issues

In spite of the sins of the past, there is still much worth protecting in New Zealand and New Zealanders are becoming more and more conscious of the need to save what is left of their unique and often breathtaking natural environment. Large areas of land are protected as national or forest parks and laws have been passed that force developers to consider the ecological aspects of any projects they are planning. Recycling is becoming more commonplace throughout the country and environmentally friendly products are appearing more frequently on supermarket shelves. Unleaded petrol has been available in New Zealand since 1988.

New Zealand follows an anti-nuclear policy and refuses to allow nuclear-powered or armed ships into its ports. The government has also protested against nuclear testing by the French in the Pacific. The greenhouse effect and the destruction of the ozone layer in the earth's atmosphere are also matters of grave concern. New Zealand is relatively close to Antarctica where ozone depletion is especially dramatic.

The All Blacks & Rugby Union Football

Ever since the first New Zealand rugby team went overseas in 1884, they have struck fear and admiration in the hearts of their opponents.

That first team played in Australia, chalking up a spectacular record of eight wins in eight matches. At least as impressive was the team that toured Great Britain in 1924. They did not loose a single match and, appropriately enough, have gone down in the annals of rugby history as 'the Invincibles'.

In the early days of international rugby, New Zealand's national team wore dark-blue jerseys and dark knickerbockers. It was not until 1901 that the players' uniform changed to all black with the famous silver fernleaf adorning the jersey. However the name 'All Blacks' under which the team has become famous, was not used until the 1905 tour of Great Britain. Though the origins of this sobriquet might appear obvious, it seems that it derives from a printer's error. Instead of printing 'all backs' (as a journalist who wanted to describe the speed with which the entire team played intended), an 'l' crept in — and the new name stuck.

Over a period of roughly a hundred years, the All Black's have built up a record in international matches that is surpassed only by that of South Africa's Springboks. In the first Rugby World Cup tournament held in 1987 it was the All Black team that emerged as victorious in the final against a French side.

However the days when rugby was considered almost a religion in New Zealand are gone. The rise of new, more individualistic forms of sport since the 1970's, and a not quite so brilliant record in international competition in recent years, are contributing factors. Nevertheless a test match against such formidable opponents as the Wallabies (Australia), the South African Springboks or the British Lions still attracts fervid national interest, and Rugby Union is still a major winter sport.

The object of the game is to get the ball across the other team's goal line, whether by kicking it over the goal posts or by touching it down behind the goal line. Those who want to know more will probably find that the game is best explained by visiting a match or chatting with a local over a beer in the pub.

In recent years, seven-a-side competition has become very popular. The All Blacks won the Hong Kong Sevens tournament in 1994, 1995 and 1996. In 1998 they lost to reigning champions Fiji in the semi-finals. Fiji eventually won the cup against Samoa.

Top of the page: Coromandel
landscape with native toi-toi
grass in the foreground

Above: Kowhai flowers

Right: One of New Zealand's 180
species of fern

Below: South Island rainforest

A variety of marine mammals frequent the country's coastal waters and visitors have a good chance of seeing fur seals, dolphins and, in the vicinity of Kaikoura, even whales. All of New Zealand's land mammals have been introduced. Red deer, wapiti, chamois and wild pigs are just a few of the introduced animals that may be hunted for sport.

New Zealand's only poisonous spider is the katipo. It is found on beaches all over the North Island (but mainly on the west coast of the North Island) and as far south as Dunedin. Though its bite can be fatal, relatively few deaths have ever been recorded. Like the North American black widow spider, to which it is related, the katipo is black with a red mark on its back. Only the female is dangerous and as, the spiders are shy, it is unlikely that you will have any unpleasant encounters.

Food and drink

In recent years the quality and variety of restaurants in the larger towns and cities has improved greatly. Auckland, Wellington and Christchurch have a particularly cosmopolitan range of restaurants: Italian, Indian, Mexican, Thai and Chinese are just a few of the international cuisines to choose from. However, in the smaller settlements the basic sausage and chips establishments, where the price is right but the ambience non-existent, are still quite common.

Food

The traditional take-away foods are fish and chips (French fries) and meat pies. Meat pies are sold in dairies (small corner shops which sell milk, bread and a little bit of everything else) and also in some pubs and tearooms. Chinese takeaways are also very popular and can be great value for money. American fast food chains such as **McDonald's** and **Kentucky Fried Chicken** are found in many of the larger towns and cities. New Zealand restaurant chains include **Georgie Pie** which specialises in filled pastries, and **Death by Chocolate** where customers can treat themselves to delicious desserts.

Some excellent seafood is available in New Zealand and it is worth trying such local delicacies as whitebait, oysters, paua (abalone) and crayfish (lobster). Among the tastiest fish caught in New Zealand coastal waters are snapper, tarakihi and a deep-sea fish known as orange roughy. Not a seafood but a New Zealand classic is roast lamb with mint sauce.

Those who are catering for themselves will find the shops well-stocked with a wide variety of fresh foods. Fruit and vegetables are quite cheap during the summer and invariably of excellent quality. Try the kumara, a delicious variety of sweet potato that many Kiwis like to serve with their roast meals. The large supermarket chains such as New World, Pak 'n Save and Write Price are of course the cheapest places to go shopping.

Drink

A strong cup of tea in the morning and a cold beer after work is still a fairly accurate summary of the drinking habits of most New Zealanders. Though there used to be a lot of private breweries, almost all the local beer is now brewed by just two companies. Among the more popular brands are **DB** and **Lion**, but it is worth seeking out such famous local brews as **Black Mac** (a dark beer) and **Pink Elephant**, both of which come from the Nelson-Marlborough area. Places where beer is brewed and consumed on the premises (often referred to as boutique breweries) include the **Purangi Winery** near Whitianga on the Coromandel, **Shakespeare Tavern & Brewery** in Auckland and **The Loaded Hog** in both Auckland and Christchurch. Ask the locals for other tips.

Wine consumption is growing in New Zealand and some of the country's white wines rank with the best in the world. Good places to go wine tasting include the **Blenheim** region in the South Island and the **Hawke's Bay** and **Gisborne** regions in the North Island.

Common abbreviation used throughout this book:
BYO — Bring Your Own. (See FactFile under Restaurants).

A worthwhile investment for all those who like to conclude an evening with a good glass of wine and an appetising meal is *Michael Guy's Eating Out Guide*, which is updated annually. It is available in local bookshops.

Geography and Geology

New Zealand is located in the South Pacific, approximately 1,243 miles (2,000km) to the south-east of Australia from which it is separated by the **Tasman Sea**. Stretching 994 miles (1,600km) from north to south, New Zealand consists of two main islands (North Island and South Island) and a number of smaller islands, the largest of which is **Stewart Island** at the southern end of the South Island. The country's total land area exceeds that of Great Britain and is only slightly less than that of Colorado in the USA. Together the North and South Islands have nearly 4,350 miles (7,000km) of coastline.

Earthquakes and volcanoes

According to the theory of plate tectonics, the earth's surface is divided up into a number of separate plates which are constantly moving. New Zealand lies in a region where the Pacific plate collides with the Indo-Australian plate. The tremendous pressures that are built up in this collision zone are released in the form of sometimes violent seismic and volcanic activity. This explains New Zealand's susceptibility to earthquakes and the impressive volcanoes and geothermal activity which visitors can see in the area of **Rotorua** and **Tongariro National Park**.

Mountains, lakes and glaciers

The colliding tectonic plates are also responsible for the formation of the South Island's most distinctive geographical feature, the **Southern Alps** or **Main Divide** — New Zealand's highest range of mountains. The Southern Alps extend along virtually the entire length of the South Island and are continuing to rise at the rate of about $\frac{1}{2}$ inch (10mm) per year. The hills and mountain ranges that extend through the North Island from Wellington to East Cape are also a part of this mountain-building process, but the North Island's highest mountain, **Mt. Ruapehu**, was formed by volcanic activity.

During the Ice Ages much of the country was covered by a thick mantle of snow and ice. Relics of those times are most clearly evident in the South Island. They include the beautiful lakes near Queenstown and the magnificent fiords of **Fiordland National Park** which were, like the lakes, gouged out by vast rivers of ice. Among the most well-known of the glaciers that still exist in the South Island are **Fox** and **Franz Josef Glaciers** on the West Coast and the mighty **Tasman Glacier**, which is New Zealand's largest.

National Parks

New Zealand's first national park was created in 1887 and at present there are thirteen, each of which is discussed in the main text. The central purpose of these parks is to preserve New Zealand's remaining wilderness areas in their natural state, but public access is allowed and encouraged in so far as it is consistent with the aims of preservation.

New Zealand's nineteen forest parks offer a lesser degree of protection for some of the country's most beautiful forest and mountain scenery. As is the case with the national parks they are open to the public for recreational purposes, but a certain amount of selective logging

for native timbers and other strictly-controlled commercial activities, is also allowed.

Apart from the national and forest parks, there are also three maritime (two on the North Island, one on the South Island) and two marine parks (both on the North Island) and a variety of other, generally much smaller, scenic reserves.

The maritime and forest parks and above all the national parks, are a major attraction for outdoor enthusiasts from all over the world. Most of the parks offer a well-marked network of hiking trails and provide accommodation in the form of simple huts. A visit to one of these parks is a must for all those who want to appreciate New Zealand's natural beauty in its most untouched form.

> **Common abbreviation used throughout this book: DOC — Department of Conservation.**

Politics and Economy

Politics

New Zealand is a constitutional monarchy with Queen Elizabeth II of Great Britain as head of state. Her representative in New Zealand is the **Governor-General** who is appointed on the recommendation of the New Zealand government for a five year period. However, the governor-general's functions are only ceremonial and the real power lies in the hands of the prime minister and a cabinet of government ministers.

Above: At Cape Reinga the Pacific Ocean meets the Tasman Sea

Left: Bungy Jumping, Kawarau Suspension Bridge, Queenstown

Below: Mount Ngauruhoe has, like Mount Egmont, a nearly perfect volcanic cone

The two main political parties are **National** (conservative) and **Labour**. Among the more significant of the smaller parties are **New Zealand First** and the **Alliance**, a five-party coalition whose principal members are the Greens and a Labour splinter group known as New Labour. Elections take place every three years and all those who are over 18 years of age are eligible to vote.

New Zealand's government is modelled on the British parliamentary system, but in New Zealand the upper house was abolished in 1950.

All legislation is now passed through the **House of Representatives** (formerly the lower house of parliament) which usually consists of 120 members. Another important component of the governmental system is an independent judiciary. Like Great Britain, New Zealand has no written constitution.

Prior to 1996, seats in the House of Representatives were allocated on a simple majority of the vote basis. With the advent of a new voting system in 1996, seats are now divided according to the principle of proportional

New Zealand's MMP System

Growing dissatisfaction with what had been in effect a two-party system of government, greatly increased the desire for electoral reform. In the 1993 elections the question of proportional representation was put to the vote and the public decided overwhelmingly in its favour. The 1996 elections were held using a limited form of proportional representation (known as MMP or Mixed Member Proportional) based on the electoral system in Germany.

Space precludes a detailed description of this system in which, as opposed to the former model, every citizen has two votes (an indirect Party Vote and a direct Electorate Vote for the candidate in your electorate). Suffice it to say that the system combines constituency (the old First Past the Post system) with proportional representation and is designed to enable parliaments in which the number of seats each party holds more accurately reflects the total percentage of the vote it actually receives. As was the case in the previous system, 5 Maori Electorates have been reserved for Maori voters, thus ensuring Maori representation in parliament.

As the German model has shown, this will not only give the minor parties a greater chance of winning a seat in parliament but will probably make majority governments, once the rule, a rare thing in the future. The 1996 elections resulted in a coalition government between National and the New Zealand First Party. Labour is the most important of the parties in opposition.

representation. This new voting model is supposed to give small parties a fairer chance of gaining representation in parliament.

Economy

New Zealand is an agricultural country and its highly mechanized farms are among the most efficient in the world. Though only about 10 per cent of **GDP** is generated by agriculture, somewhat more than 50 per cent of the total land area is set aside for pastureland.

The main exports are meat, wool and dairy products. However there has been an effort in recent decades to diversify exports, and commodities produced by the forestry, horticultural, manufacturing and fishing industries are of growing significance. Due in part to the country's lack of suitable raw materials, heavy industry has never been of any significance. Main imports include machinery, cars, electrical goods, crude oil, plastics, iron and steel, pharmaceuticals and chemical products.

The principal trading partners are Australia, the European Union, Japan and the United States. Trade with the Middle East, Eastern Europe and Asia is also important. Britain, New Zealand's main trading partner in the 1970's, now accounts for only 6 per cent of foreign trade. The influence of tourism on the economy has increased dramatically in recent years and the tourist industry is now one of the main earners of overseas funds.

Economic Reforms

When Britain joined the EC in the 1970's the country lost its most important market for agricultural goods. The economy went into decline and by the mid-1980's the country had accumulated a huge foreign debt. Matters came to a head in 1984 when a foreign exchange crisis became the catalyst for a series of far-reaching reforms which changed the world's first welfare state into a country now acclaimed as a shining example of economic liberalism.

What was once one of the most regulated economies outside the former Soviet bloc organised itself along free-market principles at such a pace that even the reforms of Thatcher's Britain seem modest in comparison. Masterminded at first by Labour's finance minister Roger Douglas, the reforms were later accelerated by National's finance minister Ruth Richardson. Financial and labour markets were deregulated, state-owned enterprises were privatised, state subsidies were abolished, protectionist trade barriers were largely removed and there were drastic cuts in social welfare spending. All this, and more, has taken place in not more than a dozen years and though the rate at which change is occurring has slowed, it has by no means stopped.

Though at first the changes had some negative results, such as a rise in unemployment, the current upturn of the economy seems to suggest that they are working. Inflation is under control and unemployment has dropped from more than 10 per cent in 1991 to under 7 per cent in 1998. However it should not be overlooked that drastic cuts in the area of social welfare, including the abolition of the state-funded health insurance system, have hit low income groups especially hard.

Opposite page: The spectacular Fox Glacier on the West Coast

Above: Abel Tasman is one of the country's most beautiful national parks

Right: The Beehive, Wellington

Below: Sheep farming is still a mainstay of the economy

Income inequality has grown along with poverty and crime. In spite of this, New Zealand has generally earned much international acclaim for the reforms which have been described as the most comprehensive and far-reaching in the world in recent decades.

Population

At present New Zealand has a population of 3.71 million which is expected to increase to 4.53 million by 2039. However even then the country's total population will still be less than that of cities like New York or London! Population density is relatively low with only 13 people per square kilometre. In comparison, the UK has 92 per sq miles (239sq km) and the USA 11 per sq mile (128sq km). As in many industrialised countries, the number of elderly people is increasing in relation to the rest of the population. It has been projected that by 2051 half of all New Zealanders will be older than 46 years, as compared to an average of 33 years in 1996.

Nearly two thirds of all New Zealanders live on the North Island. Though most visitors are first struck by the rural nature of the landscape, the country is in fact highly urbanised with around 85 per cent of the population living in towns. **Auckland** (population 1,057,000) alone is home to 28 per cent of the population. It is followed in size by **Wellington** (345,000), **Christchurch** (309,000) **Dunedin** (120,000) and **Hamilton** (105,000).

Although New Zealand was first settled by the Maori, a Polynesian people, close to 80 per cent of all New Zealanders are now of European (largely British) descent. Around 15 per cent of the population is Maori. Other ethnic groups include immigrants from the Pacific Islands, Chinese and Indians.

Maori-Pakeha Relations

For many years New Zealand considered itself to be a land without racial problems. There was no segregation or open discrimination of the kind that could be seen in South Africa or the United States. Maori children went to school with children of European extraction, they could apply for the same jobs and there were seats in parliament that were especially reserved for Maori politicians. However, this overly positive impression that white New Zealanders had of their country began to crumble in the 1950's.

Prior to World War II the Maori population was largely rural based. They lived within traditional tribal structures and contact with the Pakeha (New Zealander of European descent) majority was relatively superficial. However, after the war the population became increasingly urbanised. In order to escape rural poverty, many young Maori went to the cities in search of work. For the most part they found only relatively low paid jobs in factories or in the transport industry. By the 1960's some Auckland suburbs already had large Maori populations.

Though many urban Maori successfully adjusted to their new living circumstances, there were nevertheless obvious discrepancies between the Maori and Pakeha populations. Maori children tended to do less well in school than their

Pakeha fellows, few Maori had leading positions in government or business and a disproportionate number of Maori were locked away in New Zealand jails.

Maori leaders perceived these problems as having their roots in the colonial past. Defeated, colonised and forced to adapt to a foreign culture, many Maori had lost their sense of cultural belonging. The Pakeha had followed a policy of assimilation with the goal of completely integrating the Maori within Pakeha society.

For many years the education system had played an important role in this respect, ignoring Maori cultural values so successfully that few Maori were even able to speak their own language. However, the increased sense of cultural difference that came from living within Pakeha society eventually led to a revival of **Maoritanga** (Maori culture). This in turn brought about a new political consciousness that articulated itself primarily in the demand for the return of Maori Land.

In the **Treaty of Waitangi** (1840), the British Crown had promised the Maori undisturbed possession of their lands and all the rights and privileges of British subjects. These promises were repeatedly broken and, over the years, Maori land was either confiscated by the government or lost in the course of shady land deals.

Beginning in the 1970's and continuing into the present decade, the Maori have actively protested for the return of their land. Land occupations and protest marches were used as a way of forcing the government to recognise past injustices. And they have enjoyed some measure of success. Large areas of land have been returned to some tribes as have lucrative fishing rights. In 1994 the government offered a $1 billion dollar settlement for all outstanding land claims. Though some tribes have entered into negotiations with the government, it remains to be seen whether or not this will finally resolve the problem.

The struggle for land has been at the same time a struggle for cultural equality. The government has long since abandoned its policy of assimilation and has accepted the bicultural nature of New Zealand society. Much more attention is given to Maoritanga on television and radio than was the case in the past. In the field of education there is now a much greater emphasis on the special needs of Maori students. Maori is being taught at school and university level. In special schools such as the **Kohanga Reo** (language nests), Maori children are taught within a framework based on Maori culture and values as opposed to the formerly ethnocentric ideals of the past.

Though the problems between Pakeha and Maori are still a long way from being solved, relations between the two peoples can be described as good, if not perfect. As in other former colonies it has been necessary to come to terms with the past in order to build a successful future.

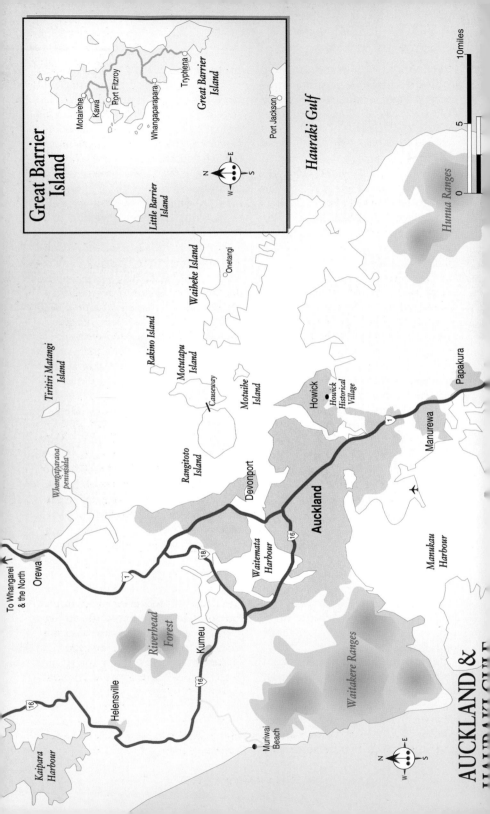

Great Barrier Island

Motairehe
Kawa
Port Fitzroy
Whangaparapara
Tryphena
Great Barrier Island

Little Barrier Island

N
W   E
S

Port Jackson

Hauraki Gulf

10 miles
5
0

Tiritiri Matangi Island

Rakino Island

Motutapu Island

Causeway

Motuihe Island

Waiheke Island

Onetangi

Whangaparaoa peninsula

Rangitoto Island

Devonport

Waitemata Harbour

Howick
Howick Historical Village

Hunua Ranges

To Whangarei & the North
Orewa

1

18

16

Helensville

Riverhead Forest

Kumeu

16

Muriwai Beach

Waitakere Ranges

Auckland

16

Manukau Harbour

Manurewa

Papakura

1

N
W   E
S

AUCKLAND &

1 AUCKLAND & HAURAKI GULF

For most foreign visitors, Auckland is the gateway to New Zealand. It is also the country's largest city and nowhere else in the world are there as many Polynesians living together in one place. But the city is not just a sprawling metropolis of concrete and glass; Aucklanders are blessed with two beautiful Harbours and there are more than 100 beaches within an hour's drive of the heart of the city. With the sparkling waters of the Hauraki Gulf more or less lapping at the doorstep it is not surprising to find that many of the locals are keen yachtsmen or women, a fact that has earned Auckland a nickname as 'the City of Sails'.

Auckland City Tour

Queen Street

A good place to start a walk around the city is on **Queen Elizabeth II Square** at the foot of Queen Street. There is a branch of the **Auckland Visitor Centre** located here where visitors can arm themselves with a free map and whatever other information they might need before setting off. Just a little north of the Square is the waterfront from where boats depart on a variety of cruises around the **Harbour** and into the Hauraki Gulf.

Located in the former Chief Post Office in Queen Elizabeth Mall is the **Waterfront 2000 Display Centre**. Here visitors can inform

Above: Auckland Harbour

Sky City Complex

A close look at Auckland's newest architectural feature involves a detour off Queen Street to the corner of Federal and Victoria Streets. The monumental Sky City complex houses a casino, a 344 room hotel, four restaurants and a theatre. Attached to the complex is the 1,076ft (328m) tall **Sky Tower**, one of the highest lookout towers in the world. Excellent views from the top, of course, but you have to pay for the pleasure.

themselves about the various projects that (pending final approval) will eventually transform Auckland's waterfront. These developments will take place over the next decade and are estimated to cost billions of dollars. As some projects that have been planned will affect the public transport system, visitors are advised to check timetables and departure points of trains and buses.

Not far from the information kiosk, on Queen Elizabeth II Square, is the **New Zealand National Maritime Museum** on Hobson Wharf. This interesting 'hands-on' museum offers visitors a fascinating insight into the country's seafaring history. There are exhibits explaining how the Maori migrated across the Pacific to New Zealand, as well as on the country's European discoverers, Abel Tasman and Captain James Cook. On display here is the world's first jet boat, the *Hamilton Jet*, which was invented by the New Zealander William Hamilton in 1957. In the museum workshops sailmakers, woodturners and boat-builders can be seen at work. Cruises on the Harbour aboard the scow *Ted Ashby* take place at 12.30pm daily.

Looking towards Auckland's busy main shopping street from Queen Elizabeth Square, it is hard to imagine that in the 1840's Queen Street was no more than a bush-covered gully. It is certainly worth the stroll uphill from here, if only to browse through *Whitcoull's Bookshop* with its good selection of New Zealand literature, or one of the various souvenir shops. Only a short way up the street, on the left hand side of the road, is **Vulcan Lane**. If it is time for a cup of coffee then one of the sidewalk cafés here might be just the thing.

Aotea Centre

Continuing on up Queen Street one eventually passes Aotea Square where the Aotea Centre is situated. The Centre is a venue for performances of classical music and much else besides. Nearby are the **Force Entertainment** and **Civic Theatre** complexes which are due for completion towards the end of 1999. They will house the main **Auckland Visitor Centre** office, as well as a **Planet Hollywood** restaurant, **IMAX** giant screen cinema and a modern live performance theatre.

From the Square the road climbs somewhat more steeply past the palms of Myers Park (right-hand side of road) and a few very inviting little ethnic restaurants on the left-hand side. Especially popular are the

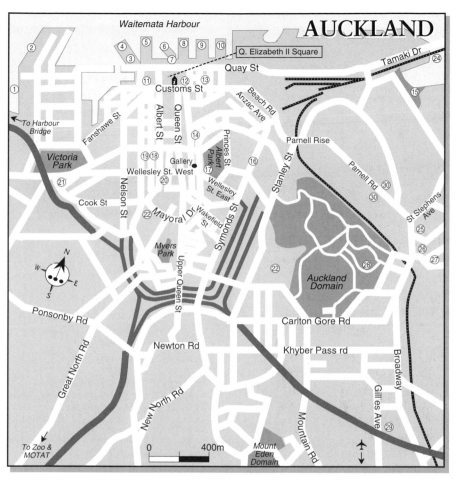

AUCKLAND

Waitemata Harbour

Q. Elizabeth II Square

Tamaki Dr

Quay St

Customs St

To Harbour
Bridge

Beach Rd

Anzac Ave

Fanshawe St

Albert St

Queen St

Victoria
Park

Parnell Rise

Parnell Rd

Gallery

Princes St

Albert
Park

Wellesley St. West

Stanley St

St Stephens
Ave

Wellesley
St. East

Cook St

Nelson St

Symonds St

Mayoral Dr

Wakefield
St

Myers
Park

Upper Queen St

Auckland
Domain

Ponsonby Rd

Carlton Gore Rd

Great North Rd

Newton Rd

Khyber Pass rd

Broadway

New North Rd

Gilles Ave

Mountain Rd

To Zoo &
MOTAT

0   400m

Mount
Eden
Domain

KEY   AROUND AUCKLAND CITY

①	Westhaven Boat Harbour	⑯	University
②	Wynyard Wharf	⑰	Art Gallery
③	Maritime Museum	⑱	AA
④	Hobson Wharf	⑲	Sky City
⑤	Princes Wharf	⑳	CPO (Chief Post Office)
⑥	Ferry Berth	㉑	Victoria Park Market
⑦	Ferry Building	㉒	Central Police
⑧	Queens Wharf	㉓	Hospital
⑨	Captain Cook Wharf	㉔	To Kelly Tarlton's
⑩	Marsden Wharf	㉕	Holy Trinity Cathedral
⑪	Downtown Airline Terminal	㉖	Kinder House
⑫	Waterfront 2000 Display Centre	㉗	Ewelme Cottage
⑬	Downtown Bus Terminal	㉘	Auckland Museum
⑭	Vulcan Lane	㉙	Highwic
⑮	Parnell Rose Gardens	㉚	Parnell Village

International Cuisine

Apart from the Myers Park section of Queen Street, there are many other areas in Auckland where it is possible to try good food, in conducive surroundings and at a reasonable price. What is rather astonishing is the sheer number of restaurants offering exotic cuisine in a country where, only a decade before, a portion of crinkly *pommes frites* with steak was considered the culinary ne plus ultra. Whether Middle Eastern, Vietnamese, Mexican, Turkish, Indian or Japanese; it is all here.

Caravanserai Tea House and Hasan Baba, both of which offer good food at reasonable prices.

K. Road

More of Auckland's cosmopolitan character can be discovered by turning right near the top of Queen Street into Karangahape Road (also known simply as 'K. Road'). Here it is possible to find greengrocers' shops catering to the taste-buds of the city's Asian and Polynesian population, as well as a few seedy sex shops and massage parlours. At 283 K. Road the Polynesian Bookshop has some excellent titles for those with a deeper interest in Polynesian culture. Popular cafés in K. Road include Urbi et Orbi and the Verona Café. The Vesuvio restaurant has been recommended for its good Italian food.

The Domain

To reach the peace and quiet of the Auckland Domain, which is the largest area of parkland close to the City Centre, continue back along Karangahape Road, cross the

Grafton Bridge, and follow Park Road. Buses to the Domain (Nos 63, 64 or 65) leave from the Downtown Bus Terminal on Custom Street, only a short distance from the information kiosk at the foot of Queen Street.

Auckland Museum

Located within the Domain is the excellent Auckland Museum which houses the largest collection of Maori artefacts in the world, along with some fine displays of art and culture from the South Pacific region. Of particular interest in the Maori section is a magnificent 82ft (25m) war canoe and a carved meeting house which originally stood near Thames on the Coromandel Peninsula. A highlight of the natural history section is a model of the extinct giant moa.

If possible it is a good idea to try and make sure a visit to the museum coincides with one of the concerts put on by the Pounamu Cultural Group. These performances of traditional Maori songs and dances take place at 11.15am and 1.30pm. Visitors who arrive early enough can combine the concert with one

Above: *Auckland is New Zealand's largest city*

Right: *Excellent restaurants offering Japanese and Thai cuisine reflect the influence of Auckland's significant Asian population*

Auckland & Hauraki Gulf

of the very informative guided tours of the Maori galleries that take place at 10.30am and 12.45pm.

Parnell

To the north-east and east of the Domain is the old suburb of Parnell. Here a number of Auckland's historic buildings have managed to escape the developers' bulldozers and the energetic might like to continue the walk through **Parnell Village** before returning to Queen Street via the University and Albert Park. Otherwise Parnell can be saved for later as it is only a short bus trip from the inner city.

If, however, the legs allow it then leave the Domain along Domain Drive and head for Ayr Street, just off Parnell Road. Situated here are **Ewelme Cottage** (1864) and **Kinder House** (1858), two fine old Victorian homes that are both open to the public. Further along Parnell Road the **Holy Trinity Cathedral** is also worth a look and from here it is not far to Parnell Village.

Albert Park

Those who have not continued through Parnell can leave the Domain via Stanley Street and then follow Grafton Road and Alfred Street through the university grounds to Albert Park. Next to the park, on the corner of Kitchener Street and Wellesly Street East, is the **Auckland City Art Gallery**.

The gallery's collection of New Zealand art is the largest and most comprehensive in the country and includes works by such early colonial painters as Gottfried Lindauer (1839-1926) and Charles Goldie (1870-1947). Goldie is famed for his detailed portraits of Maori wearing traditional mokos (tattoos) and Lindauer's scenes from traditional Maori life are regarded as being accurate, if artistically unimaginative, representations. The British and European collections include works by Gainsborough, Turner and Bassano.

A short distance away from the main building is the **New Gallery**. It is devoted to contemporary New Zealand art and features a collection of works by Colin McCahon, one of New Zealand's most important modern painters. From Albert Park it is no longer far to Queen Street and the start of this walk at Queen Elizabeth Square.

Parnell Village

The Village is a cluster of colonial buildings along Parnell Road that have been restored as a trendy shopping complex, complete with a quaint Victorian atmosphere. There are a number of handicrafts shops here as well as some nice, if somewhat pricey, cafés and restaurants. An additional plus for all those who are spending the weekend in town, is that all the shops are open seven days a week. From the Village it is about a half hour on foot back to Queen Street.

40

Auckland Suburbs

Getting about

Because Auckland sprawls over a huge area that includes most of the islands of the Hauraki Gulf as well as the Auckland isthmus itself, it is not surprising that a number of attractions lie outside the scope of an inner city walk and are best visited by either bus, car or boat. With this in mind it is worth considering getting either a *Busabout Pass* or the *United Airlines Explorer Bus Pass*. Both these all-day bus passes cost only $10 and save the hassles of parking. Fullers Cruises offer an all-day boat pass they call the *Harbour Explorer* which is also good value (see Additional Information).

The **Museum of Transport and Technology (MOTAT),** on Great North Road, is a 10 minute drive from downtown Auckland via the North Western Motorway. Among the many machines on display are two aircraft designed by pioneer aviator Richard Pearse, who, it is claimed, became airborne in 1902, ahead of the Wright Brothers. At **MOTAT 2,** a separate site a short distance away, there is an impressive collection of historic aircraft.

A vintage tram links MOTAT with **Auckland Zoo,** where the local stars are the kiwis and tuataras but lions, elephants and other animals are also present. A feature of the zoo is a large walk-through aviary where visitors may view native birds.

Devonport

The picturesque suburb of Devonport with its beaches, cafes and quaint 19th century atmosphere is situated on the other side of **Waitemata Harbour**. Though Devonport can be reached by bus it is much more interesting to do the 15 minute boat trip from the **Ferry Building** on Quay Street.

Many people do not get much further than the area in the near vicinity of the ferry dock, as it is here that most of the restaurants, cafes and arts & crafts galleries are concentrated. Certainly the view from the waterfront promenade back across to the city skyline is already quite good, but more commanding views can be had from the top of **Mt Victoria** and **North Head**. Both these hills are old volcanic cones with Mt Victoria being the higher of the two.

What it lacks in height North Head makes up for in historical interest, as it was once fortified towards the end of last century as a result of (unfounded) fears of a Russian invasion. Extended during World Wars I and II, the fortifications have since been dismantled but a few old guns remain to be seen. Not far from North Head the lovely **Cheltenham Beach** offers the chance of a swim and a tan.

Above: City from North Shore, Auckland

Main picture: Cruises around the Hauraki Gulf depart from the piers next to the Ferry Building, downtown Auckland

For many, an even greater attraction than the zoo is **Kelly Tarlton's Underwater World**, only 3 miles (6km) from the city on Tamaki Drive. Here one has the unique opportunity of experiencing what it is like to go diving in New Zealand's coastal waters and to travel in Antarctica, without getting wet or freezing in the process! In the main aquarium section, a moving walkway goes through a clear acrylic tunnel that allows visitors to experience the sensation of having schools of fish and even sharks swim around them.

Also part of the complex is the **Antarctic Encounter**. In this experience, a trip through the south polar ice is vividly simulated with an animated killer whale and a snow storm adding to the thrills. All in all, Kelly Tarlton's is probably the closest most of us will ever come to one of the world's most extreme environments.

Auckland Isthmus

Though it may not look like it now, the narrow neck of land over which Auckland spreads itself was also what one might call an extreme environment. Only a few tens of thousands of years ago, the Auckland isthmus was formed by the ash and lava spewed forth by over 60 volcanoes. Though, in the course of time, many of the smaller cones have disappeared, the larger peaks have been preserved and today they provide excellent viewpoints over Auckland and its surroundings.

One Tree Hill

Perhaps the best known of Auckland's extinct volcanoes is **One Tree Hill** (600ft/183m). Like many of the other volcanic cones it was once the site of a fortified Maori settlement or pa. It has been estimated that this pa could hold around 4,000 defenders and its massive earthworks are still clearly visible. The lone pine tree that now stands on the summit next to an obelisk, was planted to replace the original totara tree that gave the hill its name. This totara, which was sacred to the Maori, was cut down by vandals during the early period of settlement.

At the foot of the hill, in Cornwall Park, is **Acacia Cottage**. Built in

The Coast to Coast Walkway

The following points of interest can be reached by bus; however, it is also possible to visit a number of them by walking the Coast to Coast Walkway. The route is clearly signposted, begins by the Ferry Building on **Waitemata Harbour** and ends at **Manukau Harbour**. It takes about 4 hours to complete (there are plenty of opportunities to catch a bus if you get tired) and takes in Albert Park, Auckland Domain, One Tree Hill and Mt Eden. The Auckland Visitor Centre has pamphlets describing this and other walks in and around the city.

1841 it is the city's oldest building. Though not as old, two other Victorian homes worth visiting are **Alberton,** to the north-west of One Tree Hill at 100 Mt Albert Road, and **Highwic,** at 40 Gillies Avenue, a short distance south of the Auckland Domain. Further afield, more of Auckland's colonial past can be seen at **Howick Historical Village,** a restored military settlement about a twenty minute drive south-east of the City Centre.

A bit further north of One Tree Hill and only a five minute drive from Queen Street is the volcanic cone of **Mount Eden** (643ft/196m). Though there are also the remains of a pa on the hill's slopes, it is the best view in Auckland that leads most people to the summit. From here one can look out over the entire Auckland isthmus and towards the islands of the Hauraki Gulf beyond.

Hauraki Gulf Maritime Park

The sheltered waters of the Hauraki Gulf are dotted with islands, forty-seven of which fall within the boundaries of the maritime park. Though a number of the islands can be easily reached from Auckland, some require special permission from the Department of Conservation (DOC) before they can be visited and others are strictly off limits. The reason for such restricted access is that a few of the more remote islands serve as a last refuge for plants and birds that are now very rare or no longer present on the mainland.

Most boats to the islands leave from near the Ferry Building on the Auckland waterfront, not far from the foot of Queen Street. **Fullers** runs regular trips to Waiheke, Rangitoto, Great Barrier, Motuihe and Rakino Islands. **Gulf Trans** operates from Wynyard Wharf to Great Barrier and the schooner *Te Aroha* sails during the summer from Captain Cook Wharf to Little Barrier and Tiritiri Matangi Islands — both wharfs are within walking distance of the Ferry Building.

Waiheke Island

Not included in the maritime park, but only a half hour away from Auckland, is Waiheke Island. Its accessibility, great beaches and a good range of accommodation, make this the most visited island in the Gulf.

Sea kayaks can be hired on the island and there are some good walking trails for those who prefer to stay on dry land.

On top of all this, fourteen vineyards ensure that Auckland's fastest growing wine region has no shortage of good vintages with which to toast the efforts of the day.

The small resident population consists of artists, farmers, pensioners and a few enviable business people who commute to Auckland City.

The Islands of Rangitoto & Motutapu

Included within the maritime park and joined to each other by a causeway are Rangitoto and Motutapu Islands. Of the two, it is Rangitoto that is the more interesting. This bush-clad island was formed by a series of volcanic eruptions, the most recent of which took place only 250 years ago. Since then, the volcano has been a picture of tranquillity and people have been coming here for picnics and to walk through a beautiful forest of red-flowering pohutukawas for close to a century.

A 'must' when on the island is the walk from the wharf to the island's summit which takes about an hour. The views from the crater rim are spectacular. Another track branches off the summit walk to some interesting lava caves (30 minutes return). As the volcanic terrain is very rough, good walking shoes are essential. For those who want to stay longer, the only accommodation is a simple campsite on Motutapu Island.

Great Barrier Island

About a two hour boat trip from Auckland, Great Barrier is the largest island in the Gulf. With its fine beaches and unspoiled stands of native forest, this sparsely inhabited island is the perfect escape for all those who love the outdoors. Popular activities on Great Barrier, or Aotea as it is known by the Maori, include mountain biking, tramping, scuba diving, surfing and sea kayaking.

Though a wide range of accommodation is available, the eating out possibilities are mainly limited to Tryphena, the island's main town. There are, however, a few stores (at Tryphena, Claris and Whangaparapara) where foodstuffs and other basic necessities can be bought.

Authors' Tip

The only electrical power on Great Barrier is provided by privately run generators. As there is no street lighting, visitors should bring a flash light with them. Note also that there is no scheduled bus service and that the roads are mainly unsurfaced. Hire cars are available, but many visitors prefer to rent a mountain-bike for excursions around the island.

Little Barrier Island

Whereas only parts of Great Barrier are included within the maritime park, Little Barrier Island enjoys complete protection as it has the last significant area of native forest unaffected by introduced animals in the country. Among the rare native birds that have found refuge in Little Barrier's virtually undisturbed rainforest, are the flightless kakapo parrot and the stitchbird. As there is no ferry service, and access is anyway very restricted, it is probably easiest to get there on a nature tour with the schooner Te Aroha (see Activities section).

Tiritiri Matangi

More easily accessible is the island of Tiritiri Matangi. This wildlife sanctuary offers the unique opportunity of seeing some of New Zealand's, and the world's, rarest birds in the wild. Endangered native birds that may be spotted here include the flightless takahe, saddlebacks, red-crowned parakeets and New Zealand's rarest species of duck, the brown teal.

The unspoiled beaches of Great Barrier Island and the Coromandel are only a short flight away from Auckland City

Fullers' mail run

Motuihe and Rakino Islands, with their fine sandy beaches, can be visited on Fullers' very popular mail run. This leisurely cruise takes you around the islands and bays of the inner gulf and lasts the whole day. For a description of Kawau Island, see the following section on Northland.

NOW if one has had one's fill of Auckland but not of beaches, sea and sun, then there is only one thing for it: cross Auckland's Harbour Bridge with its 'Nippon Clippons' (two extra lanes on both sides added by Japanese engineers) and head for sunny Northland.

ACTIVITIES

Auckland

Adventure Activities

Auckland Adventures
☎ 528 3036
Offer camping, winery and cultural tours.

Auckland Wilderness Kayaking
☎ 630 7782
Guided kayak tours to remote areas. Half or full day, also overnight trips.

Bush and Beach Ltd
☎/Fax 478 2882
Tours into the Waitakere Ranges and to the gannets at Muriwai Beach. Highly recommended.

Cliffhanger Tours
☎ 815 1851
A one day abseiling and bushwalking tour in the Waitakere Forest.

Ferg's Kayaks
☎/Fax 529 2230
Tours around Rangitoto Island and Kawau Island.

Harbour Trips & Hauraki Gulf Cruises

Most of the boats and cruises depart from Quay St, next to Ferry Building.

Devonport Ferries
Are operated by Fullers and depart daily from the city to the picturesque suburb of Devonport, on the other side of Waitemata Harbour. The scenic crossing takes 15 minutes. Boats depart from the Ferry Terminal, Quay St on a half hourly basis 6.15am-7pm.

Fullers Cruises
Offers a variety of trips around the Harbour and to various islands in the Hauraki Gulf (Rangitoto, Waiheke, Great Barrier and a few smaller islands). Boats depart from the piers near the Ferry Building. Tickets and information are available from Fullers Cruise Centre, ground floor of Ferry Building, Quay St. ☎ 367 9102 for information or 367 9111 for reservations.

Fullers Harbour Explorer is an all day or half day boat pass that allows passengers to get on and off at the various stops. The boat stops at Kelly Tarlton's, Rangitoto Island and Devonport. Boats depart daily at 9.30am, 11am, 2pm & 4pm.

Fullers Mail Run is an all day trip that takes in many of the islands and bays of the inner gulf. The boat departs Sat, Sun & Wed at 9.30am and arrives back in Auckland at 5.45pm.

Kestrel (Jazz Ferry)
Does trips from Auckland's Ferry Terminal to Devonport on Friday and Saturday evenings. A jazz band entertains passengers and a reasonably

priced ticket allows you to go back and forth as often as you like. Those who wish to dine on board should make reservations. It runs from 7pm to 1.15am ☎ 367 9111.

Pride of Auckland Company
Offers lunch and dinner cruises aboard their yachts. They depart from the pier next to the Ferry Building (☎ 377 0459).

Te Aroha
Natural history cruises of the Hauraki Gulf are offered by Adventure Cruising Co. Ltd., PO Box 338, Auckland 1 ☎ 444 9342. The cruises take place aboard the historic schooner *Te Aroha* and vary in length from a single day to four days. Cruises are offered from Nov-April and depart from Captain Cook Wharf, Downtown Auckland.

Ted Ashby
Free cruises on the scow at 12.30pm daily. Departure point is the Maritime Museum.

Mountain Biking
Adventure Cycles
Fort Street
☎ 309 5566
Hire mountain and touring bikes.

Desert Coast Mountain Biking
☎/Fax 411 8612
Mountain bike tours.

Pedaltours
164 Parnell Road
☎ 302 0968 Fax 302 0967
Organise bike tours throughout New Zealand.

Scenic Flights
Balloon Safaris
☎ 415 8289
Fly over Auckland in a hot-air balloon. Champagne and snacks are included.

Scenic Air Safaris
☎ 298 5210

The Helicopter Line
☎ 377 4406

Great Barrier Island
Adventure Activities
Stray Possum Lodge
☎/Fax (09) 429 0109
Run a large number of activities from their hostel. They include mountain biking, sea kayaking, snorkelling and tramping. They also offer cheap backpacker-style accommodation in the lodge, or one can choose a more expensive self-contained chalet.

Mountain Biking
For those who are not actually doing one of the excellent walking tracks, then the best way to get around Great Barrier is by mountain bike. Bikes can be hired on the island at **Tryphena** or (quite often) from the place you are staying.

ACCOMMODATION

*See pages 288 and 300 in the FactFile for the accommodation and
restaurant rating guide*

**Auckland City
Garden Lodge $**
(Backpackers)
25 St Georges Bay Rd, Parnell
☎ (09) 302 0880
Fax (09) 309 8998
Historic villa. Very quiet
and clean. Well equipped
communal kitchen.

**Downtown Constitution
Hill Backpackers $**
6 Constitution Hill
☎ (09) 303 4768
Located in a park, 5 mins
walk from City Centre.

**Downtown Queen Street
Backpackers $**
4 Fort St
☎ (09) 373 3471
Fax (09) 358 2412
Central location. Busy and loud.

**International
Backpackers Parnell $**
"Alan's Place"
8 Maunsell Rd, Parnell
☎/Fax (09) 358 4584
Quiet location.

Aachen House $$
(Bed & Breakfast)
39 Market Rd, Remuera
☎ (09) 520 2329
Fax (09) 524 2898
Edwardian mansion,
2$\frac{1}{2}$ miles (4km) to City Centre.

**Aspen Lodge Bed
& Breakfast Hotel $$**
62 Emily Place
☎ (09) 379 6698
Fax (09) 377 7625
Central location. Child's
play area.

**Harbourview
Station Hotel $$**
131 Beach Rd
☎ (09) 303 2463
Fax (09) 358 2489
Close to City Centre,
opposite railway station.

**Freeman's Travellers'
Hotel $$**
(Bed & Breakfast)
65 Wellington St
☎ (09) 376 5046
Fax (09) 376 4052

Kiwi International Hotel $$
411 Queen St
☎ (09) 379 6487
Fax (09) 379 6496
Toll free: 0800 100 411
Restaurant and free parking.

First Imperial Hotel $$$
131-139 Hobson St
☎ (09) 357 6770
Fax (09) 357 6793

Hyatt Auckland Hotel $$$
Cnr Princes St & Waterloo
Quadrant
☎ (09) 366 1234
Fax (09) 303 2932

EATING OUT

Caravanserai Tea House $
(BYO)
430 Queen Street
☎ (09) 302 0244
Middle Eastern cuisine.

Death by Chocolate $
42 Jervois Road, Ponsonby
☎ (09) 360 2828
Only desserts.
Also at 92 Tamaki Drive,
Mission Bay and
55 Victoria Road, Devonport.

Hasan Baba $
(BYO)
466 Queen St
☎ (09) 358 5308
Turkish cuisine.

Konditorei Boss $
305 Parnell Rd
Parnell Village, Parnell
☎ (09) 377 8953
German cakes, pastries
& light fare.

Poppadom $$
(BYO/Licensed)
55 Customs Street
☎ (09) 379 8661
Good Indian
food.

**Thai
Friends $$**
(BYO)
3/311
Parnell Rd,
Parnell
Village,
Parnell
☎ (09) 373
5247
Good Thai
food.

Vesuvio Restaurant $$
(BYO/Licensed)
Karangahape Plaza 501,
Karangahape Road
☎ (09) 379 4769
Excellent view over city,
Italian-style cuisine.

Cin Cin $$$
99 Quay St
☎ (09) 307 6966
New Zealand specialities
and waterfront location.

Japanese Restaurant Daikoku $$$
Cnr Quay St & Downtown Square
☎ (09) 309 8151
This branch of the Daikoku
specialises in sushi and sashimi.

**Kermadec Ocean
Fresh Restaurant $$$**
Kermadec Brasserie and Bars
1st Floor Viaduct Quay
Cnr Hobson & Quay Sts
☎ (09) 309 0412 (restaurant)
☎ (09) 309 0413 (brasserie)
Perhaps the best seafood
restaurant in Auckland.

Café, Herne Bay, Auckland

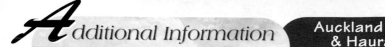

GENERAL INFORMATION

Auckland, Area Code: ☎ (09)

Consulates

Australia
Union House,
32-38 Quay St
☎ 303 2429

Canada
9th Floor, Jetset Centre,
48 Emily Place
☎ 309 8516

USA
General Building,
Cnr Shortland & O'Connell Sts
☎ 303 2724

UK
Fay Richwhite Building,
151 Queen St
☎ 303 2973

Important Telephone Numbers

Automobile Association	☎ 377 4660
Emergency Chemist	☎ 520 6634
Emergency Dental	☎ 520 6609
Emergency Medical	☎ 524 5943
Taxis	☎ 300 3000

International Airlines

Air New Zealand	☎ 357 3000
British Airways	☎ 367 7500
Canadian Airlines	☎ 309 0735
Japan Airlines	☎ 379 9906
Qantas Airways	☎ 357 8700
Singapore Airlines	☎ 303 2129
Thai Airways	☎ 379 6455
United Airlines	☎ 379 3800

Post Offices

The main post office and poste restante service is located in the Bledisloe Building, Wellesley Street. Post offices are open Mon-Fri 9am-5pm.

TRANSPORT

Airport Transport

The Airbus departs from the Downtown Airline Terminal, cnr Quay & Albert Sts. The first bus leaves at 6.10am, the last bus at 8.50pm. From Auckland International Airport the first bus leaves at 6.20am and the last one at 8.20pm. The journey takes about 40mins. For timetables ☎ (09) 275 7685 or for general enquiries ☎ 275 9396.

There are also shuttle buses offering door to door service:
Super Shuttle ☎ 307 5210 or 0800 727 747,
Johnston's Shuttle Link ☎ 275 1234.

Bus Services & City Tours

The Downtown Bus Terminal is on Custom Street. Airport & Sightseeing buses depart from Downtown Airline Terminal and Old Ferry Building, Quay St.

Please note that the proposed redevelopment of the Britomart area scheduled for 1999 (completion in 2001) will affect bus departure points and timetables.

For information on buses, trains, ferries and carpooling phone **Rideline** on 366 6400.

Those travelling on will find that the InterCity (☎ 357 8400) and Newmans (☎ 309 9738 or freephone: 0800 777 707) long distance buses depart from Sky City Coach Terminal, Sky City, 102 Hobson St. Reservations can also be made by calling at the Auckland Visitor Information Centre or at any accredited Travel Agent.

Apart from the **Explorer** and **Busabout** buses mentioned below, many other companies also offer sightseeing tours around Auckland and further afield.

United Airlines Explorer Bus: includes a number of Auckland's major attractions on its route and passengers can get on and off whenever they wish. The **Explorer All Day Bus Pass** may be purchased at the Ferry Building, end of Queen St. It departs the Ferry Building on an hourly basis, 10am-4pm daily.

Busabout All Day Bus Pass: valid on Auckland's Yellow Buses. Information and timetables available from information kiosk, Downtown Bus Terminal or ☎ Buz-A-Bus 366 6400. The **Busabout Pass** is available from the driver. It allows unlimited travel from 9am weekdays and at all times on the weekend and public holidays.

Trains

Long distance trains depart from Auckland Central Railway Station, Beach Road. Freephone: 0800 802 802. Reservations are taken from 7am-9pm daily. Tickets can also be booked at the Visitor Information Centre, 24 Wellesley Street.

NIGHTLIFE & ENTERTAINMENT

For up-to-the-minute information on local events, concerts and so forth contact the Auckland Visitor Centre. The Saturday edition of the New Zealand Herald newspaper also provides daily updates on what is going on in the city.

Most of the city's nightlife is concentrated in the central city area. A number of pubs offer live music on weekends, many staying open until the early hours of the morning. **Shakespeare Tavern & Brewery** in Albert Street has live music on weekends as does the **Civic Tavern** on Wellesly Street West. Here the British Isles are well represented in the form of an Irish, a Scottish and an English Bar.

The place to go for live jazz and blues (every night) is the **Java Jive**, at 12 Pompallier Terrace, Ponsonby. Also recommended is **Kitty O'Brien's Irish Pub** at 2 Drake Street, Freemans Bay where the Guinness is downed to the accompaniment of live Irish folkmusic.

Performances of classical music as well as ballet, opera and musicals take place at the **Town Hall** and **Aotea Centre** (☎ 309 2678). Live theatre venues include the Galaxy Theatre (☎ 302 0095), Mercury Theatre (☎ 303 0693) and Maidment Theatre (☎ 379 3685).

Note that the buses stop running at about 10.30pm on weekdays and 7pm on Sundays.

PLACES TO VISIT

Entry fees are payable unless otherwise stated.

Historic Places

Alberton
100 Mt Albert Rd

Ewelme Cottage
14 Ayr St, Parnell

Highwic
40 Gillies Ave, Epsom
Open: the above are open daily
10.30am-12pm, 1-4.30pm,
except Xmas & Good Friday.

Howick Historical Village
Bells Road, Lloyd Elsmore Park,
Pakuranga
Bus: Howick bus from
Downtown Bus Terminal.
Open: daily 10am-4pm.

Kinder House
2 Ayr St
Open: Mon-Fri 12-3pm.

Parnell Village
Parnell Road, Parnell
A picturesque cluster of shops
in colonial style.
Bus: Busabout, United Airlines
Explorer and buses 63, 64 & 65
from Downtown Bus Terminal.

Markets

Otara Markets
Newbury St (off East Tamaki Rd),
Otara
Unique Polynesian atmosphere.
Food, clothes, arts & crafts.
Open: Sat 6am-12 noon.

Victoria Park Market
Opposite Victoria Park
Victoria St West
Art galleries, fashion
boutiques, jewelry,
souvenirs, cafes & restaurants.
Open: daily 9am-7pm.

Museums

Auckland City Art Gallery
Main Building
Cnr Kitchener & Wellesley Sts
Open: daily 10am-4.30pm. Entry
to Ground Floor collection is free.
Free guided tours 2pm Wed-Sun.
Paintings from the 19th and early
20th centuries.

New Gallery
Cnr Wellesley & Lorne Streets
Open: daily 10am-4.30pm.
Collections of contemporary
New Zealand art.

Auckland Museum
Auckland Domain
Open: daily 10am-5pm (except
Xmas day & Good Friday).
Perfomances of Maori Songs and
Dances on most days at 11.15am
& 1.30pm. Admission is charged
for concerts. Further details
☎ 838 7876. Admission to
museum is free.

Top of the page: *Picturesque marine views are just one of Auckland's many attractive features*

Above: *Two tramping huts on Great Barrier provide simple accommodation*

Right: *Auckland Harbour Bridge from Westhaven Marina*

MOTAT & NZ Science Centre
Great North Road
Western Springs
Bus: ARC (Pt Chevalier)
bus 045 departs Customs St,
downtown Auckland approx.
every 15 minutes.
Open: Mon-Fri 9am-5pm
(except Xmas Day). Weekends
& public holidays 10am-5pm.
☎ 846 0199

New Zealand National Maritime Museum
Hobson Wharf
Intersection of Quay
& Hobson Sts
Open: daily 9am-6pm.

Rugby Hall of Fame
187 Queen Street
Open: 9.30am-5pm daily.
This modern interactive museum
is a MUST for rugby fans.

Other Attractions

Great Barrier Island
For Great Barrier connections refer
to Regional Transport. Cruises to
various other islands in the Gulf are
mentioned in Activities.

Harrah's Sky City Casino
Cnr Victoria & Federal Sts
☎ (09) 912 6000 or 0800 888 711
97 gaming tables, slot machines
and a Keno lounge.
Open: 24 hours.

Kelly Tarlton's Underwater World & Antarctic Encounter
23 Tamaki Drive,
Orakei
Bus: No 72, 73, 74 & 75
departing Downtown Terminal.
Also Busabout bus and United
Airlines Explorer Bus.
Open: daily 9am-9pm.

Muriwai Beach and Gannet Colony
Approx. 10kms from
Auckland city.
The beach provides good
surfing and it is possible to
get quite close to the birds.
A campground is located next to
beach (☎ 411 7426/7763). Also
close-by is an 18 hole golf course.

Pavilion of New Zealand
Montgomerie Road,
Mangere (near
International Airport)
Audiovisual shows provide an
introduction to New Zealand's
past and present. Also live
entertainment, kiwi fruit farm
tours, horse riding and fishing —
they guarantee you'll catch one!
Bus: Airporter buses depart
Downtown Airline Terminal and
stop at Montgomerie Rd, only
3 minutes walk from Pavilion.
Open: 10am-4pm.

Waterfront 2000 Display Centre
Queen Elizabeth Mall
(in former Chief Post Office
building)
Open: Mon-Fri. 9am-5pm.
Weekends 10.30am-4pm.

Zoo
Motions Road,
Western Springs
Bus: Busabout bus or Pt Chevalier
bus 045 from Customs St.
Open: daily except Xmas Day
9.30am-5.30pm (last admission
4.15pm).

*A*dditional Information

REGIONAL TRANSPORT

Great Barrier Island

Air
Great Barrier Airlines flies daily to Great Barrier from Auckland International Airport's domestic terminal and North Shore Airfield. The flight takes 30 minutes ☎ 275 9120 or 0800 900 600. There are also a few smaller airlines servicing the island.

Boat
Gulf Trans, Wynyard Wharf, Auckland operates a regular car and passenger ferry service to Great Barrier Island. The crossing takes 6 hours. For details ☎ 373 4036. More expensive but quicker (2 hours) is Fullers service to the island.

For connections to other islands in the Gulf refer to the heading 'Auckland' under Activities.

VISITOR INFORMATION & PARK VISITOR CENTRES

Auckland
(Main office):
Bledisloe House
24 Wellesley Street
Auckland 1
Open:Mon-Fri 8.30am-6.00pm.
Sat, Sun & public holidays
9am-5pm.
☎ (09) 366 6888
Fax (09) 366 6893
e-mail: reservations@aucklandnz.com
The office is located just off Queen Street behind the Civic Theatre. Around April 1999 the visitor center will move to new premises in the nearby Civic complex.

Queen Elizabeth Square
1 Queen Street
Open: Mon-Sun 9.30am-5pm.
☎ (09) 366 6888

Auckland International Airport
Auckland Airport Visitor Centre
Arrivals lounge
Open: Mon-Sun from 5am
until last flight.
☎ (09) 275 6467

Great Barrier Island
Fullers Office
Tryphena
☎ (09) 429 0004
Apart from information they can also help arrange accommodation. The main tourist office in Auckland also has information on the island.

DOC Office
Port Fitzroy
☎ (09) 429 0044
Fax (09) 429 0071
Information on Great Barrier's walking tracks.

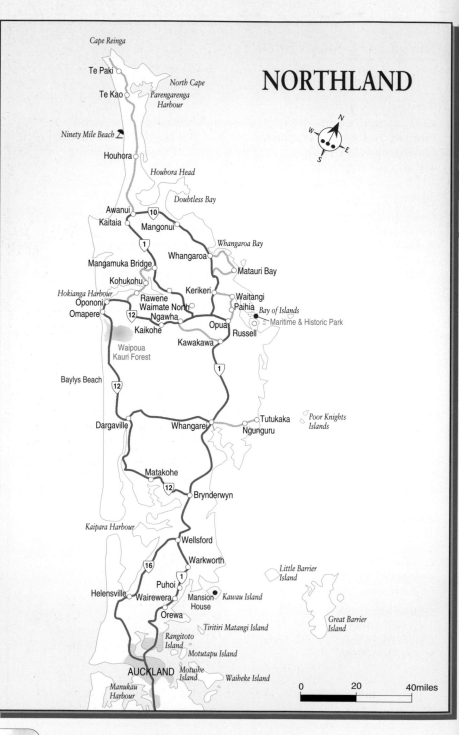

NORTHLAND

Cape Reinga

Te Paki

North Cape

Te Kao

Parengarenga Harbour

Ninety Mile Beach

Houhora

Houhora Head

Doubtless Bay

Awanui

10

Kaitaia

Mangonui

1

Whangaroa Bay

Whangaroa

Mangamuka Bridge

Matauri Bay

Kohukohu

Kerikeri

Hokianga Harbour

Rawene

Waitangi

Opononi

Waimate North

Paihia

Omapere

12

Ngawha

Bay of Islands

Opua

Maritime & Historic Park

Kaikohe

Waipoua

Kawakawa

Russell

Kauri Forest

1

Baylys Beach

12

Dargaville

Whangarei

Tutukaka

Poor Knights

Ngunguru

Islands

Matakohe

12

Brynderwyn

Kaipara Harbour

Wellsford

Warkworth

Little Barrier

Island

16

Puhoi

1

Helensville

Wairewera

Mansion

Kawau Island

House

Orewa

Tiritiri Matangi Island

Great Barrier

Island

Rangitoto

Island

Motutapu Island

AUCKLAND

Motuihe

Waiheke Island

Island

Manukau

Harbour

0   20   40miles

2 NORTHLAND

Northland is the region stretching north of Auckland. Not only is it one of the most picturesque parts of New Zealand, but the subtropical climate makes its superb beaches attractive even in winter. Among the many scenic attractions are the Bay of Islands, Ninety Mile Beach and Waipoua Kauri Forest. Boat trips around the Bay of Islands, yachting, scuba diving and big game fishing are popular activities of visitors to this region.

• ROUTE 1 •
NORTHLAND

State Highway 1 (SH1) winds its way north in a leisurely fashion, passing through small farming towns and pockets of forest, with brief forays to the coast, on its unhurried path to the sun-soaked **Bay of Islands** and **Kaitaia** in the far north of Northland.

Auckland to the Bay of Islands

Not far from Auckland, both **Orewa** and **Waiwera** on the Hibiscus Coast beckon with lovely white-sand beaches, but Waiwera can offer thermal springs as an additional

Above: Off the beaten track, Matauri Bay offers visitors a splendid beach

attraction. To get to the excellent beaches on **Whangaparaoa Peninsula**, leave the highway at Silverdale.

Only a bit further up the road from Waiwera, the village of **Puhoi's** atmospheric pub, with its photos and memorabilia from the pioneer days, is a great place to quench the thirst after a day on the beach. From tiny Puhoi, it is another 31 miles (50km) to Warkworth.

Warkworth is not much bigger than Puhoi, but the satellite station located near here gives the place a certain degree of importance. Once again there are plenty of nice beaches in the vicinity, but it is the possibility of an excursion to **Kawau Island** that recommends a longer stop. The boat leaves from **Sandspit**, just east of Warkworth. The island was once home to the colonial Governor and Premier Sir George Grey and his old residence, **Mansion House** (1844), can be visited.

From Warkworth the road turns inland to Wellsford, after which it continues north, briefly skirting the coast between Waipu and Ruakaka, before arriving in Whangarei.

Whangarei

With a population of 44,000, **Whangarei** is already a city by New Zealand standards and is Northland's largest and most important commercial area. Less reliant than other towns in this region on tourism, the city is a deep-sea port with oil refining, glass-making and ship building among to its main industries. The best views over the city and bay are from Mount Parahaki.

Down by the attractive waterfront, the **Clapham Clock Museum** has a collection of over 500 clocks, the oldest of which date back to the seventeenth century. The **Whangarei Museum** (Northland Regional Museum) lies about 3 miles (6km) south-west of town on the road (SH14) to Dargaville. Set in a large park the complex includes an **Exhibition Centre** with a fine collection of Maori artefacts, a **Kiwi House** and the historic **Clarke Homestead** which was built in 1885.

Popular beaches within reach of Whangarei are at **Ngunguru** and **Sandy Bay**. On the road to Ngunguru it is worth stopping for a look at the picturesque **Whangarei Falls**.

Best scuba diving

An excursion to the **Poor Knights Islands** can be thoroughly recommended for scuba diving enthusiasts. Departure point is **Tutukaka**, only a short distance north of Ngunguru. The waters around these islands are teeming with exotic, brightly-coloured fish and offer a diving experience scarcely to be rivalled anywhere else off the New Zealand coast.

Some 34 miles (55km) north of Whangarei, the town of **Kawakawa** is unusual in that it shares its main street with the railway. In summer a vintage steam train does regular trips from here to **Opua**.

An attraction only a short distance south of town are the glow-worms in the **Waiomio Caves**. From Kawakawa a secondary road leads to the coast and **Paihia**.

The Bay of Islands

The Bay of Islands was named by Captain Cook in 1769 and it was not all that long before it became the site of New Zealand's first European settlement — a rough, brawling port known as **Kororareka** (Russell). The brothels and grog shops of yore have, of course, long since disappeared and the Bay townships are now characterised by the bustling activities of boat tour companies, kayak hire firms and the thousands of tourists they serve. And who can blame them all for coming? With its sheltered waters being ideal for boating, fishing and swimming, and with a wonderful climate on top, the Bay is the kind of place that many a tourist dreams of.

A large number of the 150 or so islands to be found in the Bay are included within the **Bay of Islands Maritime and Historic Park**. For information about walks and camping in the park, which not only includes the islands but also stretches of coastal land, it is best to contact the Park Information Centre in Russell or the **DOC** office in **Kerikeri**.

Paihia

Paihia is the traditional base for tourists who wish to explore the Bay of Islands. From here one can either embark on a big game fishing trip or simply enjoy a leisurely island cruise. Probably the best of these cruises out of Paihia or Russell is the daily **Cream Trip**, a 5$^1/_2$ hour tour of the lovely Bay and its many islands. The tour recalls the days when milk and cream were collected by boat from isolated island farms. Other tours that can be recommended are the **Cape Brett Trip** and a romantic cruise aboard the sailing ship R. Tucker Thompson.

There is not a great deal to see in Paihia itself, though **Kelly Tarlton's Shipwreck Museum** is certainly worth a closer look. The museum is housed appropriately enough in an old sailing ship, and displays an interesting assortment of booty salvaged from the many wrecks to be found in New Zealand waters. The café on board offers light meals but is a bit pricey.

Waitangi

Waitangi lies across the bridge over the Waitangi River, a short distance north of Paihia. It was here, in 1840, that the controversial **Treaty of Waitangi** was signed and New Zealand became a part of the British Empire. In return for handing over sovereignty to the British Crown, the Maori chiefs were granted the rights of British subjects and were also guaranteed continued possession of their lands and other resources. Unfortunately, the promises in print were not carried out in fact and the treaty has been a point of contention between Maori and Pakeha (white New Zealander) ever since. Although the signing of the treaty is still celebrated as **Waitangi Day** (February 6), many Maori people feel little cause to rejoice over past injustices. Ironically enough the name 'Waitangi' can be translated as 'weeping water'.

Above: *Waka (canoe), Waitangi, Bay of Islands*

The treaty was signed on the lawn in front of the **Treaty House**, which was built as a home for the British government official James Busby in 1833. Kept inside the lovely old colonial dwelling are various historical artefacts, photos and a copy of the treaty. Nearby is a Maori meeting house, the interior of which is decorated with superb carvings. Also a tribute to the Maori wood-carver's skill is the huge carved war canoe, which is lowered to water once a year on Waitangi Day. The whole complex is entered via a Visitor's Centre where it is possible to view a half hour audio-visual on the history of the place.

Thoroughly to be recommended for those with an interest in natural history is the **Waitangi Mangrove Walk**. This nature trail goes through one of the few mangrove forests in New Zealand. The trail leads to the pretty **Haruru Falls** and requires about 2 hours. A brochure describing the walk is available at the Visitor's Centre.

Russell

Russell can be reached by launch from Paihia but those who want to take their cars have to travel a little further south to **Opua**, where there is a car ferry (daily 6.40am-8.50pm; Friday until 9.50pm). There is an unsealed road that goes via Karetu and Waihaha to Russell but the trip takes much longer along this route.

Once known as Kororareka, Russell was New Zealand's first European settlement. The earliest settlers, who began arriving around 1809, were a rough, brawling mixture of whalers, sealers, escaped convicts and adventurers. Such was the state of lawlessness in those wild colonial days that Kororareka was soon known as 'the Hell Hole of the

Pacific', and one shocked missionary described it as "a dreadful place — the very seat of Satan". Rather than have the nation's first capital in a town more noted for its grog shops than law and order, Captain William Hobson (who became New Zealand's first governor) decided on a spot further south at **Okiato**. Hobson chose the name of Russell for his new capital but it was not long before he transferred it to the more favourable site of Auckland (1840) — the capital was finally moved to **Wellington** in 1865, because of its more central location. The original Russell was eventually abandoned and in 1845 it was decided that Kororareka should shed the stigma attached to its old name by assuming that of Hobson's first short-lived capital.

Below: *Magnificently decorated interior of the meeting house at Waitangi*

Today this picturesque township flourishes as an area for yachting and big game fishing. Those visitors who prefer a quieter visit, will find it makes a good alternative to Paihia as a base. Not many buildings from the original settlement are left to recall the colonial days but the few that still remain can be discovered in the course of an easy stroll.

One reminder of more violent times is the bullet-holed walls of **Christ Church**, which survived the destruction of town by the Maori chief Hone Heke in 1845. Built in 1835, it is the country's oldest surviving church. Down on the waterfront, **Pompallier House** (1842) was originally built to house the printing presses of New Zealand's first Catholic mission. Now the house functions as a working museum with its own vintage printery and tannery.

Flagstaff Hill

For the great Maori leader Hone Heke, and other chiefs who had quickly become disenchanted with the Treaty of Waitangi, the Union Jack flying from Flagstaff Hill (Maiti Hill) behind Russell was a symbol of exploitation and broken promises. Hone Heke chopped down the flagpole four times and conducted a spirited resistance against British troops before he was finally defeated. A short, steep path leads up to this historic site from where a lovely panoramic view unfolds over the Bay.

Still on the theme of history, the **Captain Cook Memorial Museum** has a large-scale model of the great navigator's ship *Endeavour* as its most interesting exhibit. The **Duke of Marlborough Hotel** also has a lot of history behind it, but visitors who have worked up a healthy thirst need not despair: it is still a fully functioning pub and no museum. As a place to eat, many people recommend the venerable **Old Gables Restaurant** which was founded way back in 1847.

Kerikeri

The road onward leads north from Paihia to **Kerikeri**. The town is set near a picturesque inlet and is surrounded by orchards growing kiwifruit along with a mouth-watering variety of other subtropical fruits. Apart from its orchards, Kerikeri is also renowned for its arts and crafts. Anybody looking for original souvenirs might well strike it lucky in a local handicraft shop.

Two of New Zealand's oldest buildings are situated a couple of kilometres further north, right next to the inlet. **Kemp House** was built in 1821 as a mission house and is the country's oldest surviving building. Still furnished in the style of the nineteenth century, it is open to the public. Next door the **Old Stone Store** was built in 1833. It has retained its function as a shop but also has a small museum upstairs.

Other things to see around Kerikeri include **Rewa's Village**, a very interesting reconstruction of a pre-European Maori village on the other side of the inlet from the Stone Store, and **Rainbow Falls**, roughly $2^{1}/_{2}$ miles (4km) outside of town.

The Bay of Islands to Cape Reinga

Continuing along SH10 pass through Waipapa and Kapiro but then, if times allows, turn off before Kaeo for an excursion to **Matauri Bay**. The asphalt road soon changes to gravel but then the bumps and jolts are a small price to pay for a chance to get off the beaten track.

The road down to the coast from Matauri Bay township offers some terrific views, while the bay itself is graced with a lovely sandy beach. On a nearby hill is a memorial to the Greenpeace ship *Rainbow Warrior*. In an attempt to prevent the testing of nuclear bombs by the French at Mururoa Atoll, the boat had regularly taken part in protest actions within the testing zone. On July 10th 1985, French agents sabotaged and sank it in Auckland Harbour. A camera-man was killed in the incident.

The coastal road passes close to a number of secluded beaches at **Wainui** and **Tauranga Bay** before arriving at **Whangaroa**. Lacking the crowds of the Bay of Islands, this little town and its pretty bay is the ideal place to get away from it all for a few days. Big game fishing fans can try their luck here, but a relaxing pleasure cruise can also be highly recommended.

Mangonui lies further north, beautifully situated at the southern tip of **Doubtless Bay**. The sea aquarium has an interesting display of living corals, sponges and other aquatic life from local waters. Doubtless Bay is lined with some magnificent beaches, though it is **Coopers Beach** that is most popular with the holiday crowds. The beach is fringed by ancient pohutakawa trees which make a stunning backdrop when, at Christmas, they flower bright red.

Awanui on SH10 is the point where the tour buses from Paihia or Kaitaia turn off for the trip to **Cape Reinga** and **Ninety Mile Beach**. The road is tar-sealed as far as Te Paki, but it is not recommended that inexperienced motorists attempt the trip along the sands of Ninety Mile Beach.

The road to the Cape skirts **Aupouri Forest** on its way up the narrow Aupouri Peninsula. This man-made forest is composed of fast-growing pine trees that were planted to secure drifting sand dunes. Shortly before Houhora, a road branches off to **Houhora Heads**. The 3 miles (5km) detour is especially worth it in good weather as there is some good picnicking around the inlet. Another reason for this side trip is the excellent **Wagener Museum**, which has an extensive collection of Maori artefacts among its many interesting exhibits. Nearby is a camping ground and an old homestead built in the 1850's. At the old kauri gum-digging town of **Houhora** is New Zealand's northernmost pub — an excuse for a drink if ever there was!

Te Kao

Over half-way to the Cape, Te Kao is the largest Maori settlement on the peninsula. The town's humble skyline is dominated by the twin towers of the **Ratana Temple**. Though derived from the Christian faith, the Ratana Church is deeply imbued with elements of Maori culture and pre-European spiritual belief.

Further north the entrance to **Parengarenga Harbour** is the site of an impressive natural spectacle. In late February and early March, thousands upon thousands of bar-tailed godwits gather here before leaving on their epic 7,000-mile (12,000-km) journey to Siberia.

The Kauri: Giant of the Forest

The giant kauri (*Agathis australis*) can live for over 2,000 years, attain a girth of more than 65ft (20m) and exceed 164ft (50m) in height. Together with the American redwoods (sequoias), it is not only one of the largest conifers on earth but also one of the largest trees that has ever existed.

Ancestors of the kauri already dominated the primeval forests of the Mesozoic era, over 200 million years ago. In New Zealand the kauri is only found in the north of the North Island, but related trees of the same genus, *Agathis*, are also found in Southeast Asia and elsewhere in the South Pacific.

Though the Maori valued the mighty kauri for their dug-out canoes, large-scale commercial exploitation did not begin until the arrival of the Europeans. The tree's long straight, branchless trunk was used for ships' masts and the durable timber was also highly prized for building and furniture.

By the 1820's the kauri timber industry was well established and the trees were felled on a scale that would have left today's environmentalists in state of nervous shock. The rainforests (the 'kauri forest' was actually a mixed forest made up of many different species, not just kauris) which once covered nearly all of Northland, were devastated. In this region the original kauri forests now cover only 1 per cent of their former area.

Apart from the wood, the kauri was also valued for its gum, which was used in the production of varnishes and linoleum. It provided the basis for a flourishing export industry and at the height of the gum boom (late nineteenth century) hundreds of gum diggers flocked to the gumfields of the Coromandel and Northland. They either tapped the gum directly from the tree or dug for fossilised gum that had been deposited by ancient forests many thousands of years ago. The gum trade reached its peak around 1900 and then slowly petered out as synthetically-based varnishes began to dominate the market.

Tane Mahuta, Waipoua Kauri Forest

Cape Reinga

After Te Paki Station (the surroundings are managed by the government as Te Paki Coastal Park), where there are some simple camping sites, there is no other sign of human habitation until the lighthouse at **Cape Reinga**. Though the lighthouse is not open to the public, visitors are compensated by the beautiful panoramic views; in good weather it is possible to see as far as the **Three Kings Islands**, which were sighted by Abel Tasman in 1643.

Below the lighthouse, on a wave-battered promontory of rock, is an ancient pohutukawa — it is said to be over 800 years old. Maori tradition has it that the spirits of the dead depart through the roots of the tree into the ocean, on their final journey to the spiritual homeland of Hawaiki.

There is plenty of good walking in the area of the Cape and **Te Paki Coastal Park**. Information about the latter can be obtained from the Ranger at **Waitiki Landing**, or at the Information Centre in **Kaitaia**. The **Cape Reinga Walkway** is described in the book *Guide to Walkways — North Island* published by the AA. The town of **Kaitaia** is situated near the southern end of Ninety Mile Beach and is a good base for trips in the far north of the Northland region. Originally a Maori village, Kaitaia started to expand with the arrival of Dalmatian (Croatian) gum diggers towards the end of the nineteenth century. More information about the gumfields is available at the **Far North Regional Museum** which features an impressive display of polished kauri gum. Apart from the Cape Reinga tours, there are also organised excursions to the historic gumfields starting from Kaitaia.

The return journey

The route back to Auckland follows SH1 as far south as **Mangamuka Bridge** from where it takes a more scenic road to **Kohukohu** on the north shore of Hokianga Harbour. However, those who wish to visit

Ninety Mile Beach

Despite the name, Ninety Mile Beach stretches 'only' some sixty miles from west of Kaitaia to a point just short of **Cape Maria Van Diemen** in the far north. An unbroken stretch of white sand facing the Tasman Sea, the beach is also home to the toheroa, a prized New Zealand delicacy. These shellfish are protected and can only be harvested when populations have reached a satisfactory level.

The most comfortable way to appreciate the beautiful coastal scenery is on one of the bus tours starting from Kaitaia or the Bay of Islands. Private motorists must inform themselves about the tides before setting out. It should also be noted that most car rental firms do not allow their vehicles to be driven along the beach.

the historic mission station at **Waimate North** will have to continue along SH1 in the direction of Ohaeawai. This alternative also allows a dip in the hot springs near **Ngawha**, a short distance north-east of Kaikohe.

Omahuta Forest Sanctuary

A good place to get first impressions of the giant kauri tree is Omahuta Forest Sanctuary. The signposted access road is just half a mile (1km) south of **Mangamuka Bridge** — from the turn-off it is 8 miles (13km) to the car park. A half-hour walk through native bush leads from here to a grove of kauris, the largest of which, 'Hokianga', rises to a height of 177ft (54m).

This sanctuary, along with the neighbouring *Puketi Forest*, is also home to rare native birds such as kokakos, kaka parrots and kiwis. A splash of colour is sometimes provided by rosella parakeets, originally natives of Australia.

The road to Kohukohu enters a part of Northland virtually untouched by tourism. Here the clocks seem to tick slower, though Hokianga Harbour was once the scene of a lively kauri timber industry. However the majority of trees had already been felled by the early 1900's and with them went the region's prosperity. Once an important timber settlement, **Kohukohu** now sits somewhat forgotten on the shore. A car ferry links this small town to Rawene on the opposite side.

Rawene has a lovely setting near the bay and is worth a brief stop if only to see **Clendon House**, a colonial building dating from the 1860's. Those with an interest in colonial history might also find the trip to **Mangungu Mission House** well worthwhile. Built by Wesleyan missionaries around 1838, it occupies an elevated site commanding wonderful views over the sea. The mission house lies between Horeke and Rangiahua at the northern end of Hokianga Harbour.

The road south continues via the beach resorts of **Opononi** and **Omapere** before it enters **Waipoua Kauri Forest**, the largest remnant of the great forests that once covered Northland. Waipoua Kauri Forest is justly famed for the huge kauris that are still plentiful here. One veritable forest giant is known as *Tane Mahuta* (God of the Forest), an immense tree with an estimated age of 1,200 years, a girth of over 42ft (13m) and a height approaching 171ft (52m). It is the largest known tree in New Zealand.

No less impressive is *Te Matua Ngahere* (Father of the Forest) which is 98ft (30m) high, has a girth exceeding 52ft (16m) and could be close to 2,000 years old. Both trees are signposted from the main road. A bit further south, more kauri trees can be seen in the course of a walk through the smaller **Trounson Kauri Park**.

Above: Dawn at Ngunguru

Left: Walking on the beach, or just lazing about in the sun, the Bay of Islands with its superb scenery offers the perfect background

Below: Northland Bush-Waipoua Forest

Dargaville is yet another North-land town that owes its origins to the kauri gum and timber industry. The main point of interest is the **Northern Wairoa Museum** (Maritime Museum) with its displays from the pioneering days, Maori artefacts and maritime exhibits. For a dip in the briny, follow the road west to **Baylys Beach**.

SH12 follows the Wairoa River south of Dargaville before swinging east around **Kaipara Harbour**. The Harbour is in fact a system of drowned river valleys and its shores are worth exploring for those seeking that pretty little spot away from it all.

At **Matakohe** is one of Northland's best kauri museums, the **Otamatea Kauri and Pioneer Museum**. It boasts the world's largest collection of kauri gum in all its various forms, from unpolished lump to finely-crafted ornament.

At **Brynderwyn** SH12 joins SH1 but, rather than return directly to Auckland, it is much nicer to ease one's way back into the big city by branching off at Wellsford and following SH16 along the eastern reaches of Kaipara Harbour.

Near Helensville, Parakai Hot Springs is the ideal place to relax after a long day's sight-seeing. To Auckland it is only another 31 miles (50km) through the fruit and wine-growing country around Kumeu.

Below: Cape Maria Van Diemen (near Cape Reinga) was named by explorer Abel Tasman

ACTIVITIES

Bay of Islands

Boat Trips

The following cruises are offered by Fullers Northland but a wide variety of other trips are offered by smaller operators as well.

Cruises start from Paihia and Russell. Departures from Russell are usually 10-15 mins later. Trips can be booked at Fullers offices in Paihia ☎ (09) 402 7421, Russell ☎ (09) 403 7866 or Auckland, Bay of Islands Travel Centre in Downtown Shopping Centre (Shop 2 facing Customs St) ☎ (09) 358 0259.

The Cream Trip ($5^{1}/_{2}$ hrs): daily from October-May. Departs Paihia 10am. June-September departs Mon, Wed, Thurs & Sat.

Cape Brett (Hole in the Rock) Cruise (4hrs): daily October-May. Departs 9am & 1.30pm. Boat is a high speed catamaran.

R. Tucker Thompson (6hrs): daily November-May. Departs 9.30am. This cruise takes place aboard a sailing ship. Lunch included.

Kawakawa

Steam Train

Kawakawa to Opua (45 mins): daily except Fri in summer. In winter Sat, Sun, Mon & Tues.

Kerikeri

Boat Trips

Kerikeri River Cruise on M.V. *Belfast*: Departs Stone Store Wharf hourly ☎ (09) 407 8276.

Ninety Mile Beach

From Kaitaia & Doubtless Bay: Being closer to Ninety Mile Beach the bus tours are cheaper from either Doubtless Bay or Kaitaia than from the Bay of Islands. Operating from Kaitaia are Sand Safaris (☎ (09) 408 1778) at 221 Commerce St & Tall Tale Travel 'N Tours (☎ (09) 408 0870) at 123B Commerce St. Nor-East Coachlines (☎ (09) 406 0244) operate from Mangonui. Travel 'N Tours also offers a tour to Te Rarawa Marae, a unique opportunity to learn a bit about modern Maori culture.

From Paihia & Kerikeri: Fullers 'Cape Reinga — Wanderer' trip is an all day trip and is available all year round. Buses depart Paihia at 7.30am and Kerikeri at 8am.

Paihia

Dolphin Swimming

Swims with the dolphins are offered by Fullers Northland (Dolphin Encounters) and Dolphin Discoveries (☎ (09) 403 7350), both of which operate out of Paihia and Russell. Season: all year

Sea Kayaking

Kayak hire and sea kayak trips are offered by a number of operators. For more details contact the local Visitor Information Centre.

Russell

Dolphin Swimming

See Paihia above.

Sea Kayaking

For addresses and details contact the Visitor Information Centre.

Whangaroa

Boat Trips

Snow Cloud: This yacht does full day trips out to the Cavalli Islands. Very good value ☎ (09) 405 0523.

Sea Fever Cruises do bay cruises. For more information contact the Boyd Gallery, Whangaroa ☎ (09) 405 0230.

Sea Kayaking

For addresses and details contact the local Visitor Information Centre.

ACCOMMODATION

See pages 288 and 300 in the FactFile for the accommodation and restaurant rating guide

Paihia

Peppertree Lodge $
(Backpackers)
15 Kings Road
☎/Fax (09) 402 6122
Close to town and beach.

Abba Villa $$
(Bed & Breakfast)
21 School Rd
☎/Fax (09) 402 8066
Non-smoking, close to town.

Russell

**Russell Lodge,
Motel & Backpackers $**
Chapel St
PO Box 33
☎ (09) 403 7640
Fax (09) 403 7641
Swimming pool, central location.

Duke of Marlborough Hotel $$
The Strand
PO Box 52
☎ (09) 403 7829
Fax (09) 403 7760
Colonial style hotel directly on waterfront.

Whangarei

**Central City (Hatea House)
Backpackers $**
67 Hatea Drive
☎ (09) 437 6174
Fax (09) 437 6141
Kayaks for rent, cave tours.

Whangarei Falls Caravan Park $
Ngunguru Road
Tikipunga
☎ (09) 437 0609
3 miles (5km) from town.
Tent sites, cabins and bunkrooms.

Aaron Court Motel $$
22 Wolfe St
☎/Fax (09) 438 9139
Freephone 0800 730 731

Above: Dune Riders, Ninety Mile Beach

Left: Waitangi Golf Course

Below: Big-game fishing trips start from Paihia and Russell

Below: R Tucker Thompson, Bay of Islands

EATING OUT

Paihia

Café Over the Bay *
(BYO/Licensed)
Waterfront
☎ (09) 403 7080
Overlooks wharf and bay.
Seafood and snacks.

Bistro 40 ***
40 Marsden Road
☎ (09) 402 7444
Excellent seafood. In the same
building **Only Seafood** is also
good.

Russell

The Gables ***
The Strand
☎ (09) 403 7618
Set in an historic building built in
1847. Cuisine is of a high
standard.

Whangarei

Reva's Pizza Parlour *
(BYO/Licensed)
15 Dent Street
☎ (09) 438 8969
A mixture of Italian
and Mexican food.

Le Grand Monet ***
(BYO/Licensed)
The Grand Hotel
2 Bank Street
☎ (09) 438 6282
The menu here has
a French influence.

Above: *Café, Town Basin, Whangarei*

Left: *Poor Knights Islands — ready to dive*

PLACES TO VISIT

Dargaville
Northern Wairoa Museum
(Maritime Museum)
Harding Park.
Open: daily 9am-4pm.

Helensville
**Parakai Hot Springs
(Aquatic Park)**
2¹/₂ miles (4km) south of town at
Parakai. Open: daily 10am-10pm.

Horeke
Mangungu Mission House
Open: 12noon-4pm weekends
& summer school holidays.

Houhora Heads
Wagener Museum
Open: daily 8am-5.30pm.

Kaitaia
Far North Regional Museum
Commerce Street
Open: Mon-Fri 10am-5pm.
Weekends 1pm-5pm.

Kawau Island
Ferry departs several times daily.
Earliest sailing is at 7.45am and
last sailing at 2pm. Fullers Kawau
Ferries Ltd also offers a variety of
longer cruises on a daily basis in
summer. The Royal Mail Run
(NZ's longest by boat) departs at
10.30am daily. Departure point is
Sandspit, east of Warkworth. For
further information and
reservations ☎ (09) 425 8006.
Fax (09) 425 7650.

Kerikeri
Kemp House & Old Stone Store
Kerikeri Basin
Open: daily 10am-12.30pm,
1.30-4.30pm except Xmas
& Good Friday.

Rewa's Village
Kerikeri Basin
Open: daily 10am-5pm.

Matakohe
**Otamatea Kauri
& Pioneer Museum**
Open: daily 9am-5pm.
Refreshments at Gumdiggers
Tearooms.

Paihia
**Kelly Tarlton's Shipwreck
Museum**
Next to bridge, 550yds (500m)
south of Treaty House.
Open: 10am-10pm. Cafe.

Rawene
Clendon House
Open: daily 10am-4pm except
Xmas & Good Friday.

Russell
Pompallier House
Open: daily 10am-5pm except
Xmas & Good Friday.

Russell Museum
(Captain Cook Memorial Museum)
York Street.
Open: daily 10am-4pm.

Waimate North
Te Waimate Mission House
Open: daily 10am-12.30pm,
1.30-4.30pm except Xmas
& Good Friday.

Waiwera
Waiwera Thermal Pools
Open: daily 9am-10pm,
Fri & Sat until 11pm.

Waitangi
National Reserve
Open: daily 9am-5pm.
Admission for children is free.

Whangarei
Clapham Clock Museum
Town Basin, Quayside
Open: daily 10am-4pm.

Northland Breweries
104 Lower Dent Street
Open: 9am-6pm Mon-Sat. Free
beer tasting and tours available.

Whangarei Museum
(Northland Regional Museum)
On Road to Dargaville, SH14.
Open: daily 10am-4pm

VISITOR INFORMATION & PARK VISITOR CENTRES

Bay of Islands Maritime Park
Visitor Centre, The Strand,
PO Box 134, Russell
Open: daily 9am-5pm.
☎ (09) 403 7685

Dargaville
Normanby Street
☎/Fax (09) 439 8360

Kaitaia
Northland Information Centre,
Jaycee Park, North Road
☎/Fax (09) 408 0879

Paihia
Information Bay Of Islands,
Marsden Road, PO Box 70
Open: daily 8am-5pm.
☎ (09) 402 7426
Fax (09) 402 7301

Waiheke Island
2 Korora Road, Oneroa
☎ (09) 372 9999
Fax (09) 372 9919

Waipoua Kauri Forest
Waipoua Forest Visitor Centre,
Private Bag, Dargaville
☎ (09) 439 0605

Whangarei
Tarewa Park, Otaika Road
Open: daily 8.30am-5pm.
☎ (09) 438 1079
Fax (09) 438 2943
Also information about scuba
diving around Poor Knights
Islands.

COROMANDEL, WAIKATO & KING COUNTRY

N
W—E
S

Port Jackson
Mount Moehau
Port Charles
Colville
Kuaotunu
Opito Bay
Cooks Beach
Coromandel
Whitianga
Hahei
Kaimarama
Whenuakite
309
Coroglen
Tairua
Pauanui
Waiheke Island
Tapu
Coromandel Forest Park
25
25
Auckland
Firth of Thames
Kauaeranga
Whangamata
Thames
Hot Springs
Miranda
25
Coromandel Forest Park
Waihi Beach
26
Waihi
Historical Maritime Park
Paeroa
1
Waikato River
2
27
Te Aroha
2
Huntly
Morrinsville
Waihou River
Raglan
23
Piako River
Hamilton
26
Tauranga
Te Mata
Cambridge
Matamata
Waipa River
29
Kawhia
1
Te Awamutu
31
Waikato River
Putaruru
3
Otorohanga
Kiwi House & Native Bird Park
1
Waitomo Caves
Hangatiki
Te Kuiti
To New Plymouth
Te Tokanganui-a-Noho

0   10   20kmiles
0   10   20kms

3 COROMANDEL, WAIKATO & KING COUNTRY

Rugged, wild and densely forested, the Coromandel Peninsula pokes into the sea like a gnarled finger raised admonishingly at the urban sprawl of Auckland on the other side of the Hauraki Gulf. Settlement on the peninsula is relatively sparse and limited to the ragged coastal fringes where, especially on the east coast, the visitor can find some excellent beaches.

Though the peninsula has retained much of its natural grandeur and is now protected as a forest park, it did not escape nineteenth century New Zealand's hunger for gold, kauri gum (used in varnish) and timber. The gold and gum booms were relatively short-lived, but the tree-fellers only stopped after they had decimated the once extensive kauri forests. The peninsula still has large deposits of gold, silver, zinc and lead and some locals fear that commercial interests could again threaten an ecosystem that is still recovering from the excesses of the past.

The Waikato encompasses the area to the south of Auckland and the Coromandel Peninsula. In contrast to the Coromandel, it is an area of broad fertile plains which support some of the richest farmlands not only in New Zealand but in the world. Though mostly famed for its highly productive dairy farms, horticulture has also become important in recent years. Hub of the region is **Hamilton** on the banks of the Waikato River

Above: Sea kayaking is an ideal way to explore the lovely Coromandel coastline

which, with a total length of 264 miles (425km), is the longest river in New Zealand.

The **King Country**, which lies to the south of the Waikato, gets its name from the Maori King Movement. This movement was formed by a number of North Island tribes who felt that the only way to stop further European encroachment on their lands was to stop feuding among themselves and to unite under a common leader. Potatau I was proclaimed the first Maori King in 1858. Today the movement is led by Queen Te Ata-i-rangi-kaahu, who has her base at Ngaruawahia. During the land wars, the King Country was a refuge for those Maori who were struggling against colonial rule and for many years afterwards it was strictly off-limits for any Europeans. It was not until the 1880's that local chiefs finally allowed the region to be surveyed and the first European settlers were able to enter the area without fear for their safety.

Physically, the King Country has more in common with the Coromandel than the Waikato. The terrain is very rugged with many areas still covered by a luxuriant blanket of native forest. The principal towns are Otorohanga, Te Kuiti and Taumarunui.

• ROUTE 2 •
AROUND THE COROMANDEL PENINSULA

From Auckland the route to Coromandel follows SH1 over the Bombay Hills then turns east along SH2 and SH25 to Thames, gateway to the Coromandel.

Touring Note

This tour of the Coromandel Peninsula is also suitable for cyclists. The sections that each can be cycled comfortably in a day are as follows: Thames to Coromandel; Coromandel to Fletcher Bay; Coromandel to Whitianga via the 309 Road; Whitianga to Tairua; and Tairua to Whangamata. Many towns on the Peninsula have outlets where cycles can be hired. See Additional Information for addresses.

Thames

The largest settlement on the peninsula can look back on an eventful history as a gold rush town. In 1867 the rich 'Shotover' strike on the nearby Kuranui stream, initiated a rush to the Thames area that reached its peak in 1871. For those who want to look for reminders of the gold rush days, the Information Office in Queen Street can give tips about gold-mining relics in the vicinity. Among these remainders is the gold mine and stamper battery at the north end of town. In view of the wide variety of gemstones that are to be found on the peninsula, an interesting place to visit is the **School of Mines Museum**. It claims to have the most comprehensive collection of mineral samples in the country. Roughly 18½ miles (30km) west of Thames, at **Miranda**, is a popular thermal springs complex.

A good place to start exploring the rugged hill-country of Coromandel Forest Park is the **Kauaeranga Valley**, a few miles south-east of Thames. There is an Information Centre here where visitors can learn about the old kauri logging industry and the ecology of the area. Some of the shorter signposted tracks in the valley can be walked in twenty minutes, others would require five hours or more.

Before travelling north, self-caterers should bear in mind that Thames is perhaps the best place on the Peninsula to buy supplies. The **Goldfields Shopping Centre** with the Pak 'N Save supermarket is comparatively cheap and has a wide range of both fresh and canned produce. It is located off Brown Street.

Coromandel

Avoiding the rugged interior, the road to Coromandel hugs the coast, passing on its way enticing sandy beaches and idyllic little bays dotted with yachts.

Coromandel township has managed to retain some of its colonial character in a few lovely old buildings from

Short cut to Whitianga

At **Tapu** a narrow, largely unsealed scenic road branches off the main route to traverse the Coromandel Range in the direction of Coroglen. This route would make an interesting short-cut to Whitianga for those in a hurry to get to the peninsula's best beaches. The many tree-ferns and nikau palms lining the road give a real subtropical feeling to the forest here.

One signposted walk leads off the road to a 1,200 year old kauri that is something of a curiosity with its nearly square trunk. Also worth a stop along the way are the beautifully land-scaped **Rapaura Water Gardens**.

the Victorian era. It was here that gold was first discovered in New Zealand in 1852, but today the town's prosperity rests in its function serving the surrounding dairy farms and as a popular holiday resort. Stores selling handicrafts, along with potter's workshops hint at the lifestyle that has attracted many artists and crafts-people to this quiet part of the country.

Not that 'dropping-out' means being impractical: the potter Barry Brickell originally built himself a little railway to transport clay to his workshop, but now helps make it pay by offering rides to tourists. The **Coromandel School of Mines Museum** recalls the gold rush days

Above: A rugged chain of hills form the backbone of the Coromandel Peninsula

and a working stamper battery just north of town shows how gold was separated from quarz. Of all the larger settlements on the Peninsula it is Coromandel that has the most relaxed atmosphere.

North of Coromandel

The area north of Coromandel is only sparsely settled. The last chance to buy supplies for those travelling to the tip of the peninsula is at **Colville**. A dusty gravel road skirts the flanks of **Mt. Moehau** which lies within an area sacred to the Maori. The strenuous climb to the top (8 hours return) begins by **Te Hope Stream** and is rewarded with the best views on the entire peninsula. In the course of this hike there is a (slight) chance of spotting a very rare native frog, *Leiopelma archeyi*. It is the most primitive of all known frogs and is strictly protected; on no account should it be disturbed! After winding its way through spectacular coastal scenery the road eventually arrives at **Port Jackson** which greets visitors with a fine beach and camping site. Camping is also possible at **Fletcher Bay**, just a little further on at road's end.

Those without a tent can stay at Fletcher Bay Backpackers, a good base for mountain biking, fishing, snorkelling and sea kayaking (bookings essential ☎ (07)868 8898 or 868 8808). Sheltered by pohutukawa trees, the bay is not only picturesque but also the starting point for the **Coromandel Walkway** to Stony Bay, a beautiful coastal track (6 hours round trip).

To get to the beaches at **Port Charles** on the east coast, branch off the Port Jackson road at Whangaahei, a short distance north of Colville. The road back to Coromandel goes via Waikawau and Kennedy Bay.

Coromandel to Whitianga

There are two possibilities for continuing on from Coromandel to Whitianga, both of which involve crossing the rugged **Coromandel Range**. SH25 is the longer (1¼ hours) route. It offers some fine views over the coastal scenery, especially from its highest point (1,138ft/347m), and actually touches the coast at intervals between Te Rerenga and Kuaotunu. Though also only partly sealed, it is certainly easier to drive than the '309' Road described below, which offers no seascapes.

On the SH25 route, the township of **Kuaotunu** is worth a mention as it is popular for its beaches and fishing spots. A scenic drive known as Black Jack Road leads from here to secluded **Opito Bay**.

Those who do not mind narrow, winding, unsealed roads will find the '309' Road to Whitianga just as scenic as SH25 and it certainly gives you a better idea of the Coromandel's hilly, bush-clad interior. Like the Coroglen Road, it goes through some beautiful stretches of regenerating native forest.

The shortest route to Whitianga (around 45 minutes) also offers a number of attractions along the way. First up is **Harmony Gardens**, a privately owned garden with an idyllic setting alongside the Waiau River. **Waiau Waterworks** is a short distance further on and features

Below: *View from Castle Rock, off the '309' road*

Touring Note

The 309 Road combined with SH25 between Whitianga and Coromandel makes an interesting loop. Starting from Coromandel, follow the 309 to Whitianga and then SH25 back to Coromandel. The trip will be a pleasant day's outing and gives you a very good impression of the Peninsula's varied scenery.

various kinetic sculptures and machines, all of which are worked by water.

Castle Rock requires a detour off the 309 just beyond the Waterworks. A one mile (2km) drive up through pine forest leads to the start of the walking track. The hill is in fact the core of an old volcano (a volcanic plug). It requires about 1¼ hours to the top and back.

Further along the road, **Chiltern Reserve** is a good picnic spot whereas the bush-fringed pool at the foot of **Waiau Falls** offers the chance of a dip. Remnants of the Coromandel's once extensive Kauri forest can be seen at the **Kauri Grove**. A short walk through native bush leads to the trees.

After **Egan Park**, where you can also go picnicking or swimming, the 309 Road joins SH25 to Whitianga.

Whitianga is especially favoured as a holiday resort among big-game fishing enthusiasts. For other holiday-makers, the town offers fine beaches, seafood restaurants, launch trips and a variety of other

water-based activities. A ferry regularly crosses the narrow waterway to **Ferry Landing**, the site of an old stone wharf built in 1837. From the wharf it is possible to do a few pleasant walks.

Ferry Landing and a number of other interesting places can also be reached by road via **Coroglen** — the turn-off is a short distance further on at Whenuakite.

Cooks Beach

Cooks Beach is so named because it was here that Captain Cook hoisted the British flag and formally took possession of the country in the name of King George III. The purpose of Cook's stay was not, however, merely to expand the British Empire.

While here, he and his party observed the transit of Mercury and, to mark the significance of these scientific investigations, he named the bay **Mercury Bay**. There is a memorial to Cook's visit on **Shakespeare Cliffs**. You can drive to the top of the cliffs where the view is simply magnificent. A flight of steps hewn from the rock leads down to the untouched shores of **Lonely Bay**.

East of Cooks Beach, **Hahei** not only has a lovely beach, but also offers a chance to stretch the legs in the course of a 40 minute scenic walk to **Cathedral Cove**. The cove lies to the north of Hahei beach and is only accessible at low tide.

Hot Water Beach is situated to the south and is not to be missed! At low tide, bathers dig shallow holes and then bask in the thermally heated water which rises through the sand. Either borrow a spade or hire one from Hot Water Beach Store.

Whitianga to Paeroa

Further south along SH25 is Tairua. This beautifully located beach resort looks across Tairua Harbour to the more expensive resort of Pauanui. The drive, or walk, up to Paku summit is a must when in Tairua as the views are fantastic. Guided tours starting from Pauanui include trips into the Coromandel Range and to abandoned gold mines. Visitors who simply want to give themselves a real treat could spend a night or two at Pauanui's luxury Puka Park Lodge.

The next resort on the coast is perhaps the liveliest of them all. Whangamata has the best surfing on the entire peninsula, and in summer, half the population seems to be made up of bronzed, board-carrying surfies. With the emphasis on the outdoors, holiday-makers can choose between scuba diving, cycling, canoeing and fishing trips. Those without the gear can hire it here.

Waihi

After Whangamata the road winds inland to Waihi. This is the last major stop on the Coromandel Peninsula and, in view of the region's gold mining past, it is perhaps appropriate that the tour ends here at the site of the biggest gold find in New Zealand's history.

The original Martha Mine was discovered in 1878 and by 1908 it was one of the world's richest. After closing down in 1952 the mine was reopened in 1988 as new techniques made the extraction of gold profitable again. However, the reopening was preceded by a protracted conflict with environmentalists who wanted to prevent further despoliation of the region due to commercial mining interests. It is estimated that over a period of twelve years, the new Martha Mine will produce about 300,000 ounces of silver and 55,000 ounces of gold annually.

The Waihi Arts Centre and Museum illustrates the history of the mine with photos, maps and models. The mine itself can be visited as part of a conducted tour. During the summer months, an added attraction is provided by the Goldfields Steam Train Society which runs a vintage railway between Waihi and Waikino.

An excursion to the highly popular Waihi Beach can be done as part of a round trip. Follow the signposted road east to Waihi Beach, where there is excellent swimming and surfing, then return via Athenree Gorge and Waimata. Route 4 can be joined by following SH2 south via Waimate and Katikati to Tauranga.

Paeroa

The Karangahake Gorge links Waihi to Paeroa and was once alive with gold mining towns that have since faded or vanished completely. Following a disused railway through the gorge is the Karangahake Gorge Historic Walkway, a great way to come in closer contact with the history of the area.

Paeroa is best known in New Zealand as the home of 'Lemon and Paeroa', a soft drink made using the waters of a local mineral spring. North of town it is worthwhile visiting the **Historical Maritime Park**. A number of old boats have been restored here to their former glory, including a vintage paddle steamer. Otherwise Paeroa serves as departure point for an exploration of the Waikato: follow SH26 south-west to Hamilton.

• ROUTE 3 •
THROUGH THE WAIKATO & KING COUNTRY

Hamilton

The main road south from Auckland (SH1) leads direct to Hamilton, New Zealand's largest inland city. At the heart of rich farming country, the city has grown rapidly along the banks of the **Waikato River**. Lovely riverside parks and a lake near the City Centre are among the city's chief attractions.

Recalling the days when the Waikato River was an important transportation route, is the *Rangiriri Riverboat* in **Memorial Park**, near the river's eastern bank. However, the best way to experience some of the romance of the old riverboat days is to take a trip on the paddle steamer *M.V. Waipa Delta* which departs from Parana Memorial Park.

Further insight into the region's past is offered by the **Waikato Museum of Art and History**. Along with its collections of fine art, the museum's most interesting exhibit is the magnificent Maori war canoe *Te Winika* (1838). Contemporary Maori carving is also on display and there is a museum shop offering work by local craftspeople.

The direct route to **Te Kuiti** at the end of this tour follows SH3 south from Hamilton. However a more scenic alternative is to make a detour to the west coast via Raglan and Kawhia and to rejoin SH3 at Otorohanga.

The SH3

Of interest on the direct route is the National Agricultural Heritage complex at Mystery Creek. Signposted from the main road, this museum complex presents a fascinating panorama of New Zealand farming from the earliest days to now. Visitors can try their hands at milking cows, stroll through a colonial village or take rides on wagons drawn by huge Clydesdale horses.

Further south, Te Awamutu is also worth a longer stop. St John's Anglican Church (1854) is one of the oldest churches in the country, while next door the modern New Parish Church of St John (1965) can

Above: *Relaxing on Hot Water Beach*

Below: *Disused petrol pumps on the Port Jackson Road: after Colville there
are no more chances to tank the car*

to Te Kuiti

claim an original and
interesting interior. An
excellent, if small, museum
is the Te Awamutu and
District Museum. Exhibits
deal with the Waikato Land
Wars between Maori and
white settlers and the
pioneer days in general.

At the Aotearoa Centre,
visitors can not only watch
Maori carvers at work but
also have the opportunity to
buy their finished products.
Tours of the Otawhao
meeting house, where there
are more examples of con-
temporary Maori carving to
be admired, are arranged
by the Aotearoa Centre.

Raglan to Kawhia

First stop for those who have decided on the longer scenic route is Raglan, nearly 31 miles (50km) to the west of Hamilton on SH23. Outside the busy holiday season, this seaside resort is a haven of peace with a pretty natural bay providing lots of additional charm.

The road to **Kawhia** goes south from Raglan via Te Mata — please note that this road is sealed only as far as **Te Mata**. An attraction on the way is **Bridal Veil Falls**. The waterfall is signposted from the road and is accessible along a short track through dense bush.

Kawhia is a wonderfully isolated little town, mainly visited by local holiday-makers who value the picturesque seclusion of the place. A special attraction is **Te Puia Beach**, where hot water springs rise up through the sands. Friends of down-to-earth food might like to know that **Kawhia Takeaways** is acclaimed for the best fish and chips in the area. If you like your fish fresh, then fishing trips start from the wharf.

From Kawhia SH31 winds its way through rugged hill country to join SH3 at **Otorohanga**. A must for those with an interest in wildlife is the **Kiwi House** and **Native Bird Park**. Here it is possible to get close up views of the shy and semi-nocturnal kiwi. Other native birds can be seen in a walk-through aviary.

Te Kuiti

Te Kuiti lies 12½ miles (20km) south of Waitomo Caves on SH3.

Visiting

Near Hangatiki, turn west off SH3 to **Waitomo Caves**. This extensive system of limestone caves is one of New Zealand's most famous attractions.

Most of the attention focuses on the **Waitomo Cave** with its glow-worm grotto, entered by boat on an underground river. Unrelated to their European counterparts, the glow-worms use light to trap insects on long sticky threads they dangle below themselves. Though found throughout the country, it is only at Waitomo that they shine in such impressive numbers.

Nearby **Aranui Cave** is mainly interesting for its spectacular limestone formations. To avoid crowds during the holiday season it is best to plan a visit for the early morning or late afternoon.

For thrill-seekers, Waitomo has a few other unique attractions in the 'not to be missed' category. The **Lost World Trip** consists of being lowered 328ft (100m) by rope into the depths of the **Mangaopu Cave**. Those who have not fainted on the way down can then take part in a five hour walk through an awe-inspiring subterranean world. If that was not enough

Waitomo

to still the thirst for adventure, then a bit of black water rafting in **Ruakuri Cave** might be just the thing. Equipped with protective hat, torch and rubber tube you are whisked through the cave by a swift flowing stream.

Among the less strenuous alternatives to the above activities is a visit to the **Waitomo Museum of Caves**. The museum has a collection of fossils found within the caves along with very informative displays offering a fascinating insight into the natural history of the area.

Unrelated to the topic of caves, but nonetheless interesting, is **Ohaki Maori Village and Weaving Centre**. Here it is Maori culture that takes pride of place; traditional weavers can be watched at work and visitors can wander through a reconstructed pre-European Maori pa.

Visitors who have decided to spend a day or two at Waitomo could consider an excursion to the spectacular **Marokopa Falls**, further west of Waitomo on the road to Marokopa. Closer at hand is the **Waitomo Walkway**. This half-day walk starts by the museum and goes through some beautiful bush scenery.

Of particular interest here is the beautifully carved meeting house **Te Tokanganui-a-Noho**. It was built in 1878 by followers of the famous Maori guerilla leader Te Kooti (circa 1830-93), who found refuge here from colonial troops. Permission must be obtained before entering the building but it is worth the effort as one seldom has the chance of seeing a carved meeting house of such historical and artistic significance. Inquire at the tourist office.

South-east of Te Kuiti, **Pureora Forest Park** encompasses one of the North Island's last significant stands of podocarp forest; in other words, a forest made up of native trees like miro, rimu, totara, and matai. It is also home to a large variety of native birds, including the very rare kokako. A good place to see kokakos is at the end of Bismarck Road, though this means rising very early in the morning. The Park Visitor Centre is on the Waimiha Road which branches off SH30 between Te Kuiti and Mangakino. The **Totara Walk** nature trail as well as other walks can be undertaken from here.

Onwards

From Te Kuiti there are a number of possibilities for the onward journey: SH3 provides a very scenic connection to **New Plymouth** on Route 5, SH30 leads to the thermal region of **Rotorua** and SH4 leads directly south to the volcanoes of **Tongariro National Park**.

Above: Glow-worm cave, Waitomo

Below: Breeding champion thoroughbreds is a lucrative activity in a country where betting on the horses is an extremely popular form of gambling. This bloodstock farm is located near Cambridge, Waikato

Opposite page: Brian Boru Hotel, Thames

ACTIVITIES

Coromandel

Sea Kayaking

Papa Aroha Holiday Park
Colville Rd
☎/Fax (07) 866 8818
Kayaks for hire

Fletcher Bay

Sea Kayaking

Fletcher Bay Backpackers
PO Box 8,
Colville
☎ (07) 868 8808 or 868 8898

Hahei

Boat Trips

Hahei Explorer
12 Beach Rd
☎ (07)866 3910
Also snorkelling trips.

Hamilton

Boat Trips

M.V. Waipa Delta
Memorial Park, Memorial Drive
☎ (07) 854 9415
Morning Tea Cruise Sundays
10am. Daily Luncheon Cruise
12.30pm, Afternoon Tea Cruise
3pm & Moonlight Cruise 7pm.

Kauaeranga Valley

Tramping

Sunkist Lodge Shuttle
Thames
506 Brown St
☎ (07) 868 8808
Sunkist Lodge offers a shuttle
(on demand) from Thames to
the walking tracks of the
Kauaeranga Valley.

Kawhia

Fishing Trips
Details at wharf ☎ (07) 871 6305

Pauanui Beach

Tramping

**Sharon Johansen Outdoor
Guiding Services Ltd**
Settlement Rd
☎/Fax (07) 864 8731
Half day or full day treks through
Coromandel's wilderness areas.

Thames

Agatha Christie Weekends

Brian Boru Historic Hotel
Cnr Richmond & Pollen Sts
☎ (07) 868 6523
Fax (07) 868 9760
Twice monthly, guests can take
part in a murder mystery à la
Agatha Christie. The charming
old hotel, established in 1868,
offers the perfect background.

Mountain Biking
Price & Richards
430 Pollen St
☎ (07) 868 6157
Mountain bike hire.

Sea Kayaking
Coromandel Kayakers
122 Tararu Creek Rd
☎ (07) 868 7037

Waihi

Steam Train
Goldfields Steam Train
Wrigley Street
Open: daily between Waihi
and Waikino. Trip takes 1 hour.
☎ (07) 863 8251

Tramping
Goldfield Treks & Tours
16 Clarke St
☎ (07) 863 7699
Organised treks in the
Coromandel region.

Karangahake Walkway Shuttle
30 Mackay St
☎ (07) 863 8511
Operates summer weekends &
school holidays, every half to
one hour. Runs from Waikino
Station, Owharoa Falls & Crown
Battery to the walkway.

Whitianga

Dolphin Swimming
Dolphin Quest
c/o Whitianga Information Centre
☎ (07) 866 5555
Apart from swims with the
dolphins, their glass-bottom
boat tours are a good alternative
for those who want to view
the underwater world without
getting wet.

Fishing Trips
Ocean Adventures
8 Laura Place,
☎ (07) 866 5005
Fishing, big game fishing and
diving. Fishing tackle and bait
included in price.

Waipounamu Sportfishing
Ferry Landing
☎ (025) 924 899
Also dolphin & whale watching.

Mountain Biking
Power Cycle Rentals
Whitianga Sports Centre
32 Albert St
☎ (07) 866 5295
Motorised mountain bikes are
also available from a number of
other locations on the Coromandel.
☎ (07) 868 8488

Whitianga Mowers & Cycles 1987
15 Coghill St
☎ (07) 866 5435
Mountain bike hire.

Sea Kayaking
Mercury Bay Sea Kayaks
17 Arthur St
☎/Fax (07) 866 2358

Waitomo

Cave Adventures
Black Water Rafting
PO Box 13
☎ (07) 878 6219
Depart: Museum of Caves.
3-6 hour trips through caves.

Lost World Adventures Ltd
Lost World & Haggas
Honking Holes
PO Box 29
☎ (07) 878 7788
Depart: Museum of Caves

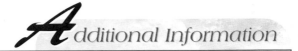

Waitomo Down Under
PO Box 24
☎/Fax (07) 878 6577
Depart: Taware House next to
Museum for cave rafting and
caving (abseil into cave)
adventures.

Whangamata

Mountain Biking
All Terrain Mountain Bike Tours
652 Port Rd
☎ (07) 865 8096

ACCOMMODATION

See pages 288 asnd 300 in the FactFile for the accommodation and restaurant rating guide

Hamilton

Hamilton East Tourist Court $
61 Cameron Road
☎ (07) 856 6220
Also camping.

Parklands Travel Hotel/Motel $$
(Bed & Breakfast)
24 Bridge Street
☎/Fax (07) 838 2461

Thames

Sunkist Lodge $
506 Brown Street
☎ (07) 868 8808
Fax (07) 868 7426
Freephone: 0800 800 838
Bookings for Fletcher Bay
Backpackers at the northern tip of
the Peninsula can be made at the
Lodge.

**"The Thames"
Backpacker's Resort $**
Dickson Holiday Park
Victoria Street
☎ (07) 868 7308
Fax (07) 868 7308
Also camping.

Brian Boru Hotel $$
Pollen Street
☎ (07) 868 6523
Fax (07) 868 9760

Waitomo

Juno Hall $
(Backpackers)
$^2/_3$ mile (1km) before Waitomo
☎ (07) 878 7649

THC Waitomo Hotel $$
Middle of town
☎ (07) 878 8228
Fax (07) 878 8858
An historic hotel built in 1908.

Whitianga

Buffalo Beach Tourist Resort $
Cnr Eyre St & Buffalo Beach Rd
☎/Fax (07) 866 5854
Tent sites and tourist flats.

Anne's Haven $$
Bed & Breakfast
119 Albert Street
☎ (07) 866 5550

Cosy Cat Cottage $$
Bed & Breakfast
41 South Highway
☎ (07) 866 4488
Eccentric decor!

EATING OUT

Coromandel

Coromandel Café $
(BYO)
36 Kapanga Road
☎ (07) 866 8495

Success Café $$
(BYO/Licensed)
Kapanga Road
☎ (07) 866 7100
Specialises in seafoods.

Hamilton

No.8 $$
(BYO)
Alma Street
☎ (07) 838 0631
Non-smoking,
Italian cuisine.

Left Bank Café $$$
Marlborough Place
Victoria Street
☎ (07) 839 3354
One of the best
in Hamilton.

Thames

Majestic Family Restaurant $$
(BYO)
640 Pollen Street
☎ (07) 868 6204
Seafoods are a specialty.

Old Thames Restaurant $$$
705 Pollen Street
(07) 868 7207
Popular among the locals.

Waitomo

Roselands Restaurant $$$
Fullerton Road
☎ (07) 878 7611
Outdoor and indoor dining.

Whitianga

PJ's Bistro & Bar $$
31 Albert Street
☎ (07) 866 5249

The Back Porch $$
111 Buffalo Beach Road
☎ (07) 866 5637
Seafood, New Zealand cuisine.

PLACES TO VISIT

Coromandel

Driving Creek Pottery & Railway
Driving Creek Road
Open: Trains run daily at 2pm
& 4pm. During summer also
at 10.30am. Trip takes 1 hour.

School of Mines Museum
Rings Road
Open: daily 10am-12noon
& 2-4pm during summer.

Hamilton

**Waikato Museum of
Art & History**
Cnr Victoria and Grantham Streets
Open: daily 10am-4.30pm except
Good Friday & Xmas Day.

Miranda

Hot Springs
Front Miranda Road
Open: daily 10am-9pm.

Mystery Creek

National Agricultural Heritage
Close to Hamilton Airport,
on Mystery Creek Rd
Open: daily 9am-4.30pm
This large museum complex
incorporates the Clydesdale
Museum, National Dairy
Museum, Heritage Village
and much else besides. Jet
boat tours on Waikato River
are also offered.

Otorohanga

Kiwi House & Native Bird Park
Alex Telfer Drive
Open: daily 10am-5pm.
June to August closes 4pm.

Paeroa

Historical Maritime Park
Located on SH2
Open: daily all year
except Xmas Day.
Tapu-Coroglen Road

Rapaura Water Gardens
Open: daily 10am-5pm.
Refreshments are available.

Te Awamutu

Aotearoa Centre
1 Factory Rd
Open: Mon-Thurs 9am-4pm,
Fri 2-4pm.

Te Awamutu & District Museum
Roche Street
Open: Tues-Fri 10am-4pm, Sat,
Sun and public holidays 2-4pm.

Thames

Gold Mine and Stamper Battery
Northern end of town
Open: 9am-4pm (summer).
Tours of mine twice daily.

School of Mines Museum
Cochrane St
Open: daily 11am-4pm.
Extensive mineral collection.

The '309' Road

Harmony Gardens
Open: daily 9am-5pm (summer).

Waiau Waterworks
Open: daily 9am-5pm (summer).

Waihi

Waihi Arts Centre & Museum
Kenny Street
Open: Mon-Fri 10am-4pm,
weekends & public holidays
1.30-4pm.

Waihi Gold Mining Co. Ltd
PO Box 190
Open: weekday tours by prior
arrangement. Tours start from
Information Centre, Seddon Street.
☎ (07) 863 9880

Waitomo

Ohaki Maori Village & Weaving Centre
$2/3$ mile (1km) before Waitomo
Open: daily 10am-4.30pm.

Waitomo Caves
Open: Tours of the Glow-Worm
Caves take place every hour on
the hour from 9am-5pm. Tours
of the Aranui Caves take place
at 10am, 11am, 1pm, 2pm &
3pm. Admission is free for
children under 5.

Waitomo Museum of Caves & Information Centre
Open: daily 9am-5pm

Whitianga

Purangi Winery
On road to Cook's Beach
Open: daily 9am-9pm.
Fruit wine tastings and a good
restaurant. Winery also organises a
$1^{1}/_{2}$ hour cruise on Purangi River.
☎ (07) 866 3724

REGIONAL TRANSPORT

Coromandel Peninsula

Air

Air Coromandel has daily flights from Auckland to Thames Coromandel, Whitianga and Pauanui. They also fly three times a week from Whitianga to Great Barrier Island.
Freephone 0800 275 912 or (09) 275 9120.

Boat

During the summer months there is a boat service between Tryphena on Great Barrier Island and Fletcher Bay on the Peninsula.
Contact Aquaventure ☎ (09) 429 0033.

Buses

InterCity has a daily service from Auckland to Thames and **Murphy Buses** depart Auckland's downtown bus terminal Monday to Friday at 1pm. From Hamilton Tavs City Connection also has a service to Thames. On the Peninsula itself Murphy Buses (☎ (07) 868 6265) run daily from Thames to Coromandel, Whitianga, Tairua and then back to Thames. The **Whitehouse Backpackers** in Coromandel runs a shuttle service between Coromandel and Fletcher Bay ☎ (07) 866 8468. Bookings can also be made through the Coromandel Information Centre.

Coromandel Busplan

The Busplan can be used on all the various buses around the Peninsula. There are two versions of the Busplan ticket:

1. The **Full Pass** which includes travel around the Peninsula, as well as the return trip from Auckland.

2. The **Loop Pass** which includes Thames, Coromandel, Whitianga and Hahei on its loop around the Peninsula.

Both tickets offer travel 7 days a week and are valid for three months. For information and reservations ☎ (09) 373 5737
or Thames (07) 868 9088,
Fax (09) 358 3471.

All three forms of transport can be combined with the **Great Barrier & The Coromandel Pass**. This includes the two hour cruise from Auckland to Great Barrier, a 30 minute flight to Whitianga and the bus from Whitianga back to Auckland. For more information freephone 0800 767 786 or (09) 429 0109.

VISITOR INFORMATION CENTRES

Coromandel
Council Offices, Kapanga Rd
Open: Monday to Friday 9am-
5pm, weekends 10am-12.30pm.
☎ (07) 866 8598

Hamilton
Angelsea Street, PO Box 970
Open: Monday to Friday 9am-
4.30pm, weekends 10am-2pm.
☎ (07) 839 3580
Fax (07) 839 0794

Kauaeranga Valley Visitor Centre
Kauaeranga Valley Road.
Open: daily.
☎ (07) 868 6381

Otorohanga
80 Maniapoto Street,
PO Box 152
☎ (07) 873 8951

Paeroa
Public Relations Office,
Belmont Rd
☎ (07) 862 8636

Tairua
Main Road Shopping Centre
☎ (07) 864 7575

Te Kuiti
Rora Street, PO Box 404
Open: Mon-Fri 9am-5pm,
weekends 10am-4pm.
☎ (07) 878 8077
Fax (07) 878 7771

Thames
405 Queen Street, PO Box 545
Open: daily 9am-5pm, (summer).
☎ (07) 868 7284
Fax (07) 868 7584

Waihi
Seddon Street
☎ (07) 863 6715

Waitomo Caves
Museum of Caves Information Centre
Main Street, PO Box 12
Open: daily 8.30am-5.30pm.
☎ (07) 878 7640

Whangamata
Port Rd
☎/Fax (07) 865 8340

Whitianga
Albert Street
Open: Monday to Friday
9am-5pm, weekends 9am-1pm.
☎ (07) 866 5555
Fax (07) 866 2205

4 THE VOLCANIC HEARTLAND

Volcanoes, hot-pools, geysers and crater-lakes are the common denominators linking the tours within this chapter. The region offers much of the North Island's most spectacular and unique scenery, from the almost perfect volcanic cone of the now dormant Mt Taranaki (Egmont) to the sulphurous clouds hanging over the active volcano of White Island in the Bay of Plenty. With its three volcanoes, Tongariro National Park is a popular destination for trampers in summer and for skiers in winter.

A highlight for all visitors is the thermal region around Rotorua, with its numerous mud-pools and geysers. Rotorua is also the heart of Maori culture, where Whakarewarewa Village offers a rare insight into traditional Maori society. On the other hand, keen anglers will certainly want to spend a few days on the shores of Lake Taupo, famed for its rainbow trout.

Above: Emerald Lakes, Tongariro National Park

FROM THE BAY OF PLENTY TO THE VOLCANIC PLATEAU

Tauranga

Tauranga is situated on the lovely Tauranga Harbour and can be quickly reached by taking SH2 south from Waihi (Route 2) or by following state highways 1 and 29 east from Hamilton (Route 3). Near the middle of town is the **Monmouth Redoubt**, a fortified site that was built during the New Zealand Land Wars. Not far away on **The Strand** is the *Te Awanui* war canoe (1973). This beautiful replica of a traditional Maori war canoe (waka) is only paddled on certain special occasions.

Other places of interest recalling Tauranga's early history are **The Elms Mission House** (1847) in Mission Street and **Tauranga Historic Village** on 17th Avenue West. Here the colonial days are brought vividly back to life with Victorian period shops, houses, a saw mill and steam train.

A bridge over the Harbour links Tauranga to the busy port of **Mount Maunganui**. In summer the town swells with thousands of holiday-makers attracted by the golden sands of **Ocean Beach**. As it extends down the coast, there is plenty of room in spite of the crowds. An added attraction is the hot salt-water pool at the foot of the 'Mount', a 761ft (232m) hill that can be climbed for a splendid panorama of the bay.

The route (SH2) now continues a short distance inland into kiwifruit country. **Te Puke** claims itself to be the 'Kiwifruit Capital of the World' and this small furry fruit, once known as the Chinese gooseberry, has certainly done a great deal to boost the town's prosperity.

Kiwifruit

A sub-tropical fruit that originally came from China, it has been successfully grown in a number of areas in New Zealand. Although first introduced to the country in 1907, it was not until the mid-1970's that it became an export hit. In 1990 export earnings reached $450 million and, although the kiwifruit boom is now over due to strong overseas competition, it is still New Zealand's leading horticultural product. The Kiwifruit Harvest Festival is held in May.

Whakatane & White Island

After Te Puke the road returns to the coast which it follows to Whakatane. The town is mainly interesting for the excellent surfing beach at nearby **Ohope**, but there are also several excursions that can be booked here which might easily justify a longer stay.

Especially worthwhile are the scenic flights over White (Whakaari)

Island. This continuously active volcano lies about 31 miles (50km) off the coast in the **Bay of Plenty**. The clouds of ash and steam it belches forth are usually visible from many points along the coast, but nothing can compare to the fantastic experience of actually walking on the volcano itself. Its deeply-rutted, ash-covered slopes are pock-marked with boiling-hot fumaroles (temperatures inside these volcanic vents can reach 1470°F/800°C) and a look over the rim of one of the huge steaming craters allows a glimpse of the titanic forces that have shaped our planet.

Though the island is a privately owned scenic reserve, it can be visited by either helicopter or boat from Whakatane. **Vulcan Helicopters** offer a three hour excursion that includes a 40 minute flight over the Bay and a guided tour of the huge crater area. The tour by boat has the advantage of being much cheaper and includes a 1 hour guided tour of the island. Other organised trips from Whakatane include dolphin swimming, jet boat rides on the **Rangitaiki River**, whitewater rafting on the **Motu River** and big game fishing in the Bay.

Further south at **Taneatua** is the Information Centre for **Urewera National Park** (see Chapter 5). Trips into the park via either Ruatoki North or Matahi can be arranged at the Ranger Station in Taneatua. A bit further east, Route 6 can be joined at Opotiki.

Rotorua

From Whakatane, SH30 moves inland through pockets of lush native bush and past shimmering blue lakes to reach the famous tourist resort of Rotorua. The town lies directly on the shores of **Lake Rotorua**, the largest of eleven lakes in the near vicinity. Spectacular thermal activity, superb — if sadly depleted — stands of native bush, and traditional Maori culture, are the main ingredients that have made Rotorua one of New Zealand's greatest tourist attractions.

Rotorua's steaming pits and pools have been described as 'a foretaste of hell', and judging by the crowds that come to see them, the Devil could do very good business if he decided to charge for his own fire and brimstone. However, the first thing that strikes a visitor to Rotorua is not, in fact, any particular sight but rather the pungent smell of sulphur, which is often likened to the smell of rotten eggs. Caused by a perfectly harmless natural gas associated with the region's thermal activity, it does not take long to get used to.

Anybody planning to spend a day or two here — to be recommended if all the attractions are to be seen at leisure — will find that **Fenton Street** offers the greatest range of accommodation. Visitors who want to give themselves a special treat should try and get a room with a thermally-heated spa pool attached.

Whakarewarewa

One of Rotorua's main sights is at the southern end of Fenton Street: Whakarewarewa thermal area. If visitors only have time to visit one thermal area, then Whakarewarewa is the one to choose. Boiling mud pools, hot pools and geysers, draw thousands of people here every year.

With a plume rising to nearly 100ft (30m), **Pohutu** is the largest geyser in New Zealand. It is also one of the more reliable ones, so there is a good chance of seeing its spectacular eruption.

However, thermal activity is by no means the only reason for visiting Whakarewarewa. **Rotowhio Pa** is a model pa recreating the fortified settlements of the pre-European Maori. The carved gateway is especially striking. At lunchtime (12.15pm), the pa is the site of an excellent Maori folklore concert.

The **Maori Arts and Crafts Institute** next door is also worth a look. Here Maori carvers and weavers can be watched while they work. Informative guided tours through the thermal area start from the institute.

At the other end of the thermal reserve is a genuine Maori village. The villagers still use the hot pools, as the Rotorua Maori have done for countless generations, for cooking, bathing and washing. A curiosity are the graves in the village cemetery which are raised above ground because of the hot earth below.

Another pocket of Maori culture is **Ohinemutu Maori Village**, directly on the lakefront. Of particular interest is the superbly carved **Tamatekapua Meeting House** (1873) and **St. Faith's Church** (1910). The church is definitely worth entering as it is richly decorated with Maori carvings and traditional woven panels known as tukutuku.

The Legend of Hinemoa

Those who want to undertake a cruise on Lake Rotorua, will find that the boats depart from the lakefront jetty, roughly half a kilometre south of St Faith's. Popular is the trip to **Mokoia Island**.

According to what is thought to be a true story, a beautiful Maori maiden named Hinemoa lived with her tribe on the shores of the lake. She was in love with Tutanekai, a young man from another tribe who lived on the island. Unfortunately Hinemoa's parents were not in favour of them marrying. To thwart any plans their daughter might have of joining Tutanekai, they made sure that the heavy canoes were pulled ashore every evening. But at night Hinemoa could hear her lover serenading her on his flute across the broad expanse of water that divided them. Unable to stand their forced separation any longer, she stole away one night and, buoyed up by calabashes tied around her body, swam out to meet him. On hearing what Hinemoa had done to be with her lover, her parents finally relented and consented to their union.

The carved gateway at Rotowhio pa (Whakarewarewa) portrays the two lovers entwined in each others arms.

Government Gardens

Not far from the northern end of Fenton Street are the Government Gardens. What captures most attention here is the highly photogenic **Tudor Towers** (1906), a building in Elizabethan style. This former bath house is a reminder of the days when many people came to Rotorua to take advantage of the curative properties of the thermal springs. Inside the bath house is a museum with some local Maori artefacts and an art gallery. Only a short stroll from Tudor Towers, the **Polynesian Pools** offer visitors a chance to ease aching limbs in hot mineral waters.

Areas of thermal activity

Apart from Whakarewarewa there are three other major areas of thermal activity which, however, are all some distance from Rotorua.

Tikitere

A drive north-east back in the direction of Whakatane, leads to **Tikitere** thermal area (Hell's Gate) where a hot waterfall, **Kakahi Falls**, is the undisputed highlight.

Waimangu

On the road south to **Taupo**, the eerily beautiful **Waimangu Valley** is the site of the **Waimangu Cauldron**, a large boiling lake. While here, it is worth taking the launch trip across Lake Rotomohana to the **Steaming Cliffs**, and the site of the once famous **Pink and White Terraces** which were destroyed in a violent volcanic eruption over 100 years ago.

A popular full-day excursion is the **Waimangu Round Trip** which includes a visit to the Waimangu thermal area as well as a boat trip across **Lake Rotomohana** and **Lake Tarawera** to the buried village of **Te Wairoa**.

Waiotapu

Waiotapu thermal area is only a short distance further south and has the **Lady Knox Geyser** as its crowning glory. The geyser is brought punctually to life at 10.15am every day with the help of a bit of soap. The soap, it seems, reduces the surface viscosity of the water below and thus allows the super-heated steam and water deeper down to release its pent up energy by erupting through the vent! Such an eruption can last up to an hour. Also to be admired are some subtlely-hued silica terraces known as The **Artist's Palette**, the bubbling **Champagne Pool** and **Bridal Veil Falls**.

Excursions from Rotorua

Several other destinations can be reached from Rotorua in the course of a pleasant drive.

Lake Tarawera

An outing to Lake Tarawera, for instance, could be done in half a day. To get there, head north from the city on SH30 until the signposted turn-off is reached. Along the way, the **Blue** and **Green Lakes** are passed. These two lakes are famed for their contrasting colours but are best appreciated on a fine day. A little further on, the road reaches **Te**

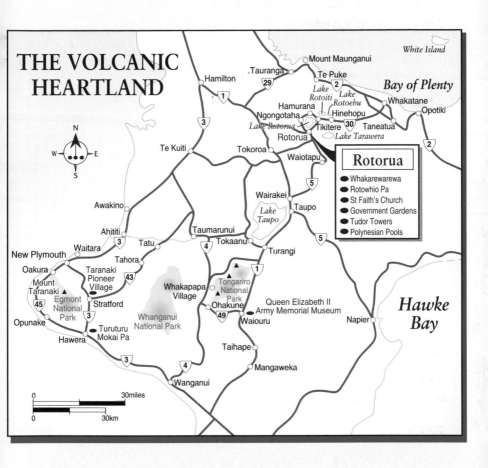

THE VOLCANIC HEARTLAND

White Island

Mount Maunganui
Tauranga
Hamilton
29
Te Puke
2
Bay of Plenty
Lake Rotoiti
Lake Rotoehu
Whakatane
1
Hamurana
Ngongotaha
Hinehopu
Opotiki
Lake Rotorua
Tikitere
30
Taneatua
3
Rotorua
Lake Tarawera
2
Te Kuiti
Tokoroa
Waiotapu

Rotorua
- Whakarewarewa
- Rotowhio Pa
- St Faith's Church
- Government Gardens
- Tudor Towers
- Polynesian Pools

Wairakei
5
Awakino
Lake Taupo
Taupo
Ahititi
Taumarunui
Waitara
Tatu
Tokaanu
5
New Plymouth
Tahora
4
Turangi
Oakura
Taranaki Pioneer Village
43
Whakapapa Village
Tongariro National Park
1
Mount Taranaki
Stratford
Ohakune
Queen Elizabeth II Army Memorial Museum
Egmont National Park
45
3
Whanganui National Park
49
Hawke Bay
Opunake
Turuturu Mokai Pa
Waiouru
Napier
Hawera
3
Taihape
4
Mangaweka
Wanganui

0   30miles
0   30km

Wairoa Buried Village, near the shores of Lake Tarawera (see also Waimangu valley).

Tarawera Landing is situated a few kilometres further on from the village and this is where boats depart for the trip across Lake Tarawera. **Mount Tarawera** itself can be seen on the eastern side of the lake.

Lake Rotorua

For the drive around Lake Rotorua itself, leave the city in the direction of Hamilton on SH5. First stop is at **Rainbow** and **Fairy Springs**. The springs have a lovely bush setting and are teeming with brown, rainbow and brook trout. The trout may be hand-fed and some real monsters can be seen through an underwater viewing window. Other attractions include wallabies, kiwis and the descendants of the pigs Captain Cook introduced over 200 years ago (known as 'Captain Cookers').

Not far away is the **Agrodome** at **Ngongotaha**. Here visitors are entertained with demonstrations of sheep-shearing and can watch sheep dogs being put through their paces. But if your taste for sheep only extends to the chops on your plate, then continue on around the lake to **Hamurana Springs**. There is another trout pool here as well as a grove of giant Californian redwoods. By making a detour north at **Mourea** it would be possible to visit **Okere Falls**, otherwise continue along the lake shore to Tikitere (see above) and then follow SH30 back to Rotorua.

Hongi's Track

The last outing from Rotorua to be described here involves a bit more walking. Follow SH30 north to **Hinehopu** at the far end of Lake Rotoiti. This is the starting point of Hongi's Track, a beautiful walk

The Maori Hangi

Rotorua is one of the best places in New Zealand to try a traditional hangi meal. A *hangi* is a Maori earth oven in which food is cooked by steam. Wood is piled over a shallow pit and then stones are placed on the wood. A fire is lit and, once the stones are hot enough, the remaining wood is removed. Water is then sprinkled over the stones and the food is placed in containers on top. Everything is now covered with a layer of leaves and dirt and left to steam for three to four hours.

Hangi food can taste delicious if properly prepared and the hangi that visitors can enjoy in Rotorua are usually accompanied by traditional Maori songs and dances. Though the large hotels provide excellent hangi meals, the tours that take people to a marae provide a more authentic background for the feast.

through magnificent native bush scenery to the shores of **Lake Rotoehu**, only 1 mile (1$\frac{1}{2}$ km) away. Hongi Hika (1777-1828), after whom the track was named, was a famous warrior chief of the Ngapuhi tribe. On his way to attack an enemy tribe, he and his warriors had to carry their canoes along this track between the two lakes.

On the way back to Rotorua, a detour could be made to **Lake Okataina**. This is the Rotorua region at its most unspoiled. No roads circle the shore of this lake which is hugged in a green embrace of sub-tropical forest. One has no choice but to leave the car and to follow one of the tracks, shaded by the delicate fronds of giant tree ferns.

Rotorua to Taupo

If SH30 and then SH1 are taken south to Taupo, a detour could be made to the fascinating thermal valley of **Orakei Korako**. The turn-off is signposted some 43 miles (70km) south of Rotorua. Access to the thermal area is via a short boat trip across **Lake Ohakuri**.

From the jetty, a path then threads its way past geysers, mud pools and some beautiful silica terraces. Just how colourful the terraces will be at any one time depends on whether enough hot water is flowing over them to create the conditions necessary for the growth of hot-water algae. These orange, pink and green algae can flourish in temperatures of up to 140°F (60°C).

Another interesting natural formation is **Ruatapu Cave** (Aladdin's Cave) with its hot pool. High-ranking Maori women once used the pool as a mirror while adorning themselves — hence the name Orakei Korako which means 'place of adorning'.

Those who take SH5 south will pass **Waimangu** and **Waiotapu** thermal areas (described above) and, shortly before Taupo, nobody is likely to miss the huge clouds of steam billowing from the **Wairakei Geothermal Station** — it can also be seen by those who follow SH1 as it joins SH5 just above Wairakei.

At **Wairakei**, geothermal energy (super-heated steam below the earth's surface that is tapped by drilling deep bores) is exploited to generate electricity. Those interested in learning more should definitely visit the complex.

The impressive **Huka Falls** are only a short drive further south. Here the Waikato River gushes through a narrow gap of rock to plunge 36ft (11m) into a pool below. Other sights in the area include the **Craters of the Moon**, a thermally active valley where visitors can have a free look at bubbling mud pools and steaming craters, and **Aratiatia Rapids**. The rapids were made dry because of a hydro-electric scheme and would have vanished for good were it not for the ensuing public outcry. They are now 'turned on' between 10-11.30am and 2.30-4pm.

Lake Taupo

Though the town of **Taupo** itself is not of great interest, it does have a magnificent setting on the shores of Lake Taupo, New Zealand's largest lake (234sq miles/606sq km). Few people would suspect it, but Taupo's waters actually fill a gigantic crater that was formed in a series of massive volcanic eruptions that belong to the most violent that the earth has ever known. The last great explosion in the Taupo volcanic area took place around 1,800 years ago and covered an area of some 8,000sq miles (21,000sq km) with volcanic debris.

These days the lake is better known for its excellent trout fishing than the cataclysmic events of the past, and anglers come from all over the world to fish in its waters or in the streams and rivers that feed it. Especially famous among anglers is the **Tongariro River** which enters Lake Taupo at its southern end near Turangi. Those who are not keen on fishing can join a cruise on the steamboat Ernest Kemp to some modern Maori rock carvings in **Mine Bay**. A couple of other boats also offer a similar trip.

Though Taupo certainly makes an excellent base for an angling holiday, there are also plenty of other activities in the area (jet boating, tandem skydiving, scenic flights, etc) to keep most people busy for a few days. With this in mind it is worth mentioning that many of the hotels, motels and even camping grounds in Taupo have hot pools attached. A short distance along the road to Napier (SH5) are the well-appointed **De Brett Thermal Pools**.

Taupo to Tongariro National Park

The drive down to Turangi on SH1 is especially pretty after Hatepe as the road now follows the lake shore. **Turangi** is mainly interesting for anglers, as the trout-rich Tongariro River flows close to town.

Trout

Trout are not native to New Zealand, but were introduced in the nineteenth century from North America and Europe. In spite of the fact that they seem to thrive in New Zealand waters, it is necessary to maintain special hatcheries as not all New Zealand's rivers and lakes offer suitable spawning grounds. However, the trout released from these hatcheries sometimes reach record sizes. A brown trout might grow to weigh as much as 35lbs (16kg)!

Of the two species it is the brown trout that is more widespread. Rainbow trout are mainly found in the lakes around Rotorua and in Lake Taupo. One of the more important hatcheries is the Tongariro National Trout Centre near Turangi.

Because trout fishing is treated purely as a sport, trout are not fished commercially and are not available on restaurant menus. If you want a trout meal you will either have to catch one yourself or make friends with an angler!

Above: *Pohutu Geyser, Rotorua*

Right: *Brown trout, Rangitaiki River*

Below: *Taupo Marina, Lake Taupo*

The direct route south is to follow SH1 to Waiouru. This stretch of the highway is commonly known as the **Desert Road** as it goes through a desolate, yet often dramatically beautiful, region of tussock grasslands bordering Tongariro National Park. There are good views of the park's volcanoes from various points along the road.

Those who want to explore the area of Tongariro National Park a bit more thoroughly, should leave SH1 at Turangi and head in the direction of National Park township by following SH47 around the shores of **Lake Rotoaira**. If the weather is fine, it might be worth stopping just before this lake for a swim in the clear waters of bush clad **Lake Rotopounamu**. A signposted walk (20 minutes) leads off the road to the lake which can be circled in about two hours. Roughly 5 miles (8km) short of National Park is the turn-off to **Whakapapa Village**, within the boundaries of Tongariro National Park.

Tongariro National Park

New Zealand's first national park, and one of the world's oldest, was the result of a far-sighted gift. To ensure that his sacred tribal lands would never fall into the hands of land hungry colonists, the Maori chief Te Heu Heu Tukino IV presented the area now covered by Tongariro National Park to the Crown in 1887. In 1991 the park was recognised by UNESCO as a World Heritage site and anyone who takes the time to explore this place of active volcanoes, will soon appreciate the significance of Te Heu Heu's unique gift.

Volcanoes

Of Tongariro Park's three volcanoes, it is **Mt Ngauruhoe** 7,513ft (2,290m) that is most continually active. When it is not actually belching out steam and ash, the volcano's almost perfect cone can be climbed for tremendous views over the entire plateau.

At 9,173ft (2,796m) **Mt Ruapehu** is the North Island's highest peak. Though it is not normally as active as Ngauruhoe, it did produce some spectacular eruptions in 1995. The ash cloud it emitted covered large areas of central North Island but fortunately no lives were lost. At its summit is a steaming crater lake.

Mt Tongariro (6,457ft/ 1,968m) may once have been cone-shaped like Ngauruhoe, but at some time in the distant past a massive explosion blew the mountain's upper section away. On Tongariro's northern flanks are **Ketetahi** hot springs.

Walking in Tongariro

Like all New Zealand's national parks, Tongariro has an excellent system of walking tracks and, if time allows, **Whakapapa Village** is a good place to start off on an exploration of this magnificent, often bizarre volcanic landscape on foot. Not only is National Park headquarters located here but there is also a range of accommodation to suit all budgets. Park headquarters has all the necessary information about tracks and huts within the park, as well as detailed walking maps and pamphlets describing shorter walks.

Starting close to park headquarters is the 4 miles (6½km) circular track to **Taranaki Falls**. A much longer walk the authors can highly recommend takes two to three days to complete but goes through some of the parks' most fascinating volcanic scenery. It starts (or ends) at the **Chateau**, skirts the nearly perfect volcanic cone of Mt Ngauruhoe and takes in the Emerald Lakes, Blue Lake, Red and Central craters and, as an essential detour, the hot springs at **Ketetahi Hut**.

Huts along the way are Mangatepopo, Oturere and Waihohonu. The track exits the park on the Desert Road (SH1) after Waihohonu Hut and transport has to be arranged from here. This walk serves as a shorter alternative to the 4-5 day **Round the Mountain Track**, which it basically follows.

Ohakune

In winter, trampers give way to skiers who flock to Whakapapa Village and the nearby ski fields on Mt Ruapehu. On the south-western flanks of the mountain, **Ohakune** assumes the role of ski village for **Turoa** ski field. This pleasantly situated little town is also a good alternative base for walking in summer.

For those who simply do not have the time to do any long walks, the **Ohakune Mountain Road** leading up to the Turoa slopes offers some compensation, as it is a beautiful drive through some of the park's finest stands of native forest. There are a number of nice spots for picnics along the way and if the hamper needs filling, supplies can be bought from **New World** supermarket in Ohakune even on Sundays. Information about the park is available from the ranger station at the start of the road.

Close to the ranger station begins the **Mangawhero Forest Walk**. It goes through beautiful bush scenery and takes about 2 hours to complete.

South to Taihape and Mangaweka

Continuing south from Ohakune it is possible to take either SH4 via Raetihi to Wanganui (see Chapter 6) or to go via Waiouru on SH1 which is the main road down to Wellington. **Waiouru** is the site of New Zealand's most important army training camp and the main point of interest here is the excellent **Queen Elizabeth II Army Memorial Museum**. The museum deals with the history of the New Zealand Army from colonial times to the present. There is a regular audio-visual display and refreshments are also available within the complex.

Taihape

Only 17½ miles (28kms) further south is the small rural township of Taihape. Because of its central position between Auckland and Wellington on SH1, the town has long been a popular refreshment stop for visitors. In fact, in spite of only having a population of around 2,500 there are some 16 restaurants and takeaways in town! The range of accommodation is almost as impressive, with prices ranging from medium to low budget.

Apart from eating and sleeping, Taihape offers visitors prepared to stay a few days outdoor activities and sightseeing away from the main tourist trail. A major attraction is **Titoki Point Garden and Nursery** to the north-west of town which has been acclaimed as one of the finest private gardens in the country. **Rongoiti Garden**, which lies to the west, is also of interest with its bush walks and native birds.

A good address for outdoor enthusiasts is **River Valley Ventures**. They organise horse treks, canoe safaris and white water rafting on the scenic **Rangitikei River**. Hunting and tramping is possible in the nearby **Kaimanawa** and **Ruahine** forest parks.

Mangaweka

Another base for outdoor adventures is Mangaweka, further south on SH1. Right next to the main road and impossible to miss is the **Aeroplane Café**, an old DC-3 plane that has been fitted out as a tearoom. It is worth stopping for a snack here if only to experience more leg-room than you will ever get in the Economy Class of any modern jumbo-jet. Beside the plane is the office of **Rangatikei River Adventures**. They are the key to a 141ft (43m) bungy jump, jet boat trips and other outdoor activities in this rugged landscape of dramatic river gorges, walled by sheer cliffs of dazzling white papa rock.

From Taihape it is just over 124 miles (200kms) down to Wellington or 1$\frac{1}{2}$ hours via Bulls to Wanganui at the start of **Route 8**.

• ROUTE 5 •
TARANAKI

Coming from the north, **New Plymouth** in the Taranaki region is best reached from **Te Kuiti** (Chapter 3), but another interesting possibility for visitors coming from **Tongariro National Park** is to first go north via **Taumarunui**, then to follow the **Taumarunui-Stratford Heritage Trail** 93 miles (150km) south-west. The road is very windy and some stretches are unsealed, but it allows visitors to see a very beautiful yet little visited area of the North Island.

Before leaving Taumarunui, it is advisable to make sure the fuel tank is full as there are not many chances to fill the tank along this route. An-other good idea is to get hold of the *Heritage Trails* booklet from the Information Centre or DOC office in town. It contains useful information about the various points of historic interest along the trail, such as old Maori pa sites and abandoned coal mines.

From Taumarunui the road first follows the **Whanganui River** west, then turns south through **Tatu** to enter the picturesque Tangarakau Gorge. At **Tahora**, at the end of the gorge, there is a motor camp. Another motor camp is located at **Douglas**, not far from Stratford. **Stratford** is named after Shakespeare's birthplace and many of the

Swimming with Dolphins

Dolphin swimming is becoming an increasingly popular activity in New Zealand and many visitors rave about this unique experience.

Not only do participants get close enough actually to touch the dolphins as they swim about in the open sea but they are also given an informative commentary about the animals and their marine environment. Non-swimmers are welcome on these trips and the chances of getting an excellent close-up photo of a wild dolphin at sea are quite high. Swimmers are provided with wet suits and snorkels and are then taken by boat to where the dolphins normally feed. Such an excursion usually lasts about 3 hours. In Whakatane, dolphin swimming is offered by Dolphins Down Under, but another recommended operator is Dolphin Mary Charters in Kaikoura (South Island).

Above: *Fullers Dolphin Encounter depart Paihia and Russell (see Chapter 2) and the cruise is well worth it for all those who have never seen these fascinating animals in their natural environment*

Right: *You can stay wet or dry for close-up views of the dolphins*

streets have Shakespearian names. Apart from this bit of borrowed glory, the town is most interesting as an alternative base to New Plymouth for exploring the vicinity of Egmont National Park. Of interest near town is the Taranaki Pioneer Village which features fifty historic buildings. Within the complex there is a café along with a souvenir and craft shop.

New Plymouth

Twenty-five miles (40 km) north of Stratford, the small coastal city of New Plymouth is the first major stop in Taranaki for those visitors who have taken SH3 south from Te Kuiti. Though most people come to this part of the country to visit Egmont National Park, there are a few places of interest in and around New Plymouth worthy of a closer look.

The **Taranaki Museum**, for instance, has a very good collection of Maori artefacts, along with exhibits on the region's colonial and natural history. The **Govett-Brewster Art Gallery** is not to be missed if you have an interest in contemporary New Zealand and Pacific art. A special section is devoted to the avant-garde artist and experimental film-maker Len Lye. Among the more important historic buildings in town are **Richmond Cottage** (1853) and **St Mary's Church** (1846) on Vivian Street, which is the oldest stone church in New Zealand.

New Plymouth is, however, most renowned for its exceptionally beautiful parks. Perhaps the most outstanding is **Pukekura Park**, only a short walk from the City Centre. A touch of almost oriental charm is provided by the bright red bridges which arch over the park's two artificial lakes; they provide a sharp contrast to the lush green of the native bush. From the lakeside tea kiosk, a splendid view of **Mt Taranaki** (Egmont) has photographers rushing for their cameras. From mid-December to early February the park is lit up with coloured lights, and hundreds of people stroll through in the evenings to enjoy the spectacles of an illuminated fountain and floodlit waterfall.

Great views over New Plymouth and the coastal surroundings can be had from the top of **Paritutu Hill**, at the western edge of town near the power station. Visible from here are the rocky **Sugar Loaf Islands** which form part of Sugar Loaf Islands Marine Park. The islands are a sanctuary for birds and also for seals which are present in their greatest numbers between August and October. In summer, boat trips can be made out to the islands. At the foot of Paritutu Hill the **Rangimarie Arts and Crafts Centre** offers visitors a chance to see Maori craftspeople at work.

Difficult to miss with its 650ft (198m) chimney, the thermal power station was originally built to burn coal but was converted to run on gas or oil after the discovery of natural gas off the Taranaki coast in 1969. This discovery of natural gas offshore, as well as an earlier find at **Kapune**, has resulted in an economic boom for the region and New Plymouth in particular. The power station is open to the public on Wednesdays and Sundays.

Two beautiful parks within short driving distance of New Plymouth are the **Pukeiti Rhododendron Trust** and **Lake Mangamahoe Domain**. The Domain is one of the author's personal preferences. Not only is it a beautiful picnic spot, but the view of Mt Taranaki (Egmont) with the lake in the foreground makes the heart of any photographer beat faster. Superb!

Egmont National Park

This national park is, as far as most visitors are concerned, Taranaki's crowning glory. It surrounds the 8,261ft (2,518m)-high **Mt Taranaki**, a dormant volcano with an almost perfect cone which is often compared to that of Japan's Mt Fuji. On those days when the mountain is not obscured by heavy white clouds (which can be rather often!), the sight of its snow-capped peak towering above the surrounding dairy lands is strikingly beautiful. A long-standing dispute as to how the mountain should be named was settled by deciding that it can be referred to by either its Maori name *Taranaki* or the European name Egmont. The park, which was created in 1900, is the second-oldest in the country after Tongariro and has, incidently, retained its European name.

Getting there

The majority of people enter the park along one of the three mountain roads.

The closest to New Plymouth is Egmont Road which leaves SH3 at **Egmont Village**. The **North Egmont Visitor Centre** is located at the top of the road and provides simple accommodation, a cafeteria and displays relating to the park.

Pembroke Road goes up the mountain from Stratford to the **Mountain House Motor Lodge** at East Egmont and the **Manganui** ski field. The ranger station is reached before East Egmont and this is the place to stop for park information.

To the west of Stratford, Manaia Road leads up to **Dawson Falls Visitor Centre**. Accommodation is available at the Tourist Lodge next door.

Walking on Mt Egmont

Skiing on the mountain is perhaps the most popular sport during the winter months but otherwise the park is the domain of trampers and climbers. The most popular walk is the 34 mile (55km), four day **Round-the-Mountain Track**. It can be easily reached from the ends of any of the mountain roads which also provide convenient starting points for shorter day walks.

Please note

The easiest route to the summit starts from North Egmont and requires about 8 hours return.

It is only 'easy' for fit trampers under favourable weather conditions. When there is a lot of snow on the summit mountaineering experience (ice axe and ropes) is essential. As the weather can quickly change anywhere in the park, even in summer, it is important to have suitable footwear and to carry warm clothing and a raincoat on any longer walks. It always pays to inquire about track and weather conditions before starting out.

On to Wanganui

There are two possibilities for the continued journey to Wanganui (Chapter 6); either follow the inland route via Stratford on SH3 or take the coastal road following SH45.

Oakura, a short distance outside of New Plymouth on the coastal road, is known for its excellent surfing and windsurfing. There is also some good swimming and surfing at **Opunake** further down the coast.

Hawera, where SH45 merges with SH3, is interesting because of a couple of unusual private museums. **Tawhiti Museum** covers Taranaki's eventful history with life-size figures cast from real people living in the area, as well as colourful dioramas. Attached to the museum is a bush railway. The other private museum has been the work of New Zealand's most devoted Elvis fan: Kevin Wasley. Although a long way from Graceland, Elvis fans should not miss the **Elvis Presley Memorial Record Room** with its collection of rare recordings and memorabilia.

A short distance north of town, the **Turuturu Mokai Pa** is regarded as one of the best remaining examples of a pre-European Maori fortification. Having said that, it should be mentioned that the only visible remains are the trenches, dug-in hut sites and food storage pits. A pamphlet put out by the local tourist office helps explain the historical significance of the place and is worth getting for those who plan a visit. Just over 56 miles (90km) south-east of Hawera is the city of **Wanganui**.

Opposite page: Mount Ngauruhoe, Tongariro National Park

Below: Maori Meeting House, Rotorua

ACTIVITIES

National Park

Kayaking/Canoeing

Plateau Outdoor Adventure Guides
☎ (07) 892 2740
Rentals and guided trips on Whanganui River.

New Plymouth

Boat Trips

Chaddy's Charters
Tickets: Chaddy's Boat Shed, Ocean View Parade.
☎ (06) 758 9133
Sugar Loaf Islands and Marine Park.

Ohakune

Kayaking/Canoeing

Canoe Safaris
☎/Fax (06) 385 8758
2 to 5 day guided trips on Whanganui River.

Yeti Tours
PO Box 140
☎ (06) 385 8197
Rentals and also guided trips on Whanganui River.

Rotorua

Boat Trips

Departure point for cruises on Lake Rotorua is the lakefront jetty at the end of Tutanekai Rd. Among the more popular are those aboard the paddle steamer *Lakeland Queen* which offers breakfast, luncheon and dinner cruises every day during the summer. *The Scatcat*, a motorised catamaran, and the *Ngaroto* both do cruises to Mokoia Island.

Cruises on Lake Rotomahana, which lies roughly 20 minutes south of Rotorua, can be done as part of the **Waimangu Round Trip** (see main text). The cruise itself takes just over an hour.

Fishing

There is good trout fishing in the Rotorua area. **Tourism Rotorua** can help arrange guides or give tips if you want to go it alone.

Jet Boating

Longridge Adventure Trips
☎ (07) 533 1515

Kayaking/Canoeing

Adventure Kayaking
☎ (07) 348 9451
Rentals and guided trips on Lake Tarawera and Lake Okataina.

Maori Hangis & Concerts

In Rotorua, many of the large hotels offer a Maori hangi and concert. The performances are well done and very popular but a more authentic setting is provided by tour operators who take visitors to a marae. Here they learn something about Maori customs before enjoying the concert and hangi. At the hotels it is some-times possible to buy a ticket for the concert only, which is of course cheaper than the combined concert and hangi.

All the following hotels offer complimentary transport within Rotorua.

Kingsgate Hotel
Eruera Street
Freephone 0800 654 685 or
(07) 347 1234
Nightly feast at 7pm,
Maori Revue at 8.30pm.

Quality Hotel
Fenton Street
Freephone 0800 808 228 or
(07) 348 0199
Hangi and concert every night
from 6.45pm. Free pick up
& drop off within Rotorua.

THC Hotel
Froude Street
☎ (07) 348 1189
Hangi and concert nightly 6pm.

Marae-Based Hangi include:
Rakeiao Marae
The Maori Experience
☎ (07) 348 8969

Tamaki Tours
PO Box 1492
Twilight Cultural Tour
Freephone 0800 500 331 or
(07) 3462 823
This is a Maori-owned company
has earned a good reputation
for its informative evening tours.
The hangi and concert take place
on a marae. They also do tours
to thermal areas.

Waiteti Marae
Maori Hangi & Concert
☎ (07) 357 2023

Scenic Flights
Several companies offer
flights over the thermal
regions. They include:

Kiwi Kopters
☎ (07) 347 7575
Helicopter flights.

Tiger Moth Flights
☎ (07) 345 4885
See the lakes and craters in
an open cockpit bi-plane.

Volcanic Wunderflites
☎ (07) 345 6079
Popular for flights over
Mt Tarawera.

Volcanic Tours
Rotorua offers the largest range
of volcanic sightseeing tours.
However, there are also some
interesting tours starting in Taupo
and Whakatane. See also Boat
Trips and Scenic Flights.

Mud 'N Mountain (Wild Trax)
Contact Tourism Rotorua
☎ (07) 345 3264
Highlights: Waiotapu Thermal
Wonderland, Mt Tarawera
& a Hot Swim.

Tarawera Volcanic Golds Tour
Contact Tourism Rotorua
☎ (07) 347 1199
Highlights: Waimangu Valley,
Rotomahana Crater Lake
& Mt Tarawera.

Waimangu Round Trip
Contact Tourism Rotorua
or PO Box 402, Rotorua
☎ (07) 347 1199
This is the oldest and
most famous volcanic tour.

Taihape
White Water Rafting
River Valley Ventures
☎ (06) 388 1444
Rafting off the beaten track.

Taumarunui

Kayaking/Canoeing

Wades Landing Outdoors
☎ (07) 895 5995
Rentals only.

Taupo

Boat Trips

The sailing-boats *Barbary* (this yacht once belonged to Errol Flynn) and *Spirit of Musick* and the steamboat *Ernest Kemp* offer 2-2$^{1}/_{2}$ hr cruises on the lake. Depart daily at 10am and 2pm. Depature point is Taupo Boat Harbour, off Redoubt Rd. Contact the tourist office or book at the wharves.

The **MV Waireka** (African Queen) does a 2 hr cruise on the Waikato River to Huka Falls. Departs daily at 10am and 2pm. Departure point is 5$^{1}/_{2}$ miles (9km) north of Taupo, along Huka Falls Rd
☎ (07) 374 8338.

Fishing

Fly fishing guides and fishing charters can be arranged at **Information Centre**. Equipment is provided.

Jet Boating

Huka Jet
☎ (07) 374 8572

Maori Hangis & Concerts

Maori hangis and concerts are offered by **De Bretts Hotel**, **Spa Hotel** and at **Huka Village**. Contact information office for details.

Volcanic Tours

Paradise Tours
☎ (07) 378 9955
A 2$^{1}/_{2}$ hour tour to Aratiatia Rapids, Craters of the Moon and Huka Falls.

Rapid Sensations
☎ (07)378 7902
Similar tour to Paradise Tours but this time on a mountain bike.

Tauranga

Dolphin Swimming

Gemini Galaxsea
☎ (07) 578 3197
Swim with dolphins from a motorised yacht.

White Water Rafting

Wet 'N Wild Rafting Company
☎ (07) 578 4093
Tongariro National Park.

Scenic Flights

Mountain Air
☎ (07) 892 2812
Offer spectacular flights over the volcanoes from Chateau Airport.

Tramping

Tongariro Crossing (part of Round the Mountains Track):
The **Tongariro Trek Shuttle** departs from Whakapapa Visitors Centre at 8am and brings trampers to the start of the track at Mangatepopo Hut. At the Ketetahi end of the track trampers are picked up at 4.30pm and 6pm.
☎ (07) 892 3897. Also contact **Alpine Scenic Tours** ☎ (07) 386 8918 for details of transport from Turangi or National Park township to the park's various tracks.

Whakatane

Boat Trips
Blue Sky Tours
'Kahurangi Cat'
☎ (07) 323 7829
Trips to White Island.
Takes 5 hours.

Dolphin Swimming
Dolphins Down Under
92 The Strand
☎/Fax (07) 308 4636
Trips are subject to weather
conditions. Wet suits and other
necessary equipment is supplied.

Jet Boating
Kiwi Jet Boat Tours
☎ (07) 307 0663

Scenic Flights
Vulcan Helicopters
PO Box 10 Waimana
☎ (07) 308 4188 or 0800 804 354
Trips to White Island volcano.
Highly recommended. Flights
depart Whakatane airport.

White Water Rafting
Motu Raft Tours
☎ (07) 308 7760

ACCOMMODATION

*See pages 288 and 300 in the FactFile for the accommodation and
restaurant rating guide*

New Plymouth

Rotary Lodge $
(Backpackers)
Willow Grove, 12 Clawton Street
☎ (06) 753 5720
Set in tranquil surroundings 15
minutes from town. Free pick-up.

Wave Haven $
(Backpackers)
780 Main South Road, SH45
Oakura
☎ (06) 752 7800
Fax (06) 752 7733
The place to stay if you
enjoy surfing.

**Aaron Court Motel
& Caravan Park $$**
57 Junction Road, SH3
☎/Fax (06) 758 8712
Freephone 0800 101 939

Balconies Bed & Breakfast $$
161 Powderham St
☎ (06) 757 8866
Good value and central.

Rotorua

Kiwi Paka $
(Backpackers)
60 Tarewa Road
☎ (07) 347 0931
Fax (07) 346 3167
Tent sites, ensuite chalets,
hot pool, courtesy coach.
Campervans are welcome.

Eaton Hall Guest House $$
39 Hinemaru Street
(Bed & Breakfast)
☎/Fax (07) 347 0366
Reservations are necessary
in summer.

Midway Motel $$
293 Fenton Street
☎/Fax (07) 347 7799
Each unit has a thermal
plunge pool.

Princes Gate Hotel $$$
1 Arawa Street
☎ (07) 348 1179
Fax (07) 348 6215
Colonial style building,
beautifully renovated.
Not outrageously expensive.

Taupo

Burkes Backpackers $
69 Spa Road
☎ (07) 378 9292
Fax (07) 378 6803
Central location and a hot
spa pool are the attractions here.

Taupo All Seasons Holiday Park $
16 Rangatira Street
☎ (07) 378 4272
Fax (07) 378 1272
Tent sites, cabins, tourist flats.
Thermal pool and spa pool.
$^2/_3$ mile (1km) from middle of
town.

Huka Lodge $$$
Huka Falls
☎ (07) 378 5791
Fax (07) 378 0427
Royalty have stayed here.
Very expensive, very luxurious!

Tauranga

Bell Lodge $
(Backpackers)
39 Bell Street
☎ (07) 578 6344
Fax (07) 578 6342
Tent sites available.
$2^1/_2$ miles (4km) from
middle of town.

Greerton Motor Inn $$
1237 Cameron Road
☎ (07) 578 8164
Fax (07) 578 3064
Swimming pool and spa pool.

St Armand Hotel $$
105 The Strand
☎/Fax (07) 578 8127
Central location.

EATING OUT

New Plymouth

Tastings Foodcourt $
City Centre, Gill Street
☎ (06) 757 8379
Various food counters selling
Chinese, seafood, wholefood
and so forth.

Juliana's Restaurant & Bar $$$
Auto Lodge,
393 Devon Street East
☎ (06) 758 8044
Stylish decor, international cuisine.

L'Escargot $$$
37 Brougham Street
☎ (06) 758 4812
French cuisine along with
international fare.

Rotorua

Alzac Cafe $
135 Tutanekai Street
(BYO/Licensed)
☎ (07) 347 2127
International dishes:
Thai chicken curry to pizza.

Tastebuds Mexican Cantina $$
93 Fenton Street
☎ (07) 349 0591

Poppy's Villa $$$
4 Marguerita Street
☎ (07) 337 1700
Good New Zealand food
in an Edwardian-style villa.

Rendezvous Restaurant $$$
116 Hinemoa Street
☎ (07)348 9273
Great lamb dishes!

Taupo

**Margarita's Tapas Bar
& Restaurant $$**
63 Heuheu Street
☎ (07) 378 9909
Good Mexican food
and a nice interior.

Edgewater Restaurant $$$
Manuels Resort Hotel
Lake Terrace
☎ (07) 378 5110
Top-notch dining with lake views.

Tauranga

Bizzari Italian Cafe $
(BYO/Licensed)
59 The Strand
☎ (07) 578 9349
Reasonably priced
Italian food.

**Harbourside
Brasserie & Bar $$$**
Old Yacht Club Building,
The Strand Extension
☎ (07) 571 0520
Dine inside or out,
innovative cuisine.

PLACES TO VISIT

Hamurana

Hamurana Springs
10½ miles (17km)
north of Rotorua
Open: daily.

Hawera

Elvis Presley Memorial Room
51 Argyle Street
Open: by prior arrangement.
☎ (06) 278 8599. No admission
fee but donations appreciated.

Tawhiti Museum
47 Ohangai Road
Open: Fri, Sat, Sun, Mon
10am-4pm. June, July,
August Sunday only.

Mount Maunganui

Hot Salt Pools
Adams Avenue
Open: daily 8am-10pm.

New Plymouth

Govett Brewster Art Gallery
Queen Street
Open: Mon-Fri 10.30am-5pm,
weekends & public holidays
1-5pm. Admission is free.

Power Station
Open: Guided tours Wed 10am
& Sun 2pm. Admission is free.

Pukeiti Rhododendron Trust
Carrington Road
Open: daily 9am-5pm.

Pukekura Park
Fillis Street
Open: Display houses daily
10am-12noon & 1-4pm.
Tea kiosk closed Tues.

**Rangimarie Maori
Art & Craft Centre**
Centennial Drive
Open: 8.30am-4pm Mon-Fri.

Above: *Government Gardens, Rotorua*

Below left: *The Round The Mountain Track, Tongariro National Park, is one of New Zealand's 'Great Walks'*

Below right: *Maori Poi Dance, Rotorua*

Richmond Cottage
Gill Street
Open: (November to May)
Mon, Wed, Fri 2-4pm; Sat, Sun,
public holidays 1-4pm.
(June to October) Fri 2-4pm;
Sat, Sun, public holidays 1-4pm.

Taranaki Museum
Ariki Street
Open: 10.30am-4.30pm
Tues-Fri & 1-5pm weekends.
Admission is free.

Ngongotaha

Agrodome
Riverdale Park, Western Road
Open: daily. Live Sheep Shows
at 9.15am, 11am and 2.30pm.
Licensed restaurant.

Orakei Korako

Thermal Region
Open: daily 8am. Last trip
leaves 4.30pm (summer),
4pm (winter). Café.

Rotorua

Polynesian Pools
Hinemoa Street
Open: daily 9am-10pm.
Café & bar.

Rainbow & Fairy Springs
Fairy Springs Rd,
3 miles (5km) from city
Open: daily 8am-5pm.
Shows at 10.30am, 1pm and
2.30pm. Licensed restaurant.

St Faith's Anglican Church
Lakefront, Ohinemutu
Open: daily 8.30am-5pm.

Tamatekapua Meeting House
Ohinemutu
(Opposite St Faith's Church)
Open: Every evening at
8pm Maori concerts are held
at the meeting house. Belonging
to the complex is a craft and
souvenir shop (normal business
hours).

**Te Whakarewarewa
Thermal Reserve &
Maori Arts & Crafts Institute**
South of the middle
of town on Fenton St
Open: daily 8.30am-5.30pm.
Guided tours hourly. Cultural
Concert 12.15pm.

Tudor Towers (Bath House)
Government Gardens
Open: daily 10am-4.30pm.

Stratford

Taranaki Pioneer Village
$^2/_3$ mile (1km) south of Stratford
Open: daily 10am-4pm.

Taihape

Rongoiti Garden & Nursery
Koeke Road - off Rongoiti Rd,
8 miles (13km) from SH1
Open: Wed-Sun 1st September
to 30th April.

Titoki Point Garden & Nursery
North-west of town
(20 mins from SH1)
Open: 10am-4pm Wed-Sun,
October to May.

Taupo

De Brett Thermal Pools
Napier-Taupo Highway
Open: daily 8am-9.30pm.

Tauranga

Historic Village Museum
17th Avenue West
Open: daily 9am-6pm summer.
Winter 5pm.

The Elms Mission House
Mission Street
Open: tours by prior arrangement.
Contact tourist office.

Te Wairoa

Buried Village
Tarawera Rd, 9 miles (15km)
east of Rotorua
Open: daily 8.30am-5.30pm.
June to August 9am-4.30pm.

Tikitere

Hell's Gate
10 miles (16km) NE of Rotorua
Open: daily 9am-5pm.

Tokaanu

Thermal Park & Pools
Open: daily 10am-9.30pm.

Turangi

Tongariro National Trout Centre
Open: daily 9am-4pm.
Entry is free.

Waimangu Volcanic Valley
SH5, 12 miles (19km)
south of Rotorua
Open: daily 8.30am-5pm.

Waiotapu Thermal Region
SH5, 18$^{1}/_{2}$ miles (30km)
south of Rotorua
Open: daily 8.30am-8.30pm.
In winter closes at 5pm.
Lady Knox Geyser erupts
daily at 10.15am.

Waiouru

Army Museum
Next to SH1
Open: daily 9am-4.30pm.

Wairakei

Craters of the Moon
Open: dawn to dusk.
Admission is free.

Geothermal Station
Information Centre
Open: daily 9am-4pm.

Huka Village
Huka Falls Rd
Open: daily 9am-5pm.
A colonial-style craft village.

REGIONAL TRANSPORT

New Plymouth to Rotorua

C Tours
43 Egmont Street, New Plymouth
☎ (06) 758 1777
Connecting services to Rotorua. On the regular buses, this west to east route through the central North Island is very time consuming.

VISITOR INFORMATION & PARK VISITOR CENTRES

Egmont National Park
Department of Conservation
(DOC)
Devon Street West, New Plymouth
☎ (06) 758 0433

North Egmont Visitors Centre
Egmont Road, Egmont Village
☎ (06) 756 8710

Dawson Falls Visitors Centre
Take Manaia Rd from Kaponga
☎ (025) 430 248

Hawera
Information South Taranaki
55 High Street, PO Box 5
☎ (06) 278 8599

Mount Maunganui
Salisbury Avenue
☎ (07) 575 5099

New Plymouth
Cnr Liardet and Leach Sts
Open: Mon-Fri 8.30am-5pm,
weekends 10am-3pm.
☎ (06) 759 6080
Fax (06) 759 6073

Ohakune
Ruapehu Visitors Centre,
54 Clyde Street, PO Box 36
☎ (06) 385 8427
Fax (06) 385 8527

Rotorua
Tourism Rotorua,
67 Fenton Street
Open: daily 8am-5.30pm.
☎ (07) 348 5179
Fax (07) 348 6044

Stratford
Miranda and Broadway,
PO Box 320
☎ (06) 765 6708
Fax (06) 765 7500

Taumarunui
Railway Station, Hakiaha Street,
Box 345
☎ (07) 895 7494
Information on Whanganui
National Park.

Taupo
13 Tongariro Street, PO Box 865
Open: daily 8.30am-5pm.
☎ (07) 378 9000
Fax (07) 378 9003

Tauranga
The Strand, PO Box 1070
Open: Mon-Fri 8am-5pm,
weekends 8am-2pm.
☎ (07) 578 8103
Fax (07) 578 1090

Tongariro National Park
Ohakune
Ranger Station, Mountain Road
☎ (06) 385 8578

Turangi
Turangi Regional Office
Turanga Place
☎ (07) 386 8607

Whakapapa Village, Mt Ruapehu
Visitor Centre,
behind Chateau Hotel
☎ (07) 892 3729

Whakatane
Boon Street
PO Box 307
☎ (07) 308 6058

5 EAST CAPE & HAWKE'S BAY

This chapter covers most of the eastern sector of the North Island, an area blessed by long warm summers and mild winters. Major attractions include the gannet colony at Cape Kidnappers, the wilderness area of Te Urewera National Park, the 'Art Deco Capital of the World', Napier, and the secluded bays and beaches around East Cape. A special attraction around Christmas is the flowering pohutukawa trees along the East Cape coastal road.

• ROUTE 6 •
THE EAST CAPE ROAD

The East Cape is an area rich in the history of the Maori people and many of the small settlements scattered along the coast still have a predominantly Maori population. The stretch of coast between Hicks Bay and Gisborne is known to the local Maori as *Tairawhiti* which means 'the coast upon which the sun shines across the water'. As much of the land along the coastal highway is privately owned, (a fact which is not always immediately obvious, i.e. no fences or signposts), it is essential to seek permission before attempting to camp outside the designated areas.

Above: *Shopping, Napier, Hawke's Bay*

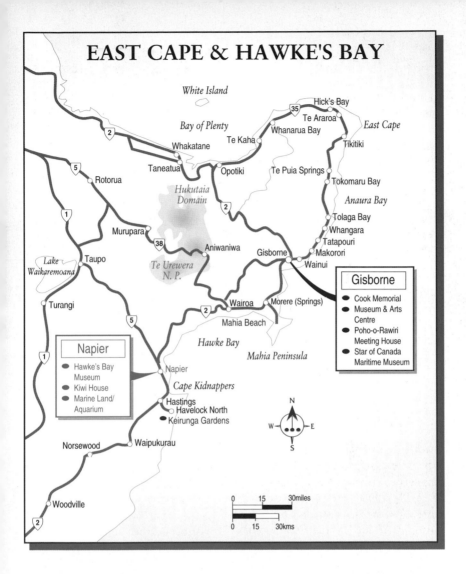

EAST CAPE & HAWKE'S BAY

White Island

2

Bay of Plenty

Whakatane

5

Rotorua

Taneatua

Te Kaha

Whakatane

Opotiki

Hukutaia Domain

2

Murupara

38

Aniwaniwa

Te Urewera N. P.

1

Taupo

Lake Waikaremoana

Turangi

5

35 Hick's Bay
Te Araroa
Whanarua Bay

East Cape

Tikitiki

Te Puia Springs

Tokomaru Bay

Anaura Bay

Tolaga Bay
Whangara
Tatapouri
Gisborne Makorori
Wainui

Wairoa Morere (Springs)
2
Mahia Beach

Hawke Bay

Mahia Peninsula

Gisborne
● Cook Memorial
● Museum & Arts Centre
● Poho-o-Rawiri Meeting House
● Star of Canada Maritime Museum

Napier
● Hawke's Bay Museum
● Kiwi House
● Marine Land/ Aquarium

1

Napier

Cape Kidnappers

Hastings
Havelock North
Keirunga Gardens

Norsewood Waipukurau

Woodville

2

N
W E
S

0   15   30miles

0   15   30kms

Opotiki

Quickly reached from Whakatane (Route 4), the small town of Opotiki is recorded in New Zealand history because of a particularly tragic event. In 1865 the Reverend Carl Volkner, who up until that time had enjoyed the trust of local tribes, was executed in his church by Maori. They belonged to the anti-European Hauhau movement. Although accounts of the killing vary, one particularly gruesome version has it that Volkner was decapitated and that his eyes were gouged out and eaten. Whether or not this account of his death is true, the fact is that Volkner had been guilty of spying and the killing can be seen as an act of revenge. The place of Volkner's untimely death is now known as the **Church of St Stephen the Martyr** and it is here that the reverend lies buried.

Organised outdoor activities that start from Opotiki include mountain bike tours through the East Cape's rugged bush-covered interior and exhilarating jet boat rides on the mighty **Motu River**. For the even more adventurous, there are also white water rafting trips through the magnificent forest scenery of the Motu River's lower gorge — one to five days of pure adventure!

A nice excursion from Opotiki, and a great spot for a picnic, is the **Hukutaia Domain**, about 4½ miles (7km) west of town. This pretty 12 acre (5 hectare) reserve contains a fine selection of native plants, many of which are identified with their botanical, common and Maori names. One of the domain's most impressive trees is an ancient puriri that is known to the local Maori as *Taketakerau*. Over 2000 years old its hollow trunk was once used as a place to inter the bones of important people.

Opotiki to Gisbourne

From Opotiki, SH35 commences its winding journey along a coastline dotted with lovely little bays and beaches.

The first place of any size is the old whaling settlement of **Te Kaha**. The last whales were harpooned here in the 1930's and since then the little town has relied mainly on farming and fishing to get by. Tourism has also done its bit to help the local economy as there are a number of fine beaches, as well as good fishing, in the vicinity. Well worth a look is the magnificently carved **Tukaki Meeting House**, though permission should be gained before entering the marae.

Continuing north **Whanarua Bay** is a particularly beautiful spot and those who wish to overnight can do so at the **Rendezvous** on the **Coast Holiday Park**. Apart from providing budget accommodation in the form of cabins and tent sites, the holiday park also offers instruction in scuba diving and they hire out boats and kayaks. From **Whangaparaoa** the road goes inland before reaching the coast again at Hicks Bay, some 18½ miles (30km) distant.

Idyllic **Hicks Bay** was named after a member of the crew on Cook's ship the Endeavour. Here visitors can spend their time fishing, swimming and bush walking in the most picturesque of surroundings. A feature of the area is the many ancient puriri trees which, in contrast to the pohutukawa, flower nearly all year round.

The road moves inland again after **Te Araroa** and the first place of interest is **Tikitiki**. Visitors should not miss seeing the Anglican Church

East Cape Lighthouse

A short journey further down the coast from Hicks Bay is the settlement of **Te Araroa**. From here it is possible to turn off along the road to the East Cape Lighthouse, supposedly the most easterly in the world. The 25 miles (40km) return trip is best done early to witness the sunrise. For those who do not have their own transport the **Hicks Bay Backpackers Lodge** (☎ (06) 864 4731) arranges 'sunrise tours' to the lighthouse.

here as it is beautifully decorated with Maori art. Further south **Te Puia Springs** is worth noting for its natural hot pools. **Tokomaru Bay** is only another 6 miles (10km) away and would be a pleasant spot to spend a few quiet days by the seaside.

Continuing south those who want to experience a really lovely stretch of coast, away from it all, should take the turn-off to **Anaura Bay**. A wonderful beach of golden sands and a panoramic walkway (2 hours) with views over the sea, are ample reward for the trip. It was here that Captain Cook made his second landing in New Zealand and there is a plaque to mark the event.

Compared to Anaura Bay and indeed to most settlements along this road **Tolaga Bay** is a sizeable town. Not only is the beach here good for swimming, it is given added distinction by the presence of New Zealand's longest wharf (2165ft/ 660m). It was built between 1926 and 1929 to enable ships to unload even when the tide was out. A few kilometres south of town the **Cook's Cove Walkway** is a great chance to stretch the legs. **Tupaea's Cavern**, a natural rock archway linking Tolaga Bay with Cook's Cove, is a highlight of the walk. The start of the track can be reached by following Wharf Road off the main highway. Closed during the lambing season (1 August- 30 September) the walk takes roughly $2^{1}/_{2}$ hours to complete.

The 34 mile (55km) drive down to Gisborne could be punctuated with stops at **Whangara**, where there is a nice beach, or at **Tatapouri** where the fishing is good and freshly caught crayfish are often for sale. Shortly before Gisborne are the superb beaches at **Makorori** and **Wainui**.

Gisbourne

Not only does the small coastal city of Gisborne get more than its fair share of sunshine, but it is also the first place in the world to see the rising sun. This is due to its proximity to the **International Dateline** and extreme easterly position. Perhaps a more important fact for some, is that all the sunshine, and suitable soils, have gone a long way to making the Gisborne region an important wine-growing area, producing some excellent Chardonnays.

The city occupies a significant place in New Zealand history as it was here, on 9 October 1769, that Captain Cook landed for the first time on New Zealand soil. The spot is marked by the **Cook Memorial** at the foot of **Kaiti Hill**, on Kaiti Beach Road. From the top of the hill, a magnificent view encompasses the city with its three rivers as well as the broad expanse of **Poverty Bay**. Near the top is a statue of Captain Cook.

The road up to the look-out on Kaiti Hill passes the **Poho-o-Rawiri Meeting House**, one of the largest in New Zealand. Although permission is required to enter (enquire at visitor information) it is well worth going inside to see some superb examples of traditional Maori carving.

Further insight into the Maori culture of the Gisborne region can be gained by visiting the small **Museum and Arts Centre**. It also deals with the period of European settlement and an old colonial cottage forms part of the complex. Next door is the **Star of Canada Maritime Museum**. An interesting fact about this museum is that it was originally the bridge of a ship wrecked off Kaiti Beach in

New Zealand Wine

In the 1820's the missionary Samuel Marsden planted what were reputedly the country's first vines. But the country's first expert viticulturist was the British resident James Busby. The explorer Dumont D'Urville found the white wine Busby offered him on his visit to the Bay of Islands in 1840, very much to his taste. This was quite a compliment coming from a Frenchman and augured well for the future of an industry that was barely twenty years old! Still, if he could have seen into the future, D'Urville would no doubt have been surprised to learn just how good New Zealand wine would one day be. In 1989 a renowned British wine magazine declared that the best Sauvignon Blanc came not from France, but from New Zealand.

With a mild sunny climate and soils that rival those of the best wine growing regions in France and Germany, it is hardly surprising that New Zealand wines continue to reap international awards. The commercial potential of these ideal growing conditions was first recognised by French, Dalmation and other European winemakers, who emigrated to New Zealand during the 19th century. With the know-how that they brought with them, they were able to lay a firm basis for what is now a flourishing industry.

In fact, the area given over to wine cultivation has increased from a mere 990 acres (400 hectares) in 1945 to over 15000 acres (6000 hectares) at present. Important growing regions are Poverty Bay, Hawke's Bay and Gisborne in the North Island and Marlborough and Nelson in the South Island.

In terms of quality, it is above all the white wine varieties such as Sauvignon Blanc and Chardonnay that enjoy the best reputation. However, the reds are steadily improving with

1912. Prior to becoming a museum it had served for many years as one of Gisborne's more unique homes.

Twenty-two miles (35km) to the north-west of Gisborne, via Ngatapa, is the **Eastwoodhill Arboretum**. It comprises the largest collection of flora from the Northern Hemisphere in the country. The best times to visit are in spring, when magnolias, cherries and horse chestnuts burst into flower, or in autumn when deciduous trees like oaks, maples and ash are aflame with colour. Another 9 miles (15km) further on, **Rere Falls** is a popular picnic and swimming spot.

Above: *Vineyard, Marlborough, South Island*

Cabernet Sauvignon, Merlot and Pinot Noir grapes producing a few good vintages.

Tourists who wish to become better acquainted with wines from Down Under can partipate in organised tours of the vineyards (for instance around Auckland) or enjoy wine tastings at wineries throughout the country. Those who want to add to their collections might consider investing in the *Buyer's Guide to New Zealand Wines* by Michael Cooper, one of New Zealand's most respected wine experts.

Gisbourne to Te Urewera

From Gisborne the road south continues via **Manutuke** on SH2, where there are two magnificently carved meeting houses. However the interior of **Toko Toru Tapu Anglican Church** is also beautifully decorated with Maori carvings. Once again visitors are reminded that meeting houses, and the *marae* on which they stand, are not only museums, but places where Maori gather socially. They are also places where ancient traditions are cultivated and preserved. It is always very important to seek permission locally before entering these Maori areas.

Another 29 miles (47km) further south at **Morere** are the **Morere Hot Springs**. Here it is possible to enjoy the thermal waters in a pretty setting of native bush. There are a number of pools, both public and private, to choose from, but nicest is the luxury of having a pool all to oneself. Several easy walks go through the surrounding forest which contains groves of nikau palms, graceful tree ferns and an abundance of native birds.

The road to **Mahia Peninsula** leaves SH2 at Nuhaka. Hilly and sparsely populated, the peninsula attracts visitors with its fine beaches and good diving and surfing conditions. The main settlement is **Mahia Beach** where there is a small golf course.

Wairoa, 20$\frac{1}{2}$ miles (33km) west of Nuhaka, is chiefly interesting as the southern gateway to Te Urewera National Park. A distinctive feature of the **Marine Parade** is a solid kauri lighthouse (1877) that was brought here from Portland Island at the tip of Mahia Peninsula.

Te Urewera National Park

Rugged, wild and unspoiled Te Urewera National Park is the third largest national park in New Zealand and protects the largest remaining area of native forest in the North Island. It is also the ancestral home of the Tuhoe people, the 'Children of the Mist', who even today live in relative isolation from the rest of the country.

State Highway 38 provides access to the park for those coming from Wairoa and also for those coming from Rotorua via **Murupara**. The northern section of the park is accessible from Whakatane via **Taneatua**. Park headquarters is located at **Aniwaniwa** on the shores of Lake Waikaremoana, but there are also ranger stations at Murupara and Taneatua.

Surrounded by primeval bush, **Lake Waikaremoana** is the main area for activities in the park. The lake itself is not only popular for swimming, boating and trout-fishing but also provides a lovely backdrop for the **Lake Waikaremoana Track** which closely follows the lake for most of its length. A highlight of this three to four day walk is the splendid view over lake and forest from **Panekiri Bluff**.

Walks in the park

There are many other excellent walks in the park varying in length from short strolls to trips of several days. In the category of 'stroll' is the walk to **Aniwaniwa Falls**, only 15 minutes from park headquarters.

Especially worthwhile is the track to **Lake Waikareiti**, a wonderfully tranquil place that can only be reached on foot. The track starts near park headquarters and about three hours is needed for the return trip.

There is a hut at **Sandy Bay** that can also be reached by rowing boat (enquire at park headquarters, Aniwaniwa) and this would be a great place to stay, if only for a single night. Here, surrounded by nothing but the silent grandeur of the forest, it is possible to imagine New Zealand as it was before the coming of man: a land of birds covered by a vast cloak of primordial green. The still of the evening is broken only by the morepork's (a native owl) call, while a multitude of insects, among them perhaps a magnificent puriri moth, are attracted by the warm glow of lantern light.

Moving on

From **Wairoa**, SH2 continues south through picturesque countryside to the coast at **Napier**.

> ## Natural History Guide
>
> The Department of Conservation (DOC) brochure, *Napier-Tutira Highway: Hawke's Bay Reserves and Walkways*, is worth getting for those with an interest in natural history.

• ROUTE 7 •
HAWKE'S BAY

For $2\frac{1}{2}$ minutes on 3 February 1931, both **Napier** and **Hastings** were gripped by one of the most devastating earthquakes ever to hit New Zealand. In that short span of time, both cities were reduced to rubble and Napier was suddenly 9,000 acres (3,600 hectares) larger, as the titanic forces unleashed by the quake heaved up land in a matter of seconds from the seabed.

Napier

Following the earthquake, Napier was mainly rebuilt in the Art Deco style of the Thirties and today the city is considered to have one of the finest concentrations of such architecture anywhere in the world. Most of the Art Deco buildings are located in the inner-city, often easily recognisable by the delicate pastel tones in which they have been painted. Good examples can be found along Emerson, Tennyson and Hastings Streets. However, one particularly splendid example, the **Rothman's Building**, is located on the outskirts of town on the road to Gisborne and Taupo. Visitors can take themselves on their own 'Art Deco walk', using the leaflet available from the Visitor Information Centre. There are also guided walks starting from the **Desco Centre** on Tennyson St.

Marine Parade

Lined with tall Norfolk pines, Napier's lovely Marine Parade lures the visitor with a variety of attractions. Performing dolphins and seals can be seen at **Marineland**, while the **Hawke's Bay Aquarium** has a fascinating collection of marine life including sharks and piranhas. New Zealand's unique tuatara is also on display here.

Close to Marineland is the **Stables Complex**. The attractions here are a waxworks museum and '*Earthquake '31*', a simulation of the great quake. They also show historic movie footage taken before and after the Napier earthquake.

Above: Gannet's Safaris, Cape Kidnappers, Hawke's Bay

Left: Anaura Bay, East Cape

Below: Te Mata Peak, Hawke's Bay

Art Deco

Popular in the 1920's and 30's in France and the US, the Art Deco style was a product of the early 20th century's optimistic belief in the virtues of technology and material progress.

Speed, glamour, elegance and sophistication were the ideals of this new industrial age. Art Deco reflected this by replacing the intricate forms that characterised its predecessor Art Nouveau with streamlined forms that symbolised those ideals and which were more suited to the machine-made objects of mass production. The hallmarks of Art Deco were simple geometrical lines and shapes (zigzags, chevrons, the rising sun), exotic colours and the use of modern man-made materials like plastic,

The influence of the Art Deco style was most apparent in furniture, fabrics, jewelry and interior design, but it also left its mark on ceramics, typography and much else besides. Its use in architecture was predominantly of a decorative nature. Outstanding international examples of Art Deco architecture include the Chrysler Building (1930) in New York City and the Art Deco District of Miami Beach, Florida.

Although Art Deco was applied to individual buildings elsewhere in New Zealand, it was only in Napier and Hastings that it came to be used as a planned feature of the townscape. After the devastating earthquake that struck both towns in 1931, architects had the unique chance of rebuilding entire streets in the styles en vogue at the time (Mediterranean styles such as Spanish Mission were also used). In the depression years of the Thirties the choice could not have been better: Art Deco buildings with brightly coloured facades and lively patterns, seemed to affirm an optimistic faith in the future. The massive rebuilding scheme also provided much needed work —
a positive side effect of the disaster. Today Napier celebrates its architectural heritage with an **Art Deco Weekend**. Featuring fancy dress, Deco tours and balls, it takes place on the third weekend in February.

During Napier's Art Deco Weekend the Roaring Twenties are brought back to life

The Napier-Hastings earthquake is also featured at the excellent **Hawke's Bay Museum**, further north along the Marine Parade. One of the best permanent exhibitions here is Nga Tukemata (The Awakening) which deals with the art of the East Coast's Ngati Kahungunu people. Other permanent exhibitions cover Art Deco, colonial history and arts and crafts in New Zealand.

North of the museum, the **Kiwi House** is unique in that it is the only such place in New Zealand where visitors can actually touch and feed a kiwi. Other creatures kept here include bush-geckoes, native land-snails, moreporks and whistling frogs.

Those in search of a great view should venture to the top of **Bluff Hill** where the look-out offers a panoramic vista of the entire Hawke Bay coastline. To get there, follow the signpost from **Lighthouse Road** at the northern end of town.

Around Napier

The biggest natural attraction in the vicinity of Napier is the colony of Australasian gannets (*Sula bassana serrator*) at **Cape Kidnappers**. This is the world's largest mainland gannet colony, the only other one being at Muriwai Beach, near Auckland. These large sea-birds usually only breed on small isolated islands, so Cape Kidnappers provides a unique opportunity to see them up close. The best time to view the birds is between early November and late February.

There are organised trips out to the colony but for those who want to walk the starting point is **Clifton Domain**, 13 miles (21km) south-east of Napier, near **Te Awanga**. The 5 mile (8km) walk runs along the beach and takes about two hours. As this route is only possible when the tide is out, it is best to start 3 hours after high tide and to return no later than $1^{1}/_{2}$ hours after low tide. Tide schedules are available from the Napier Information Centre.

Hastings

Only $12^{1}/_{2}$ miles (20km) further south of Napier, on SH2, Hastings is set in the middle of the Hawke's Bay fruit and wine-growing region. During harvest season, roadside stalls are literally brimming over with bargain-priced citrus fruits and

Hastings' architecture

Destroyed like Napier in the 1931 earthquake, the town was rebuilt in a similar fashion. There are some good examples of Art Deco architecture but it is the Spanish Mission style in particular that captures attention here. This style is fairly easy to recognise by such features as curving, rounded gables, orange roof tiles and rough-cast walls. In other words if the building looks as if it belongs on a Spanish hacienda, then it was built in the Spanish Mission style. A number of impressive buildings in this style can be seen along Russell, Eastbourne and Heretaunga streets.

Puriri (Vitex lucens)

The puriri is a sub-tropical tree with wood as hard and as durable as teak. It can reach an impressive age and if it were not for the fact that its timber has an irregular grain and is difficult to work, it might very well have been as prized as that of the kauri. The trees produce small flowers throughout most of the year and can reach a height of 65ft (20m). The puriri is only found in the northern half of the North Island.

other fresh produce. There are also several wineries producing some excellent wines, to ensure that those who follow the Hawke's Bay wine trail (contact information office for details) will have a pleasurable time.

Other places to visit include the **Hawke's Bay Exhibition** Centre, with its changing exhibitions of local, national and international art and if you are travelling with children **Fantasyland** leisure park.

In nearby Havelock North, **Keirunga Gardens** with its miniature railway is another great place to take the children. A short drive away **Te Mata Peak** (1,308ft/399m) awaits, with breathtaking views and a fine restaurant from which to enjoy them.

Norsewood

From Hastings continue south on SH2, through the sheep farming areas of Waipawa and Waipukurau, to Norsewood. This tiny place (population 330), was founded by Scandinavian settlers who arrived here in 1872. The few reminders of those early pioneering days are to be found in Upper Norsewood in the **Norsewood Pioneer Museum**. Also close by, in a glassed boat-house, is the fishing boat *Bindalsfareing*, a gift from the Norwegian government. Handy to the museum is a pleasant tearoom where you can enjoy a Devonshire tea on the porch. Woollen garments can be bought directly from the **Norsewear** factory in Lower Norsewood, opposite is an interesting crafts shop.

Moving on

Further south SH2 passes through Dannevirke, another old Scandinavian settlement, and eventually reaches **Woodville**. From here the visitor can choose between two routes to **Wellington**: either go west though the scenic **Manawatu Gorge** and then via Palmerston North and Levin to join SH1, or continue on SH2 through the little visited **Wairarapa** region (see Chapter 6).

ACTIVITIES

Gisborne

Fishing Trips

East Coast Fishing Guide Service
David Dods
☎ (06) 862 7850
Trout fishing.

Kayaking/Canoeing

Bay Kayaks Ltd
364 Ormond Rd
☎/Fax (06) 837 3737
or 837 3818
Tours on Lake Waikaremoana
and also hire.

Gisborne Health & Fitness Centre
4 Whitmore Street
☎ (06) 867 3977
Canoe hire.

Napier

Jet Boating
Hawke's Bay Jet Tours
☎ (06) 874 9703
On the Ngaruroro River.

Opotiki

Fishing Trips

Mark Draper Fishing & Outdoors
PO Box 445
☎/Fax (07) 315 7434
Trout fishing.

Jet Boating

Motu River Jet Boat Tours
☎/Fax (07) 315 8107
The same company also offer white water rafting trips.

Above: *Exhilerating jet boat rides can be enjoyed on a number of North Island Rivers*

Left: *Norsewood Pioneer Museum*

Kayaking/Canoeing

Eastland Kayak
☎ (07) 315 4839

Mountain-Bike Tours

Very popular mountain-bike tours are organised by **Dreamers and East-Capers**, ☎ (07) 315 5577. Trips include a one day ride along the Old Motu coach road which goes through some magnificent scenery and a 6 day tour which allows time for snorkelling, fishing and kayaking along the way. Those with their own bikes get a discount on all tours.

Te Urewera National Park

Tramping

Intercity buses run between Rotorua and Wairoa on Mon, Wed, & Fri.

The **Waikaremoana Shuttle** runs on demand from Tuai to the Visitor Centre and a few other destinations in the park.
☎ (06) 837 3855 or 837 3836

A ferry service operates from the Motor Camp on the shores of Lake Waikaremoana. It does a loop around the lake (with stops) twice a day in summer.

ACCOMMODATION

See pages 288 and 300 in the FactFile for the accommodation and restaurant rating guide

Gisborne

Gisborne Backpackers $
690 Gladstone Road
☎ (06) 868 1000
Fax (06) 868 4000
Originally an orphanage it now caters to homeless visitors. The recently opened **Flying Nun Backpackers** (147 Roebuck Rd, ☎ (06) 868 0461) was once a convent!

Colonial Motor Lode $$
715 Gladstone Rd
☎ (06) 867 9165
Fax (06) 867 4099

Green Gables Travel Hotel $$
(Bed & Breakfast)
31 Rawiri Street
Kaiti
☎ (06) 867 9872

Napier

Criterion Backpackers Inn $
48 Emerson Street Mall
☎ (06) 835 2059
Located in an attractive Art Deco building right in the middle of town.

Masonic Hotel $$
Tennyson Street
☎ (06) 835 8689
Fax (06) 835 2297
A lovely Art Deco building.

Pinehaven Travel Hotel $$
259 Marine Parade
☎/Fax (06) 835 5575
Small guest house with simply furnished rooms.

Opotiki

Central Oasis Backpackers $
30 King Street
☎ (07) 315 5165
A renovated Kauri villa near shops.

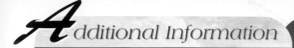

Masonic Hotel $$
Church Street, ☎ (07) 315 6115
Central location.

Tokomaru Bay

House of the Rising Sun $
PO Box 100
☎ (06) 864 5858
Close to beach, free bikes.
Pub nearby.

Whanarua Bay

**Rendezvous on
the Coast Holiday Park $**
Private Bag 1114, Opotiki
☎/Fax (07) 325 2899
Tent sites and cabins.
Hire diving equipment & kayaks.

EATING OUT

Gisborne

Café Villaggio $
57 Ballance Street
☎ (06) 868 1611
A good place to try the local wine.

Marina $$
Marina Park
☎ (06) 868 5919
Lovely old building next to the
river. Good wine list, seafoods,
lamb and game.

Pinehurst Manor $$$
4 Clifford Street
☎ (06) 868 6771
Dine within the elegant
confines of an old mansion.

Hastings

The Cat & Fiddle Ale House $
502 Karamu Road
☎ (06) 878 4111
English style pub food.

**St George Estate Vineyard
Restaurant $**
St Georges Road South
Havelock North
☎ (06) 877 5356
Nice place for lunch on
a fine summer's day.

Vidal Winery Brasserie $$
913 St Aubyns Street East
☎ (06) 876 8150
Also a good bet for a
glass of wine with the meal.

Napier

Golden Crown Restaurant $
(BYO)
38 Dickens Street
☎ (06) 835 5996
Chinese food, also takeaways.

Gumnuts Restaurant $
New Provincial Hotel
Cnr Emerson St & Clive Square
☎ (06) 835 6934
Vegetarian and seafood.

Restaurant Indonesia $$
(BYO/Licensed)
409 Marine Parade
☎ (06) 835 8303
One of the country's best
Indonesian restaurants.

Bayswater on the Beach $$$
Hardinge Road
Ahuriri
☎ (06) 835 8517
One of Napier's best.

PLACES TO VISIT

Gisborne

Eastwood Hill Arboretum
Rere Road (22miles/35km
from Gisborne)
Open: daily 10am-4pm.

Museum & Arts Centre
Stout Street
Open: 10am-4pm Mon-Fri;
Sat, Sun and public holidays
1.30-4pm.

Poho-o-Rawiri Meeting House
Open: contact tourist office
for details.

**Star of Canada
Maritime Museum**
Stout Street
Open: same as Arts Centre.

Hastings

Fantasyland
Grove Road
Open: daily .

Hawke's Bay Exhibition Centre
Eastbourne Street
Open: 10am-4.30pm Mon-Fri.
Weekends 12noon-4.30pm.

Havelock North

Keirunga Park Railway
Keirunga Park
Open: 1st & 3rd Sun of each
month 11am-4pm.

Morere

Hot Springs
Open: 10am-5pm.

Te Awanga

Cape Kidnappers Gannet Colony
Open: The season is October to
April. Transport provided by:

Gannet Beach Adventures
Charlton Rd
☎/Fax (06) 875 0898
Depart Charlton Rd on a trailer
pulled by a tractor. Booking is
essential.

Gannet Safaris
RD2, Hastings ☎ (06) 875 0511
Depart Summerlee Station,
near Te Awanga on a
4-wheel-drive vehicle.

Quadventures
☎ (06) 836 6652
Depart daily on 4-wheel
motor-bikes from Sullivan's
Motor Camp, Te Awanga.
Refreshments are provided.

Napier

Hawke's Bay Aquarium
Marine Parade. Open: daily
9am-5pm. Feeding 3.15pm.

Hawke's Bay Museum
Marine Parade
Open: daily 10am-4.30pm.

Kiwi House
Marine Parade
Open: daily 11am-3pm.
Show at 1pm. Feeding at 2pm.

Marineland of NZ
Marine Parade
Open: daily 10am-4.30pm.
Shows 10.30am & 2pm.

Stables Complex
321 Marine Parade
Open: daily 9am-5pm.

Norsewood

Norsewood Pioneer Museum
Coronation St
Open: daily 9am-4.30pm.

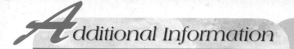
REGIONAL TRANSPORT

To get around the East Cape on the coastal road you need the services of a number of local bus companies:

Opotiki to Hicks Bay

Eastland Backpackers (☎ (07) 315 4870) operate a passenger service to Hicks Bay as do **Hicks Bay Backpackers Lodge** (☎ (06) 864 4731).

Hicks Bay to Gisborne

Fastway has a daily courier service to Gisborne ☎ (06) 868 9080.

Gisborne to Opotiki

Super Shuttle operates a daily service (except Sat.) from Gisborne to Opotiki and Rotorua ☎ (07) 349 3444.

VISITOR INFORMATION & PARK VISITOR CENTRES

Gisborne
Eastland & Gisborne District Information Centre
209 Grey Street, PO Box 170
Open: daily 8am-5pm,
longer in summer.
☎ (06) 868 6139
Fax (06) 868 6138

Hastings
Russell Street
☎ (06) 878 0510
Fax (06) 878 0512

Napier
Marine Parade
Open: 8.30am-5pm weekdays,
9am-5pm weekends.
☎ (06) 834 4161
Fax (06) 835 7129

Opotiki
Cnr St John & Elliott Street,
PO Box 591
☎ (07) 315 8484
Fax (07) 315 6102

Te Urewera National Park
For information contact the
following address:
Aniwaniwa Visitor Centre
Aniwaniwa
Postal address:
Private Bag 2213, Wairoa
☎ (06) 837 3803

DOC East Coast Conservancy
PO Box 668,
63 Carnarvon Street
Gisborne
☎ (06) 867 8531

Wairoa
Cnr SH2 and Queen Street
☎/Fax (06) 838 7440

6 WANGANUI, THE WAIRARAPA & WELLINGTON

Covered here is the capital city of Wellington with its beautiful Harbour, the 'River City' Wanganui and a thinly populated region known as the Wairarapa. Palmerston North is the starting point for exhilarating jet-boat trips through the Manawatu Gorge; Mt Bruce National Wildlife Centre is a magnet for nature lovers and Cape Palliser, the southernmost point of the North Island, is a place for those who value seclusion above all else. At the Cape there is nothing but a lighthouse, a seal colony and all the peace and quiet that anybody could ever wish for.

• ROUTE 8 •
FROM WANGANUI TO WELLINGTON

Wanganui is reached along SH3 for those coming from Taranaki (Chapter 4), but SH4 offers the most direct route if you are coming from Ohakune near Tongariro National Park. It is at Wanganui that New Zealand's longest navigable river, the Whanganui, enters the Tasman Sea and it is this river that gives the city much of its attractive character.

Wanganui

The best way to appreciate the city's location on the banks of the Whanganui is to take the elevator to

Above: The Wanganui River

Spell check

A note: According to the logic of such Maori place-names as Whakatane and Whangarei, the name 'Wanganui' should be spelled 'Whanganui'. However the 'h' has only been restored to the river and the national park. On older maps they still leave out the 'h' in the river's name.

the top of **Durie Hill**. It is reached through a long tunnel and actually ascends through the hill itself. At the top is a look-out tower with splendid views over the city to the coast and even as far as Mt Taranaki in clear weather. Not far away there are even better views from the top of the **Durie Hill War Memorial Tower**.

City Centre

Taking the elevator back down again, the City Centre is only a short walk away over **City Bridge**. Continue up **Victoria Avenue**. Wanganui's main shopping thoroughfare has undergone a complete facelift in recent years and many of the old colonial buildings have been restored to their former glory. Further along the avenue a glance to the right will reveal a hill upon which the visitor will find Wanganui's main cultural attractions.

First and foremost is the excellent **Whanganui Regional Museum**. Its Maori collection, featuring a huge war canoe that could hold 70 men, is one of New Zealand's finest. Other displays deal with colonial and natural history — note the skeletons of extinct moas in the New Zealand birds section. Also not to be missed is a collection of Maori portraits by Gottfried Lindauer (1839-1926).

Nearby the **Sergeant Art Gallery** houses a collection of paintings from the nineteenth and twentieth centuries. Important New Zealand artists represented here include J.C. Hoyte, John Gully and C.F. Goldie. Outside the building presents a rather Mediterranean aspect with its domed roof and surrounding palms.

Maori culture comes to the fore again at **Putiki Church** in Anaua Street. Though plain from the outside, the interior of the church is magnificently decorated with carvings and woven wall panels (tukutuku). However, if old river boats are more to your taste, then a visit to the wreck of the paddle steamer Waimarie, near the **Wanganui Riverboat Centre** on Taupo Quay, might be of interest. The 102ft (34m) boat is being restored and should be back on the river in 2 or 3 years.

Other attractions

There are a number of pleasant parks scattered around the city, where visitors can stretch their legs or take a picnic. Perhaps loveliest of all is **Virginia Lake**, about half a mile (1km) north of the City Centre along Great North Road (head in the direction of New Plymouth). **Kowhai Park**, with its imaginative children's playground, is on the same side of the river as Durie Hill. It spreads along the river bank near **Dublin Street Bridge** but can also be reached by crossing City Bridge and then following a path along the river.

River trip

The highlight of any visit to Wanganui — for many perhaps the highlight — is a river trip. One of the more romantic ways to do this, is to board the historic paddle steamer *Otunui* (1908). The old riverboat sails to a number of destinations along the river but the trip to **Holly Lodge Winery** is especially popular. There are also jet boats operating on the river for those who like a faster pace.

An interesting day trip from Wanganui is the excursion to **Bushy Park**, some 15 miles (24km) away. To get there drive in the direction of New Plymouth as far as **Kai Iwi**, then turn off to the right and follow the side road another 5 miles (8km). The scenic reserve features an historic homestead built in 1906 and easy walks through native bush. If you want a change from sterile motel rooms, accommodation is also available at the homestead which offers guests a unique colonial atmosphere at very reasonable prices.

The Whanganui River Road

The Whanganui River Road follows the Whanganui River from Wanganui

to Pipiriki, 49 miles (79km) north of the city. The partly unsealed road takes visitors into a remote part of New Zealand steeped in Maori and colonial history. Sprinkled along the way, tiny Maori settlements with names like Atene (Athens) and Hiruharama (Jerusalem) act as reminders of early missionary activity in the area. About 14 miles (23km) short of Pipiriki is the restored **Kawana Flour Mill**. Flour was first ground here in 1854 and the mill operated for over 50 years before falling into disuse. Next to the mill is a colonial style cottage that once belonged to the miller.

Pipiriki serves as a gateway to the rugged beauty of Whanganui National Park. In the days when riverboats regularly plied the river, the settlement boasted an elegant hotel with guests from all over the world. Fire destroyed the hotel in 1959 and at present the only place to stay is a simple campsite. The DOC office provides information about the park and a small museum housed in a colonial cottage has exhibits on the history of the river and Pipiriki. Also of interest in the village is the *MV Ongarue*, an old riverboat built in 1903 and now displayed on land.

The return trip is made by continuing north-east to **Raetihi**, then following scenic SH4 back to Wanganui. The entire journey covers 112 miles (180km) and motorists should note that there are no petrol stations between **Upokongaro** at the south end and Raetihi at the north end.

If you do not have your own transport — or even if you do — a great way to explore the **River Road** is with the "Mail Bus" which leaves Wanganui each weekday. The driver provides a commentary on places of scenic and historic interest and also stops at various points along the way.

If you are travelling under your own steam, it is well worth getting hold of the DOC pamphlet *The River Road Scenic and Historic Drive*, available at the DOC office or tourist information in Wanganui. Also available at these places is the very detailed booklet *A Motorist's Guide to the Wanganui River Road* by Judith Crawley.

Whanganui National Park

The main attraction of this park is of course the **Whanganui River**, New Zealand's second longest, which commences its 204 mile (329km) journey to the sea on the flanks of **Mt Tongariro**. But the park also protects one of the most remote areas of wilderness in the central North Island. Largely untouched tracts of podocarp-broadleaf forest, alive with native birds, are only accessible to canoeists or to those prepared to shoulder their backpacks for several days along the park's main hiking trails.

The river has a long history as a transportation route. In pre-European times the Maori used it as a link between the coast and the North Island's rugged interior.

With the arrival of European settlers, a steamer service was eventually established between the two main settlements of **Wanganui** and **Taumarunui**. The first riverboat commenced operation in 1886 and before long there was a fleet of twelve boats serving isolated farming communities along the river.

Due to the magnificent scenery tourism was also quick to develop on the river and the three day trip between the two main settlements became a must for visitors to the country. To cope with the boom the luxury hotel **Pipiriki House** was built in 1892 and in one year (1905) 12,000 guests were recorded as having stayed here. By the 1920's however the boom was over.

The decline of the riverboat industry was coupled with several factors. Erosion, difficulty of access and the sheer ruggedness of the landscape, forced many farmers along the stretch of river north of Pipiriki to abandon their farms. Rising costs and the development of road and rail dealt the final blow and steamer services ended in 1958.

Since then, however, tourism has revived on the river, with jet-boating and canoeing becoming increasingly popular activities.

Whanganui canoe tour

The canoe trip down the river from Taumarunui to Pipiriki, right through the middle of the park, is one of the most enjoyable outdoor experiences that a visitor to New Zealand can have. Riverside camping, narrow gorges and dense forest reaching right down to the water's edge, are highlights of this 4-5 day paddle tour. Because of the river's gentle gradient, the trip is also suitable for the inexperienced.

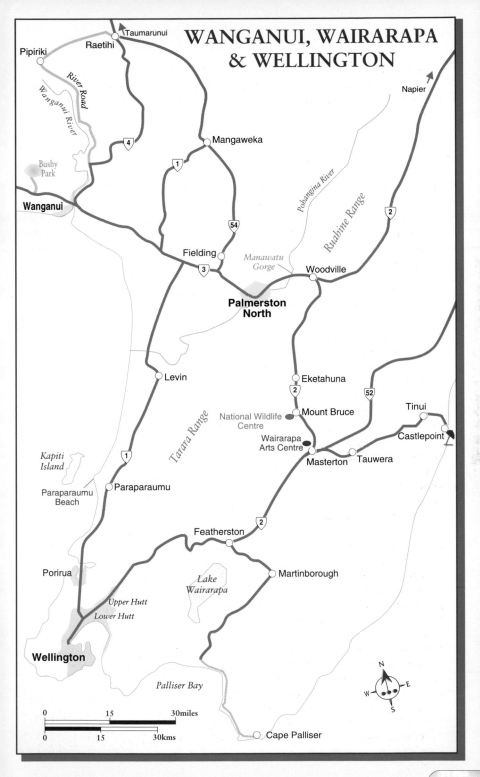

WANGANUI, WAIRARAPA & WELLINGTON

Napier

Pipiriki
Raetihi
Taumarunui

River Road

Wanganui River

Bushy Park

Mangaweka

4

1

Wanganui

Pohangina River

Ruahine Range

2

54

Fielding

3

Manawatu Gorge

Woodville

Palmerston North

Levin

Eketahuna

2

52

Tinui

Tararua Range

National Wildlife Centre

Mount Bruce

Castlepoint

Wairarapa Arts Centre

Kapiti Island

Masterton

Tauwera

1

Paraparaumu

Paraparaumu Beach

Featherston

2

Porirua

Lake Wairarapa

Martinborough

Upper Hutt
Lower Hutt

Wellington

Palliser Bay

N
W — E
S

0   15   30miles

0   15   30kms

Cape Palliser

147

Walking in the Park

Tramping in Whanganui National Park is made somewhat complicated because of the need to arrange transport. As the two main tracks either start or end on the Whanganui River, a jet boat must be arranged to pick you up or drop you off before setting out. Both the **Matemateonga Walkway** and the **Mangapurua Track** are easy 3-4 day walks. The latter is given a bit of historical interest by the 'Bridge to Nowhere'. This large concrete structure was built in 1936, at a time when many settler-farmers were already leaving the isolated Mangapurua Valley. By 1942 the valley was completely abandoned. Regenerating forest has now covered the approaches to the bridge, which remains as a poignant symbol of the settlers' vain attempt to cultivate the land.

From Wanganui, SH3 continues south to **Palmerston North**. This university town has no major attractions to hold the tourist's interest, though the **Science Centre and Manawatu Museum** is worth a visit. A jet-boat trip through the scenic **Manawatu Gorge** might also justify a longer stay. The visitor information office on The Square will have details of this and other activities in the area.

The Wairarapa

The Wairarapa region is reached by first travelling east through the Manawatu Gorge in the direction of Woodville. From here SH2 runs south through sheep and dairy farming country to the National Wildlife Centre at **Mount Bruce**.

Another 6 miles (10km) south of the National Wildlife Centre is the **Mt Bruce Pioneer Museum**. It prides itself as being Wairarapa's largest private museum with items ranging from waterwheels to gramophones.

Mt Bruce Wildlife Centre

The Wildlife Centre is fascinating for anybody who has an interest in New Zealand's unique fauna. Here it is possible to see some of the rarest birds and reptiles in the world. A track leads through beautiful forest, past large outdoor aviaries where the habitat of native birds is simulated as closely as possible. The visitor can see kokakos, saddlebacks, keas and kakapos, all of which are found no where else but in New Zealand. In the nocturnal house there are not only kiwis but also the rare tuatara, a lizard-like survivor from the age of the dinosaurs. One of the prize exhibits is the takahe, a large flightless bird that was presumed extinct until it was rediscovered in 1948. The breeding schemes and research carried out at the Centre play a vital role in the survival of the takahe and the country's other endangered species.

Masterton

Next stop is Masterton, the main area of the Wairarapa. The biggest attraction this prosperous farming town has to offer is the annual 'Golden Shears' shearing competition. Contestants come from all over New Zealand and overseas to demonstrate their skills at sheep-shearing. A top shearer can remove the wool from a sheep in less than a minute, but the judges also control the quality of the shearing and not just the speed.

Worth a longer look is the **Wairarapa Arts Centre**. Of particular interest here is the **Stidolph Museum of Early Childhood** with its collection of clockwork toys and antique dolls. There are also regular art and craft exhibitions held at the Centre.

Castlepoint

Those who want to explore a little more of the Wairarapa's rugged and sparsely populated hill country should consider making an excursion from Masterton to Castlepoint on the coast. The road goes via Tauweru and Tinui, a distance of 41 miles (66km).

The first thing visitors will notice about this little seaside settlement is the lighthouse, built in 1913 and one of the tallest in the country (75ft/23m). There is good swimming in a sheltered lagoon known as the 'Basin' and even a golf course. The annual race meeting, held in March on the sandy beach, has a tradition reaching back to last century. As there is accommodation (motel, camping grounds) and a store, Castlepoint would be a nice,

if very remote, place to escape the tourist crowds.

Featherston

Featherston lies 22 miles (36km) south of Masterton on SH2, close to the shores of **Lake Wairarapa**. Railway enthusiasts in particular, will want to pause here to see the town's **Fell Engine Museum**.

The Fell engine was designed to climb the steep **Rimutaka Incline** over the Rimutaka Range that separates Wellington from the Wairarapa. With a gradient of 1:15 to overcome, the locomotives could only manage a top speed of 3mph (5km/h) for the 3 mile (4.8km) journey up. The Fell engines were operated for 77 years, until the building of a

Cape Palliser

A side trip for the more adventurous is to the most southerly point of the North Island at Cape Palliser. To get there, continue on from Martinborough in the direction of **Lake Ferry**, a tiny fishing settlement. Shortly before Lake Ferry there is a turn-off to Whangaimoana. From now on the road is largely unsealed as it follows the rugged, exposed coastline to the Cape. Drivers should note that several streams have to be forded which can be dangerous after heavy rain. At the Cape there is a lighthouse and the North Island's largest seal colony.

Above: *Sheep Farm, Palliser Bay, Wellington*

Right: *Woodward Street, Wellington*

Below: *Wellington Harbour*

tunnel in 1955 made them obsolete. The beautifully restored engine on display is supposedly the only remaining Fell locomotive in the world.

A walkway (4 hours one way) now follows the Incline. It can be reached by taking Western Lake Road south.

To the south-east of Featherston is a wine growing district around **Martinborough**. Those who want to do their own tour of the vineyards should pick up the relevant brochure at the Information Centre in Masterton.

From Featherston the main road winds its way over the windswept but very scenic Rimutaka Range before descending into the Hutt Valley to reach Wellington.

Wellington

Tucked in between steep hills and a beautiful bay is New Zealand's capital city, **Wellington**. Nicknamed 'Windy Wellington' the weather here can be capricious to say the least. On a fine summer's day when the sunlight reflects off the waters of **Oriental Bay** and on the surrounding hills, the red or blue painted tin roofs of the houses form intense spots of colour in the crystal clear air. There can be little doubt that the city is one of the loveliest in the world.

Architecturally too the city has much to offer. It is fascinating just to walk around the downtown area, through narrow canyons formed by glass-fronted skyscrapers to be suddenly surprised by a quaint relic from the Victorian era or an impressive example of post-modernist design. Steep flights of steps climb up past boutiques and snack bars, a

spacious square provides unexpected respite from the chaos of city traffic; everywhere there seem to be nooks and crannies waiting to be explored. In fact a walk around the inner city is as easy as it is rewarding; Wellington's geographical situation has left little room for expansion except up and most places of interest are quickly reached on foot.

Parking tip

For those who have arrived by car a good place to park is near the Maritime Museum at Queen's Wharf, Jervois Quay. There is usually plenty of room here and it is not far to the City Centre. Another car park that is very handy is at the Michael Fowler Centre, Wakefield Street. Finding free parking in downtown Wellington is time consuming and for visitors probably a fruitless exercise.

City walk

If a walk around the city is started on Queen's Wharf then the first place of interest is the **Maritime Museum**. On display here is a large-scale model of the Harbour, model ships and other maritime memorabilia. A perfect way of rounding off the museum visit is to depart on a Harbour cruise with the **East by West Ferry**, only a short stroll away.

However, land-lovers might prefer to walk through nearby **Frank Kitts Park**, a nice place to sit and just watch the boats go by. From here, cross Jervois Quay — not on the

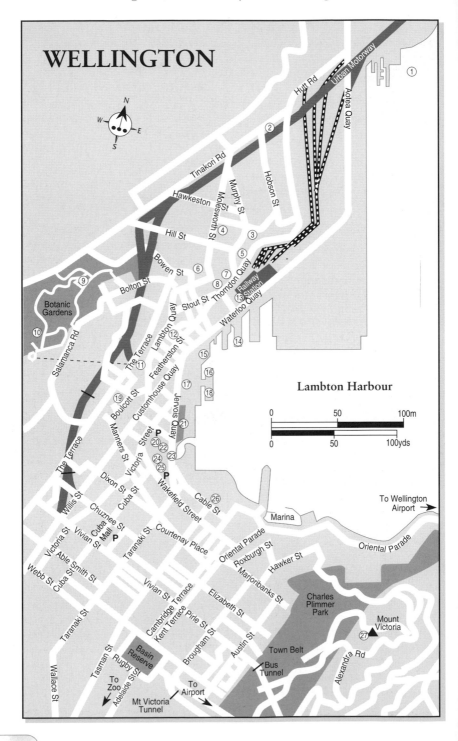

WELLINGTON

Lambton Harbour

0   50   100m

0   50   100yds

To Wellington Airport →

KEY	Wellington			
①	Cook Strait Ferry Terminal		⑫	Central Police Station
②	Katherine Mansfield's Birth Place		⑬	Post Office
③	Old St Paul's		⑭	Waterloo Quay
④	National Library & Alexander		⑮	Customhouse Quay
	Turnbull Library		⑯	East by West Ferry (Harbour Cruises)
⑤	National Archives and the Portrait		⑰	Maritime Museum
	Gallery		⑱	Queen's Wharf
⑥	Beehive		⑲	Antrim House & Dept of Conservation
⑦	City Bus Depot		⑳	Public Library
⑧	Old Gvt. Buildings		㉑	Frank Kitts Park
⑨	Lady Norwood Rose Gardens		㉒	City Art Gallery
⑩	New Zealand Astronomy Centre		㉓	City to Sea Bridge
⑪	Kelburn Cable Car		㉔	Capital Discovery Place
			㉕	Michael Fowler Centre
			㉖	Museum of New Zealand
			㉗	Mount Victoria Lookout

first footbridge but on the second, larger one. This unusually designed wooden structure is known as the 'City to Sea Bridge' and is decorated with modern sculptures. It leads to **Civic Square**, one of the city's architectural highlights.

The first thing to do in the square is to arm oneself with a free map and a few useful brochures from the Information Centre. Of interest on the square itself is the **Capital Discovery Place**, a science area designed for children, the **Michael Fowler Centre**, where concerts are held, and the **Wellington City Art Gallery**. An interesting feature of the public library, at the north end of the square, is the 'nikau palm' columns on the outside of the building. The building was designed by Ian Athfield, one of New Zealand's leading architects.

The Museum of New Zealand — Te Papa Tongarewa

The museum has been moved from its old site at Buckle Street and is now to be found on Cable Street. It can be reached by continuing south-east from the Civic Centre along Cable Street and would make a good alternative starting point for a stroll around town. Another architectural *tour de force*, the building's interior, has been designed to reflect the fact that New Zealand is a land of two different cultures. This is realised architectonically by linking the display rooms devoted to Maori and Pakeha culture by bridges, and by making the triangular room which is dedicated to the Treaty of Waitangi the architectonic heart of the building.

The museum's Maori and Pacific Island collections are outstanding and they alone would justify a visit. Especially noteworthy is a carved meeting house from near Gisborne that was built around 1842 and the exhibition of polynesian sailing vessels. In the *People of New Zealand* exhibition, light is shed on various important events in the country's colonial history.

Above: A modern skyscraper dwarfs one of Wellington's old wooden buildings

Below: Civic Square, Wellington

From Civic Square continue along Mercer Street, then turn left on Willis Street, one of the main shopping thoroughfares. After passing the imposing **Majestic Tower** building turn right, up Manners Street, to Boulcott Street. Here you can visit historic **Antrim House** (1905), an Edwardian building that is now headquarters of the Historic Places Trust. Plimmer Steps, a short distance further on, lead down to busy **Lambton Quay**.

A pleasant detour can be made from Lambton Quay by taking the cable car up to **Kelburn**. At the top there is a restaurant with superb views over the city and Harbour. An alternative place to have lunch or a snack is in the nearby **Botanic Gardens**. The Tea House is located in the Lady Norwood Rose Garden. Also in the gardens, near the upper cable car terminus, is the **New Zealand Astronomy Centre** with its planetarium. Return the same way.

Continue north along Lambton Quay, until you reach the intersection with Bowen and Whitmore Street. Across the intersection, on

the right, is the **Old Government Building**. Built in 1876 it is the second largest wooden building in the world, only a temple in Japan is larger.

On the opposite side of the road is the Parliament Buildings complex with the distinctive **Beehive**. Designed by British architect Sir Basil Spence and completed in 1981, the aptly named building houses all the ministerial offices, including that of the Prime Minister. A tour of the Beehive and the **House of Representatives** can be arranged ☎ 471-94577.

The **National Library** complex is only a short distance away, on the corner of Molesworth and Aitken Street. Apart from housing the most comprehensive collection of books in the country, the library also has a gallery where art exhibitions are held. Incorporated within the complex is the **Alexander Turnbull Library** with its important collection of historical manuscripts and photographs relating to New Zealand's colonial past.

Continue down Aitken Street to Mulgrave Street where art and the past is again the subject at the **National Archives**. Displayed here for posterity is the original Treaty of Waitangi together with other important early New Zealand documents. In the same building is the **New Zealand Portrait Gallery**.

Just a few metres up the road the penultimate stop on this walk is **Old St. Paul's** (1866). The church does not look much from outside but the magnificent wooden interior is English Gothic at its best. It is hard to believe that for a long time it was in danger of being pulled down! Today most would agree that the church that was built to replace it as a cathedral (St. Paul's Anglican Cathedral, Molesworth Street) has none of the charm of its predecessor.

By continuing along Murphy Street and then turning right into Tinakori Road you will eventually reach **Katherine Mansfield's Birthplace**. New Zealand's most famous short story writer was born here in 1888 as Kathleen Beauchamp. Though she only lived at 25 Tinakori Road for the first few years of her childhood, the house is mentioned in her stories *Prelude* and *A Birthday*. An interesting video provides background to her life and there is also a display of photographs from the period, along with excerpts from her writing.

The slightly more direct route back to the starting point is to go via Featherston Street. Otherwise return the same way along Lambton Quay where there are several good bookshops to browse through. The Quay, by the way, really did once mark Wellington's waterfront. Lack of suitable building space in the inner-city meant that land reclamation had already begun in the nineteenth century and is continuing to this day.

Around Wellington

A number of Wellington's other attractions lie somewhat further afield and are best visited either by car or bus. **Wellington Zoo** is $2\frac{1}{2}$ miles (4km) from the City Centre in the suburb of Newtown. Apart from typical zoo animals like lions and chimpanzees there are also some New Zealand originals here such as kiwis, giant wetas and tuataras.

Kapiti Island

Kapiti Island lies a short distance off the coast near Paraparaumu, a town situated on SH1 north-west of Wellington. In the early 19th century the island was a base for the marauding expeditions led by the warrior chief Te Rauparaha. Skilled in warfare and aware of the advantages of Pakeha technology, the 'Maori Napoleon' armed his warriors with muskets before embarking on a campaign of conquest that decimated rival tribes as far south as Kaiapoi, in the vicinity of Christchurch.

These days the island is a wildlife reserve with strictly limited access. As it is now virtually devoid of mainland pests such as opossums and rats, (the result of an eradication scheme carried out by the DOC over a period of many years), the native birds and vegetation have been able to regenerate. Among the rarer birds visitors may be lucky to see are kaka parrots, saddlebacks and parakeets.

Paraparaumu

Apart from being the departure point for boats to and around Kapiti Island, the seaside resort of **Paraparaumu Beach** (2 miles/3km from Paraparaumu) offers good swimming and other water activities like jet-skiing and windsurfing. Near **Paraparaumu**, the **Southward Car Museum** has a large collection of antique cars and motorcycles along with a few vintage aircraft. Special attractions include an 1895 Benz, Marlene Dietrich's Rolls and some ingenious Kiwi contributions to the art of automotive design.

Marine Drive and Mt. Victoria

Probably one of Wellington's nicest excursions is the **City Marine Drive**.

From Jervois Quay drive south towards picturesque Oriental Bay, then simply follow the coastal road to **Owhiro Bay** where the route leaves the coast and returns to the city along Happy Valley, Ohiro and Brooklyn Roads.

Popular swimming spots along the way are at **Oriental** and **Lyall Bays**. This drive also allows the possibility of an excursion up to the look-out on **Mt Victoria**. To get there climb the hill along Marjoriebanks Street, then follow signs (though it helps to have a good map). Once at the top, and no doubt battered by Wellington's infamous winds, you are rewarded with a panorama of city and Harbour second to none.

Eating out

If the day's sightseeing is to be concluded with a culinary treat then why not combine it with a dinner cruise (**Bluefin Cruises**) on the Harbour? However, if the weather makes it seem more prudent to stay on shore you can still enjoy the atmosphere, together with a delicious seafood meal, at either **Dockside** or **Shed 5** on Queen's Wharf. Otherwise take your pick; Chinese, Italian, Malaysian, Thai, Indian and even Mongolian fare can be consumed by candle-light and to a musical accompaniment ranging from classical to live jazz.

*A*dditional Information

ACTIVITIES

Palmerston North

Jet Boating
Manawatu Jet Boat Tours
☎ (06) 326 8190 or (06) 356 8657
Through spectacular Manawatu
Gorge. Minimum of 4 people.

Pipiriki

Jet Boating
**"Bridge To Nowhere"
Jet Boat Tours**
Jet Boat Tours, PO Box 192,
Raetihi
☎/Fax (06) 385 4128
On the Whanganui River

Raetihi

Boat Trips
Wakapai River Trip
RD6 Raetihi
☎/Fax (06) 385 4443 or
contact tourist offices in
Ohakune or Taumarunui.
On a **River Boat** through
Whanganui National Park.
A 5 day, 4 night adventure
package.

Wanganui
Boat Trips
Paddle Wheeler Otunui
PO Box 763
☎ (06) 345 0344 or (025) 432 997
Depart City Marina by town bridge
at 10am, 12.10pm & 1pm.

Kayaking/Canoeing
More operators offering tours on
the Whanganui River are listed
under Activities at the end of
Chapter 4.

Paterson's Canoe Hire
RD3, Wanganui
☎ (06) 343 7195

Rivercity Tours
PO Box 4224
☎ (06) 344 2554 or (025) 993 347
Guided tours on Whanganui River
and hire. Also jet-boat tours.

Whanganui River Experiences
PO Box 377
☎ (06) 345 7933 or
freephone 0800 808 686
Guided trips and hire.

Jet Boating
River City Cruises
PO Box 314
☎/Fax (06)343 9354
From Wanganui on
Whanganui River.

Mail Bus Run
River City Tours
PO Box 4224
☎ (06) 344 2554
Fax (06) 347 7888
The mail bus departs Wanganui
on weekdays for the trip to Pipiriki.
Very popular.

Whanganui National Park

Tramping
Matemateaonga Track: To walk
the Matemateaonga from
Wanganui a bit of arranging is
necessary. Take the mail bus to
Pipiriki. Catch the pre-booked jet
boat to start of track (Bridge to
Nowhere Jet Boat, address above).
To get out to Stratford at other end
either walk, hitch or arrange to be

157

Above: Demonstrations of shearing take place all over New Zealand, but a highlight of the shearing season is the annual Golden Shears competition held in Masterton (March)

Left: Wood chopping competitions may be seen at local fairs

Below: Canoes like this one, with its finely carved prow, were an important mode of transportation for the Maori

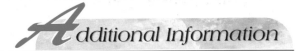

picked up by **Camp 'n Canoe**, Kaponga ☎ (06) 764 6738. The Wanganui Information Centre will be able to help with other transportation possibilities.

Wellington

Boat Trips

East by West (Trust Bank) Ferry From Queens Wharf to Days Bay. Trip takes 30 minutes.
☎ (04) 499 1273.

Blue Fin Harbour Cruises
Daytime and evening cruises. Buffet meals served on afternoon (depart 1pm) and evening (7pm) cruises. Tea/coffee & scones with morning cruise (10am). Depart from Bluefin Wharf off end Whitmore St ☎ (04) 569 8203.

Phantom of the Straits
A full day tour on board a former Whitbread Round the World racing yacht. Departs Queen's Wharf
☎ (04) 473 1223.

ACCOMMODATION

See pages 288 and 300 in the FactFile for the accommodation and restaurant rating guide

Masterton

Masterton Backpackers $
22 Victoria Street
☎ (06) 377 2228
Friendly place.

Victoria House $$
(Bed & Breakfast)
15 Victoria Street
☎/Fax (06) 377 0186
Old colonial house,
no smoking in rooms.

Palmerston North

Peppertree Hostel $
(Backpackers)
121 Grey Street
☎ (06) 355 4054
Fax (06) 355 4063

Grey's Inn $$
123 Grey Street
☎ (06) 358 6928
Fax (06) 355 0291
Nice place, they prefer
non-smokers.

Wanganui

Tamara Backpackers $
24 Somme Parade
☎ (06) 347 6300
Overlooks the river.

Grand Hotel $$
Cnr Guyton & Hill Sts
☎ (06) 345 0955
Fax (06) 345 0953
Old fashioned colonial style hotel.

River City Motel $$
59 Halswell Street
☎/Fax (06) 343 9107

Wellington

Maple Lodge $
(Backpackers)
52 Ellice Street
☎ (04) 385 3771
Non-smoking, close to City Centre.

Capital View Motor Inn $$
12 Thompsen Street
☎/Fax (04) 385 0515
Studios, units and a
penthouse. Good views
over Harbour from rooms.

Harbour City Motor Inn $$
92-96 Webb Street
☎ (04) 384 9809
Fax (04) 384 9806
Spa pool, some rooms
have cooking facilities.

Tinakori Lodge $$
(Bed & Breakfast)
182 Tinakori Road
☎ (04) 473 3478
Fax (04) 472 5554
Non-smoking, generous
buffet breakfast.

Trekkers Hotel/Motel $$
213 Cuba Street
☎ (04) 385 2153
Fax (04) 382 8873
Spa pool. Sauna, guest kitchen.
Also cheaper budget rooms.

Wellington Motel $$
14 Hobson Street
☎ (04) 472 0334
One of the city's
cheaper motels.

Hotel Raffaele $$$
360 Oriental Parade
☎ (04) 384 3450
Fax (04) 384 3652
Very good hotel,
cheaper on weekends.

James Cook Hotel $$$
147 The Terrace
☎ (04) 499 9500
Fax (04) 499 9800
Like Wellington's other
luxury hotels cheaper
on weekends.

EATING OUT

Masterton
Le Petit Café $$
(BYO)
8 Bannister Street
☎ (06) 377 5776
A small but very
good French restaurant.

Alberts Restaurant $
321 Victoria Avenue
☎ (06) 345 8408

Cables $$
51 Victoria Street
(BYO/Licensed)
☎ (06) 345 6891
Located in the old post office.
Try the venison or lamb.

Wellington
Space does not allow a complete
résumé of Wellington's cafes and
restaurants but suffice it to say
that a number of restaurants are
located along **Courtenay Place**
and **Cuba Street**.
    If you are looking for a nice cafe,
try walking along **Lambton Quay**
in the direction of the Beehive.
Try also **Plimmer Steps** (off
Lambton Quay) and **Manners
Mall** or Cuba Mall.

Angkor $
43 Dixon Street
☎ (04) 384 9423
Basic decor but the Cambodian
fare is good and the price is right.

Great India $
(BYO/Licensed)
141 Manners Street
☎ (04) 384 5755
One of the city's best
Indian restaurants.

Pico Cafe $
(BYO)
60 Ghuznee St
☎ (04) 384 9596
Vegetarian dishes,
popular among visitors.

Dockside Restaurant $$
Queens Wharf
☎ (04) 499 9900
In summer you can sit
outside while enjoying
your chargrilled swordfish.

Sala Thai $$
134 Cuba Street
☎ (04) 382 8780
Good Thai food, nice interior.

Shed Five $$/$$$
Queen's Wharf
☎ (04) 499 9069
Seafood meals inside what used to
be a woolshed. Very flash interior

which is divided between a
restaurant and cheaper cafe
and bar area. Luxury short
cruises are offered aboard
the Shed 5 launch.

Champerelle $$$
6 Edward Street
☎ (04) 385 0928
This restaurant has the
city's best wine list.

Fujiyama Teppanyaki $$$
36 Taranaki Street
☎ (04) 801 8699
Teppanyaki style
Japanese cuisine.

Grain of Salt Restaurant $$$
1st Floor
232 Oriental Parade
☎ (04) 384 8642
Very upmarket,
international cuisine.

GENERAL INFORMATION

Wellington Area Code: (04)

Important Telephone Numbers

After Hours Medical ☎ 384 4944
After Hours
  Pharmacy   ☎ 385 8810
Automobile
  Association (AA)   ☎ 473 8738
Taxis   ☎ 384 4444

Main Post Office
Railway Station
Open: Poste Restante mail can be
collected Mon-Fri 8.30am-5pm.

Public Transport

Airport Transport
An airport shuttle service is provided by **Super Shuttle** (☎ 387 8787)
and **Johnston's Shuttle Express** (☎ 384 7654). They offer either a door
to door service or a less expensive service from the railway station to
the airport. The latter service is available Mon-Fri every half hour from
7.15am-5.45pm.

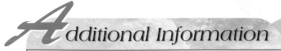
Bus Services & City Tours

Most routes start beside the railway station and the bus stop on **Courtenay Place**. Ridewell (☎ 801 7000) gives information on public transport in the Wellington region. Bus route maps and timetables are available from tourist office.

Useful to have is the **Daytripper Pass** which allows unlimited travel anywhere in Wellington city for one day. It can be bought on any **Stagecoach** bus. It is valid weekdays from 9am and at all hours on weekends ☎ 801 7000.

Long Distance Buses belonging to InterCity (☎ 472 5111) and **Newmans** (☎ 499 3261) depart from Platform 9, Wellington Railway Station.

Harbour Capital Tours: Faultline tour (1hr) departs 9am, Skyline tour (1¹/₂ hrs) at 10.30am & Coastline tour (3 hrs) at 1.30pm. Tours depart from Information Centre, Civic Centre, Wakefield St ☎ 499 1282.

Wally Hammond's City Scenic Tours: Run 10am & 2pm daily. Depart Travelworld Holidaymakers Info. Office, cnr Mercer & Victoria Sts. For Hotel pick-up & return ☎ 472 0869.

Unique Tours: Tours with an accent on Maori heritage. ☎ 383 6143 or 389 2057.

Trains

Long distance and suburban trains depart from Wellington Railway Station. For information on long distance trains (☎ 498 3413 or, freephone 0800 802 802). For information about suburban trains ☎ 801 7000.

Nightlife & Entertainment

Wellington

Of all the country's main cities it is the capital that has the best reputation for the quality and variety of its cultural offerings. Accordingly there is plenty to choose from.

Live theatre can be enjoyed at **Bats Theatre** at 1 Kent Terrace, **Circa Theatre** at 1 Taranaki Street and the excellent **Downstage Theatre** on the corner of Cambridge Terrace and Courtenay Place. **Taki Rua Theatre** at 12 Alpha Street specialises in works produced by New Zealand authors.

Concerts and other performances take place at the **Michael Fowler Centre** and **Wellington Town Hall** in Civic Square. The address for ballet and opera is the **State Opera House** in Manners Street.

The city's many pubs and nightclubs are the places to go for live music and dancing. **Bar Bodega** on the corner of Abel Smith and Willis Streets is open until late at night and serves good cocktails to the music of local bands. More upmarket is **Shed 5** at Queens Wharf and

Flanagan's on the corner of Kent Terrace and Marjoribanks Streets. Other venues include **Molly Malone's** on the corner of Courtenay Place and Taranaki Street, the **Thorndon Tavern** on Molesworth Street and the **Loaded Hog** at 12-14 Bond Street.

As always the Visitor Information Centre has a number of free publications which provide more information and addresses on what there is to see and do.

Left: Shed 5 Restaurant, Wellington

Below: Jazz Combo, International Festival of the Arts, Wellington

PLACES TO VISIT

Featherston

Fell Engine Museum
Middle of town
Open: 10am-4pm Sat and
school holidays. 10am-4pm Sun
(October-April). 1-4pm Sun
(May-September). Also by
prior arrangement.
☎ (06) 308 9777

Kapiti Island

34 miles (55km) north-west of
Wellington, near Paraparaumu
Access to the wildlife reserve is
strictly limited. Permits for a one
day visit (no overnighting) must
be obtained from the DOC office
in Wellington. As demand is high,
it is advisable to book your permit
several weeks in advance. Details
on boats out to the island are
available from the DOC:
Department of Conservation,
Wellington Conservancy, 2nd
Floor, Bowen State Building,
Bowen St, Wellington
(☎ 472 5821, Fax 499 0077)

Masterton

Wairarapa Arts Centre
Bruce Street
Open: 10am-4.30pm Mon-Fri;
weekends 1.30-4.30pm.

Mount Bruce

National Wildlife Centre
On SH2
Open: daily 9am-4pm.

Pioneer Museum
On SH2
Open: most days.

Palmerston North

**Science Centre & Manawatu
Museum**
Between Main & Church Sts
Open: daily 10am-5pm.

Paraparaumu

Southward Car Museum
Open: daily 9am-4.30pm.

Wanganui

Bushy Park
15 miles (24km) northwest
of Wanganui
Open: daily 10am-5pm.
☎ (06) 342 9879

Sergeant Art Gallery
Queen's Park/Civic Centre
Open: 10.30am-4.30pm
Mon-Fri; weekends 1-4.30pm.

Whanganui Regional Museum
Watt Street/Civic Centre
Open: 10am-4.40pm Mon-Sat;
Sun 1-4.30pm.

Wellington

Antrim House
63 Boulcott Street
Open: weekdays 9am-4.30pm.

Capital Discovery Place
Civic Square
Open: 10am-5pm Sat & Sun and
most public & school holidays.

City Art Gallery
Civic Square
Open: 10am-6pm Tues-Fri, 10am-
8pm Thur, weekends 11am-5pm.
Free entry Tues. Closed Mon.

Katherine Mansfield's Birthplace
25 Tinakori Rd, Thornton
Open: 10am-4pm. Closed Mon.

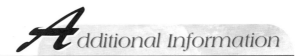

Maritime Museum
Queens Wharf, Jervois Quay
Open: Mon-Fri 9.30am-4pm;
weekends & public holidays
1-4.30pm.

Museum of New Zealand
Cable Street
Open: daily 10am-6pm.
except Thursday 10am-9pm.
This brand new museum building
was opened in 1998. Restaurants
and cafes within museum.
Admission is free.

**National Archives & New
Zealand Portrait Gallery**
10 Mulgrave Street
Open: Mon-Fri 9am-5pm
& Sat 9am-1pm.

**National Library & Alexander
Turnbull Library**
Cnr Molesworth & Aitken Streets
Open: Mon-Fri 9am-5pm,
Sat 9am-1pm.

New Zealand Astronomy Centre
Botanic Garden
Open: daily 10am-5pm.
Planetarium shows from
10.15am-4.15pm on weekends
and public holidays.

Old St Paul's Cathedral
Mulgrave Street. Open: Mon-Sat
10am-4.30pm, Sun 1-4.30pm.

Wellington Zoo
Newtown
Open: daily 8.30am-5pm
(last entry 4.30pm). Best time to
see the kiwis is 10am-12noon.

VISITOR INFORMATION & PARK VISITOR CENTRES

Masterton
**Tourism Wairarapa Visitor
Information Centre**
5 Dixon Street, PO Box 814
☎ (06) 378 7373
Fax (06) 378 7042

Palmerston North
The Square
PO Box 474
☎ (06) 358 5003
Fax (06) 356 9481

Wanganui
101 Guyton Street, PO Box 637
Open: Mon-Fri 8.30am-5pm,
weekends 10am-2pm.
☎/Fax (06) 345 3286

Whanganui National Park
Pipiriki, DOC Office
☎ (06) 385 4631

Taumarunui
Taumarunui Field Centre,
Cherry Grove
☎ (07) 895 8201

Wanganui
DOC Office
Cnr Ingestre & St. Hill Sts
Open: Mon-Fri 8am-5pm.
☎ (06)345 2402
Fax (06) 345 8712

Wellington
Department Of Conservation
(DOC)
59 Boulcott St
☎ (04) 471 0726
Information about Forest
& National Parks.

Wellington City Information Centre
Cnr Wakefield & Victoria Streets,
PO Box 2199
Open: daily 9am-5pm.
☎ (04) 801 4000 Fax (04) 801 3030

7 MARLBOROUGH & NELSON

Marlborough and Nelson belong to the sunniest regions in New Zealand. Some of the country's best wines are grown here and the local orchards can generally be counted on to produce bumper harvests of such popular exports as kiwifruit, apples and pears. Furthermore, nearly all New Zealand's tobacco and hops are grown on the small coastal plain around Motueka, on the western side of Tasman Bay.

But not all the land has been given over to agriculture: both trampers and nature-lovers will find **Abel Tasman National Park** something akin to paradise on earth. Here it is possible to combine swimming with walking on the park's splendid coastal track. Not so well known among tourists, but places of great beauty nevertheless, are **Kahurangi National Park**

(formerly North-West Nelson State Forest Park) and **Nelson Lakes National Park** further south. Over on the east coast at **Kaikoura**, visitors have the chance of getting close-up views of gigantic sperm whales. A leisurely cruise through the labyrinth of islands, bays and inlets that make up the **Marlborough Sounds** is also a fascinating experience.

Above: Alpine scenery, Nelson Lakes National Park

• ROUTE 9 •
PICTON TO ST ARNAUD

Picton

Most people arrive in Picton, at the head of Queen Charlotte Sound, with the **Cook Strait Ferry** from Wellington. Accordingly this attractive little port is used by the majority of visitors only as a short transit stop on the way to or from the North Island. However, there are a few things to see and do here and with a wide range of accommodation the town makes an ideal base for an exploration of the **Marlborough Sounds**. But perhaps an even better alternative for those who really want to get away from it all would be to stay in one of the remote lodges or farmstays elsewhere in the Sounds (see Additional Information for a few addresses). Most of them are only accessible by boat or amphibious aircraft and visitors will find the trip there as memorable as the stay itself.

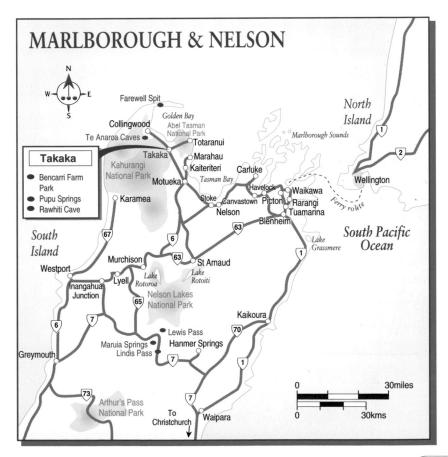

The Marlborough Sounds

The Sounds are a complex system of drowned river valleys and islands that remain as a legacy of the Ice Ages. Today, large areas are protected as the **Marlborough Sounds Maritime Park** and though passengers on the Cook Strait Ferry will already have sailed through Queen Charlotte Sound, it is only on one of the launch cruises from either Picton or Havelock that you can get a really close look at the many secluded bays and bush-clad headlands that make up the park.

One of the most popular trips on the Sounds is the 'Magic Mail **Run**' cruise. The *M.V. Beachcomber* departs Mondays and Thursdays, delivering mail and supplies to isolated homesteads scattered around Queen Charlotte Sound.

For those who want to combine a launch cruise with a hiking trip, the **Cougar Line** offers a drop-off service to the start of the **Queen Charlotte Walkway** at Ship Cove. This three to four day walk is an ideal alternative to the summer crowds on the Abel Tasman track. **Ship Cove** was, incidentally, a popular anchorage for Captain James Cook, who returned here no less than five times during his exploration of the Pacific. A memorial commemorates the explorer's visits.

In town itself, the **Smith Memorial Museum** has an interesting collection of relics from the days when whaling was a profitable industry in the Marlborough Sounds. The hull of the *Edwin Fox*, a nineteenth century sailing ship that is going to be restored to its full glory in the hopefully not-too-distant future, is located next to the ferry terminal complex. Ultimately the ship will be used as a floating maritime museum. In the meantime visitors can inform themselves about the ship's fascinating history in the adjacent **Edwin Fox Centre**.

Round trip to Rarangi

A pleasant excursion from Picton is the very windy but also very scenic coastal road via Waikawa to Rarangi. It can be made into a round trip by returning to Picton via Tuamarina on SH1, a total distance of 68 miles (110km). Around **Waikawa** there are some secluded holiday homes, tucked away in luxuriant bush and with splendid views over Queen Charlotte Sound. It is the dream of many a New Zealander to own such a holiday home which is called a 'bach' in the North Island but is also known as a 'crib' in the South Island.

Blenheim

Only 18 miles (29km) south of Picton, in the midst of a major wine-growing region, is the sun-kissed town of Blenheim. Marlborough's wines have an international reputation for excellence and the vineyards around Blenheim can offer exclusive vintages that it would be difficult to obtain elsewhere. Guided tours of the wineries with extensive tastings are conducted by **Deluxe Travel Line** (☎ (03) 578 5467), but a wine trail map is also available from the tourist office for those who want to visit the vineyards at their own pace.

Among the wineries that serve meals are **Allan Scott Wines & Estates** (a real tip for food, not just wine!), **Hunter's Wines** and **Merlen Wines**. A special treat for wine connoisseurs lucky enough to secure a ticket is the **Marlborough Wine and Food Festival**. It takes place on the second Saturday in February at **Montana Wine's Brancott Estate**, the largest vineyard in New Zealand.

Apart from the bacchanalian pleasures of food and wine, Blenheim can also offer an edifying peek into its pioneering history at the **Brayshaw Museum Park**. On display are some impressive traction engines, vintage tractors and a reconstructed colonial village.

Havelock

From Picton the route continues west along the scenic Queen Charlotte Drive to Havelock. A nice place for a picnic on this stretch of road is at **Momorangi Bay**. Shortly before Havelock the **Cullen Point** lookout provides magnificent views over Mahau Sound to the east and the rugged Richmond Range to the west.

Havelock, at the head of Pelorus Sound, is a nice enough little town and serves as a good base for boat trips or walks in the area. One of the more popular walks is the **Nydia Track**. The entire walk requires two days but it is possible to walk just the section between Nydia Bay and Shag Point in five hours. **Glenmore Cruises**, who also do the mail boat run (full day trip), can provide boat access to the track on Tuesdays and Fridays. Seafood gourmets might note that there are more than 200 mussel farms in **Pelorus Sound** and the green-lipped variety found here are a real delicacy.

Canvastown gold

The road turns inland from Havelock to pass the old gold mining settlement of **Canvastown**. Gold was discovered here in 1860 but the real rush did not take place until four years later when larger deposits were found. Many of the prospectors erected simple canvas dwellings while they worked their claims, hence the name 'Canvastown'. The rush was already over by 1865 but a few determined souls continued prospecting well into this century. Visitors who want to try their luck at gold panning can do so by inquiring at **Pinedale Motorcamp** (☎ (03)574 2349). It is claimed that enough gold can be sluiced in one day to pay for accommodation! The necessary equipment is provided.

After Canvastown the road heads towards **Pelorus Bridge Scenic Reserve**, where there are some pleasant walks, and then continues to the township of **Rai Valley** from where a short detour can be made to the old pioneer cottage (1881) at **Carluke**. Now it is just a matter of climbing over the forested Rai Saddle and passing through a few more small settlements to reach the coast and Nelson.

Nelson

Tobacco farming, orchards, forestry and fishing have all combined to make Nelson a prosperous city. Nearly surrounded by hills, Nelson enjoys an equable climate and gets more than its fair share of sunshine, as do most places in the north of the South Island. The city also has a justifiable reputation for its fine parks and an excellent beach at **Tahunanui** only a few kilometres away, adds to the natural attractions.

Focal point of the city is the rather unattractive cathedral (1925-65), which has at least a beautiful setting atop a hill at the end of the main street. Not far away the **South Street Gallery** serves as a display case for the work of some of Nelson's leading potters. The relative seclusion of this region, coupled with a more relaxed pace of life, has proved to be a magnet for many craftspeople, but especially potters have been drawn here by the excellent local clays.

Located in Queen's Gardens on Bridge Street the **Suter Art Gallery** is mainly interesting for its collection of paintings by important New Zealand artists such as Gully, Woollaston, Lindauer and Hodgkins. There is a nice restaurant here and the work of local potters can be seen in an attached craft shop.

Something of Nelson's history can be felt by visiting **Founders Park**, at 87 Atawai Drive. A few of Nelson's old buildings have been relocated here to recreate the atmosphere of a nineteenth century village. There are some more historic buildings scattered around town with **Melrose House** (1876) on the corner of Brougham and Trafalger Streets being one of the most impressive.

Stoke

Continuing on from Nelson to Motueka it is worth stopping at Stoke to have a look at the **Nelson Provincial Museum**. It is situated in the beautiful wooded expanses of Isel Park and houses a large photographic collection as well as an important collection of Maori artefacts. Nearby is historic **Isel House** (1848-1905), a lovely two-storied homestead set to advantage in the park's spacious gardens. Equally imposing is **Broad Green House** at 276 Nayland Road. It was built in the mid 1850's and is elegantly furnished according to the fashion of the time.

Another interesting stop can be made at the **Craft Habitat complex**, a short distance further along SH6. Concentrating on arts and crafts, visitors can buy directly from the craft workers' studios.

Shortly after Richmond turn right towards Appleby on SH60. From here a turn-off leads to the beach on **Rabbit Island**. Otherwise continue along the coastal road, passing more pleasant beaches at **Ruby Bay** and **Tasman** (Kina Beach), to Motueka.

Motueka

Motueka is a relaxed little town at the middle of a hops, tobacco and fruit-growing district. Apart from serving as a stepping stone to the beach and bush walks of Abel Tasman National Park, the town can be used as a base for a variety of organised outdoor activities such as

The Walk to Asbestos Cottage

In autumn the afternoon sun does not penetrate the narrow valley through which the Cobb Dam Road twists, losing itself in ever deepening shadow. There is no exit for this road which, after a laborious climb to the Cobb Reservoir, can only peter out as if spent before the vastness of Kahurangi National Park. Visitors who want to venture further into this wilderness have no choice but to continue on foot.

A well-defined track skirts the valley's side in the direction of Asbestos or Chaffey's Cottage. In summer, day-trippers take advantage of the first short section of the track which has been developed as a pleasant nature walk with signs explaining the trees and birdlife. The way leads past an abandoned asbestos mine with sulphurous green-tinged rocks. Asbestos was discovered here in 1889 at **Grecian's Creek**. This chrysolite asbestos was not high quality although it was commercially mined up until 1963.

It was the asbestos and the more glamourous lure of gold which led Henry Chaffey to choose this isolated valley as an abode in 1913 and kept him here until the start of the 1950's. He was a prospector of course, and in between working the asbestos he spent much of his time prospecting in secluded valleys for gold, often leaving his wife alone for long periods of time. This lonely life seemed to suit, however, as they rarely ventured out of the valley except for supplies.

Anne left her home only once in all their 28 years together, to go to hospital. They found solace in the chill winter evenings with the home-brew which they became addicted to. Anne nurtured a flourishing garden and blackberries and potatoes still grow by the hut.

One day, while bringing provisions on foot from the outside world, Henry Chaffey collapsed and died in the winter snow. Anne reluctantly left her home for Timaru. There she died of cancer, her grip on life no doubt lessened by the unfamiliar circumstances of town living.

Trampers who spend the night at the cottage can more easily envisage how it must have been to live in such isolation. How Anne must have warmed herself before the huge open fireplace on the evenings she was alone. How she must have fussed over the few visitors she received. With its rough-hewn furniture and the history that still clings to it there is more than just a touch of romance to the hut, one of the oldest in the park.

sea-kayaking, horse trekking and white water rafting.

The road to Abel Tasman goes north via Riwaka and **Kaiteriteri,** where there is a magnificent beach of golden sand. From here it is not far to **Marahau,** another fine beach with motor camp, at the entrance to the park.

Abel Tasman National Park

Named after the Dutch explorer who was the first European to discover New Zealand in 1642, Abel Tasman is one of New Zealand's most popular and idyllic national parks. Superb beaches, a rugged backdrop of bush clad hills and lots of sunshine draw over 30,000 people a year to the park's magnificent coastal track.

Apart from the **Marahau** entrance, the park is also accessible by road from several other points. From Takaka, in Golden Bay, a partly unsealed road leads to the **Wainui** and **Totaranui** entrances. The Coast Track can be reached by boat from Kaiteriteri or even directly from Nelson.

The Coast Track

By far the most popular walk in Abel Tasman is the Coast Track. Classified as one of New Zealand's Great Walks it runs a distance of 31 miles (51km) between Marahau at the southern end and Wainui at the northern end. It is not even necessary to walk the track in its entirety as a water taxi service picks people up or drops them off at various points along the coast. Once on the track, hikers can lounge on

magnificent beaches, cool off in the clear blue sea and no doubt spend a large amount of time scratching uncovered limbs that have been bitten by those irksome sandflies.

But the sandfly is not the only problem in paradise; all this beauty and the relative ease with which the track can be walked, means crowded huts and other hikers around every corner. The solution to the accommodation problem is to bring a tent but the best way to avoid the crowds is to visit outside the peak season (November to Easter).

Another way to be (more or less) alone with nature is to follow the coast by kayak. In fact kayaking around Abel Tasman is fast becoming a popular alternative to the Coast Track as it allows you to visit small off-shore islands and to come into closer contact with the park's fascinating marine-life; seals, penguins and dolphins might all be seen in a day's leisurely paddling.

The Inland Track

The Inland Track is rather more strenuous than its coastal equivalent but also much less crowded. It canbe started from either Marahau or Wainui and would require from three to five days to complete. A detour from the track can be made to **Harwood's Hole,** a huge vertical shaft that is over 1,214ft (370m) deep. **Visitors are warned not to approach the edge of the hole as the surrounding scree is very unstable.** The hole can also be reached along Canaan Road, a rough side road that branches off SH60 en route to Takaka.

The **Park Café** at the Marahau end of the Coast Track is a good place to fill up on homemade cooking before or after doing the track. They also serve the excellent Nelson-brewed Mac's beer. Towards the northern end of the track the **Awaroa Lodge & Café** caters to ravenous hikers and day-trippers.

Takaka

From Motueka SH60 winds up and over Takaka Hill (2,595ft/791m) to Golden Bay. The hill is also known as Marble Mountain because large quantities of marble are found beneath the softer limestone surface. As can be expected in limestone country there are plenty of caves in the area, but the **Ngarua Caves** on Takaka Hill belong to the most interesting and easily accessible. Cave features include beautiful stalactite and stalagmite formations, together with the skeletal remains of the giant moa.

Located near a number of superb beaches Takaka is the main town in the **Golden Bay** region. The town itself does not have a lot in the way of attractions but there are several places of interest in the vicinity. New Zealand's largest freshwater springs, **Pupu Springs**, bubble to the

Slippery customers

Three miles (5km) south of Takaka, at **Bencarri Farm Park**, visitors can let themselves be amazed by the spectacle of tame eels slithering out of a river to be fed!

surface in a scenic reserve about 3 miles (5km) to the north-west of town. To the south-east is the huge **Rawhiti Cave** which is over a million years old. A guided tour to the cave and back takes about three hours.

Collingwood

Collingwood lies 17 miles (28km) to the north-west of Takaka. A former gold rush town (gold was discovered in 1856 in the Aorere River) Collingwood is a base for guided tours to **Farewell Spit** and for those who plan to walk the well-known **Heaphy Track**. Other attractions in the area include the **Te Anaroa** limestone caves and isolated **Wharariki Beach** where there is a seal colony.

Farewell Spit

Farewell Spit is a narrow tongue of land, composed entirely of sand, that curves around the north-western extremity of Golden Bay. A bird sanctuary and wetland of international importance, it provides a vital habitat for many species of migratory wading birds. Towards the end of March huge flocks of bar-tailed godwits gather here prior to departing on their annual migration to the tundras of Siberia and Alaska. Other migratory birds that can be seen on the Spit include knots, turnstones and curlews.

Because of the Spit's protected status, free public access is restricted to small areas of beach at its base. The only way to travel its entire length is to book a tour with a licensed operator like **Collingwood Safari Tours**. No hobby ornithologist will want to miss their 'Gannet Tour', as it provides access to the gannet colony (and lighthouse) at the far end of the Spit. The **Collingwood Bus Service** also runs a nature tour to Farewell Spit ☎ (03) 524 8188). It takes about 6½ hours and lunch is provided.

Kahurangi National Park

The other way to come to grips with nature from Collingwood is to go on a walk through the unspoiled wilderness of **Kahurangi National Park** (formerly North-West Nelson State Forest Park). Established in 1995 and covering an area of 930,547 acres (376,572 hectares) this is not only New Zealand's second largest National Park, it is also its newest. Around 50 per cent of the country's native plant species, over 100 bird species and a labyrinthine cave system are to be found here.

The Heaphy Track

Probably the most well-known walk in the park is the Heaphy Track (6 days). The track was named after Charles Heaphy, an explorer, artist and surveyor who explored much of the region in the 1840's. It can be started near Collingwood and comes out on the West Coast near Karamea, a total distance of about 46 miles (75km). Transport is available to and from both ends of the track with Collingwood Safari Tours.

A highlight of the Heaphy is the coastal section where exotic-looking nikau palms fringe lonely beaches. The nikau (*Rhopalostylis sapida*) is the only palm tree in the world that grows naturally at such southerly latitudes. It is found throughout the North Island and in the South Island as far south as Greymouth.

The Karamea River Track

Much less travelled than the Heaphy Track, which is part of the DOC's Great Walks system, is the Leslie-Karamea (Karamea River Track). It goes through the same forest park as the Heaphy but is longer (7 to 8 days) and, in the opinion of the authors, it is a more interesting though more difficult walk.

Access to the track is along the scenic Cobb Dam Road, off SH60 near Upper Takaka. The track exits the park near Little Wanganui, a short distance south of Karamea. This last part of the walk follows a section of the Wangapeka Track. The very energetic could return to Golden Bay along the Heaphy. For more information about the track contact the DOC office at Nelson or Takaka.

From Collingwood return along SH60 to Motueka. Now take SH61 south to the junction with SH6. A side road (Upper Motueka Valley Road) branches off SH6 via Golden Downs and Kikiwa to reach **St Arnaud**, the gateway to Nelson Lakes National Park.

Nelson Lakes National Park

On first seeing **Lake Rotoiti** in 1860, the explorer Julius von Haast wrote;

"It was with the greatest delight that I looked over this beautiful lake; its deep blue waters reflected the high rocky mountain chains on its eastern and southern shores, which, for a considerable height from the water's edge (from which they rise

Above: Sea kayaking, Abel Tasman National Park

Left: Fishing boats at Picton

Below: The rainforest floor is covered by a luxuriant carpet of fern and moss

abruptly), are clad with luxuriant primeval forest. The surface of the lake swarmed with birds, giving life to this magnificent scene."

Today the great flocks of native waterfowl have, sadly, disappeared from Lake Rotoiti, decimated by introduced predators such as rats, stoats and cats and, of course, by the encroachment of man. But otherwise, over a hundred years later, the scene has hardly changed. Dense stands of beech and podocarp forest still surround the shores of both Lake Rotoiti and its larger counterpart **Lake Rotoroa.**

The ancient beech forests still resound to the song of native birds, even if a few species, like the kokako, have since disappeared. Bellbirds, native robins and the ever present fantail are commonly heard or seen along the hiking trail. Higher up in the alpine regions, New Zealand's mountain parrot, the kea, is a frequent sight. Chamois and red deer may also be glimpsed in the park, though because they are hunted they are very shy.

Situated at the northern end of the Southern Alps, the alpine regions of Nelson Lakes are more easily accessible for trampers than in the national parks further south. Without needing special alpine skills, any tramper who is reasonably fit can enjoy the solitude and beauty of these mountains.

Among the shorter walks that start from near park headquarters is the **Peninsula Nature Walk** ($1^1/_2$-3 hours return), the **Loop Track** ($1^1/_2$-2 hours return) and the **Rotoiti Lakehead Track** (6 hours return). Detailed information on these and other walks in the vicinity is available from park headquarters.

However, tramping is not the only activity in the park. In winter there is skiing at the **Mt Robert** and **Rainbow** ski fields, whereas in summer, anglers come to try their luck fishing for brown trout in the deep, clear waters of the two main lakes. Accommodation and supplies are all available in the small township of St Arnaud, which enjoys an idyllic location right next to the shores of Lake Rotoiti.

Moving on

Continue west from St Arnaud first on SH63, then on SH6, which threads its way through the picturesque **Buller Gorge** to reach the West Coast near **Westport** (see Chapter 8). On the way the road passes through the settlements of Murchison and Inangahua Junction, both of which were devastated by major earthquakes in 1929 and 1968 respectively. At **Lyell** a walkway leads to an interesting pioneer cemetery and some historic gold mines.

The Travers-Sabine Track

A popular, and very beautiful trail through the park is the Travers-Sabine Track. This five day trek starts near park headquarters in **St Arnaud**, links both main lakes via an alpine pass, and can be turned into a circular route by returning to St Arnaud from **Sabine Hut** at the head of Lake Rotoroa. It really is a magnificent walk and the authors can thoroughly recommend it.

• ROUTE 9A •
WEST COAST VIA LEWIS PASS

Instead of continuing west from Picton, this route heads south on SH1 to Kaikoura before it turns inland to reach the West Coast via Lewis Pass. Just over 18½ miles (30km) from Blenheim the road passes New Zealand's only solar salt works at **Lake Grassmere**. Sea-water is pumped into this shallow lake during the summer months where it is evaporated to obtain sea-salt. The pink colouration of some of the lake's crystallizing ponds is due to a unicellular form of algae.

Further south, after Wharanui, the road follows a wild, rocky coastline which is not only pictur-esque but also a preferred habitat for the spiny crayfish (*Jasus edwardsii*). This crustacean is similar in appear-ance to the lobster and the flesh of its tail is also valued as a delicacy. Just before Kaikoura it is some-times possible to buy freshly caught crayfish from wayside stands.

Kaikoura

Kaikoura has a lovely setting on a small peninsula with breathtaking views of the **Seaward Kaikoura Range**. The view of the mountains, which rise abruptly from the sea to heights of well over 6,561ft (2,000m), is especially beautiful in winter when snow caps the peaks. This dramatic tableau would have been enough in itself to justify a stop, but it is the chance to go whale-watching that now brings the tourists in their thousands.

There are also a few things to do in Kaikoura that do not involve spending money. A nice excursion is the drive along the peninsula to **Point Kean**, where there is a large fur seal colony. Keen nature photographers might like to follow the walkway along the seashore which starts from the carpark. Apart from close-up views of fur seals, it is also possible to see large colonies of red-billed gulls and many other seashore birds. Note that this coastal walk is only possible at low tide though. An alternative is to take the cliff-top route which allows spectacular views over the coast. A pamphlet describing various walks on the peninsula is available from the Information Centre.

Moving on

From Kaikoura SH1 goes directly south to Christchurch at the end of Route 14, but those who want to continue on to Hanmer Springs and the West Coast have a couple of possibilities open to them. The easiest road to drive is SH1 down to **Waipara**. From here SH7 can be followed over the **Lewis Pass** (2,831ft/863m) to the West Coast with a short detour to Hanmer Springs on the way.

The more direct route to Hanmer Springs is along SH70 which can be joined just south of Kaikoura. Though the fact that a long stretch of this road is unsealed and there-fore rather slow to drive, the wonderful scenery along the way is adequate recompense.

Whale Watch

Kaikoura is one of the few places in the world where sperm whales come in so close to shore. The deep waters directly off the Kaikoura coast offer an abundant supply of food, not only for whales but also other large marine animals such as dolphins (including Hector's dolphin which is the world's rarest) and seals. Visitors have a chance of seeing all these animals if they venture out in the small boats that are operated by Whale Watch Kaikoura. But the greatest thrill is when the tiny craft approach to within 984ft (300m) of the giant sperm whales.

Up to 65ft (20m) long and reaching a weight of 70 tons these behemoths of the ocean are the largest of all toothed whales. Nature lovers should on no account miss this opportunity to see at close quarters the creature immortalised in Melville's novel *Moby Dick*. Apart from sperm whales it is also possible to see killer whales (in actual fact the largest member of the dolphin family) as well as pilot, minke and humpback whales.

Because the whale watching tours only take place in good weather conditions visitors should be prepared to stay a few extra days if they want to be certain of seeing the whales. Many visitors stay longer anyway in order to go on one of the organised excursions that allow them to swim with the dolphins or seals. In winter Sea-to-Summit Safaris (☎ 319 6182 or contact Information Centre) take groups up to the recently opened Mt Lyford ski field.

Left: *The mighty tail flukes of a diving sperm whale*

Right: *Whale Watch Kaikoura's modern fleet of boats enable passengers to view the denizens of the deep at close quarters*

Hanmer Springs

With their beautiful alpine setting, the outdoor hot pools at Hanmer Springs are a glorious place to rest and soothe aching limbs. Open throughout the year, the mineral waters range in temperature from 70-100°F (36-40°C). Visitors can choose between large pools in a landscaped setting or small private pools with their own shower and change facilities. Conveniently located within the thermal reserve is a restaurant serving snacks and light meals.

Several walks go through the surrounding forest which comprises both native and exotic trees. Particularly worthwhile is the **Mt Isobel Track** (5 hours) as it goes through an area with interesting sub-alpine flora. Another good walk, the **Forest Walk** (1 hour), leads through stands of conifers and deciduous trees; it would be particularly attractive in autumn.

Other outdoor activities around Hanmer Springs include horse treks, golf, bungy-jumping, jet-boating and skiing at the nearby **Amuri** ski field. A bit further afield there is good walking through alpine scenery at the top of **Lewis Pass** (contact Information Centre at Hanmer Springs for track information), while the hot pools at nearby **Maruia Springs** provide a place to relax afterwards.

Molesworth

For those who want to return north the road through the remote tussocklands of **Molesworth Station** provides a spectacular alternative to the coastal route. This private road is only open to the public between January 1 and February 13 and links Hanmer Springs to Blenheim. With a spread of 444,798 acres (180,000 hectares), Molesworth is New Zealand's largest high country cattle station. The scenery is quite magnificent and well worth the small fee payable for using the road. Those who do not want to take their own vehicles along this unsurfaced road can join one of the safari tours starting from either Hanmer Springs or Blenheim.

Touring Note

Visitors who have continued south to Christchurch can still join Route 10 on the West Coast by crossing the Southern Alps via Arthur's Pass to Greymouth or Hokitika. From Christchurch the start of Route 11 at Wanaka is joined by following state highways 72, 79 and 8 south via Mount Hutt, Tekapo and Omarama - see also Route 14.

ACTIVITIES

Abel Tasman National Park

Tramping

For up-to-the-minute timetables and information as to the various transport possibilities, please contact the Information Centres in either Motueka or Nelson.

By Bus/Minibus: Skyline Connections, Wallace St, Motueka depart from Nelson and Motueka for Marahau daily (entrance to park). Also depart Takaka for Wainui/Totaranui (northern entrances to park) ☎ (03) 528 8850.

Abel Tasman National Park Enterprises, Old Cederman House, Main Road, Riwaka have a daily bus service to both ends of the park. Departs from Nelson, Motueka & Takaka ☎ (03) 528 7801.

Bayways Book-a-Bus
Takaka also operate on demand to Abel Tasman ☎ (03) 525 9864.

By Boat: Abel Tasman Seafaris (☎ (03) 527 8083) depart Marahau and drop hikers off, or pick them up, at various points in the park. Also day cruises.

Abel Tasman National Park Enterprises (see above) depart Kaiteriteri. Offer similar service to Seafaris. Also day cruises.

Spirit of Golden Bay (a catamaran) provides a daily ferry service from Tarakohe Harbour (near Takaka) to various points around coast of Abel Tasman and on to Nelson ☎ (03) 525 9135.

Collingwood

Nature Tours

Farewell Spit Bird Sanctuary
Collingwood Safari Tours Ltd
Tasman Street,
Collingwood, Golden Bay
☎ (03) 524 8257
Offer the 'Original Farewell Spit Safari Tour'. Departures are daily on demand and the tour takes 5 hours. The slightly longer tour to the gannet colony takes place twice a week.

Collingwood Bus Service
c/o Post Office
☎ (03) 524 8188
Their 'Farewell Spit Nature Tours' run daily for groups of 5 or more people. Bookings essential. Apart from this they also operate a 5 hour 'Mail Run Tour' which is also good value.

Hanmer Springs

White Water Rafting

Rainbow Adventures
Jack's Pass Road
☎ (03) 315 7444

Havelock

Boat Trips

Pelorus Mail Run

Glenmore Cruises
☎ (03) 574 2276
Departs: Havelock Tues, Wed, Thurs at 9.30am. Returns Tues 5.30pm, Wed 6.30pm & Fri 5pm. The boat follows a different route on each of these days. Free tea & coffee. Bring your lunch. In summer booking is essential.

*A*dditional Information

Sea Kayaking
Te Hoiere Sea Kayaks
PO Box 33
☎ (03) 574 2610
Rentals & Trips

Kahurangi National Park

Tramping
Heaphy Track: Collingwood Safari Tours have an on demand service from Collingwood to Heaphy Track and/or return. They can also arrange air transport
☎ (03) 524 8257

Heaphy & Cobb Tracks: Bayways **Book-a-Bus** (see Abel Tasman National Park above) also provide transport to Heaphy and Cobb (Leslie-Karamea) tracks.

Kaikoura

Dolphin Swimming
All the necessary equipment for the following trips to the dolphins and seals is provided by the operators.

Dolphin Mary Charters
Booking office in the middle of town
☎ (03) 319 6777
The best time to visit the dolphins is the early morning. The trip takes about 3 hours.

Kaikoura Wildlife Centre
Whaleway Station Road
☎ (03) 319 6622
Offer swimming trips with dolphins and fur seals.

Seal Swimming
Dive & Sports Centre
Yarmouth Street
☎ (03) 319 6444
Apart from swims with seals also various diving trips.

Graeme's Seal Swim
Book at Visitor Centre
☎ (03) 319 5641
This swim with the seals has been recommended.

Whale Watching
Whale Watch Kaikoura Ltd
The Whaleway Station
Freephone 0800 655 121 or
☎ (03) 319 6767
Season: up to 4 sailings daily, throughout the year.

Bookings are essential and should be made at least 3-4 days in advance. In the course of the 3 hour trip you may see sperm whales, orcas, dolphins and seals.

A number of operators offer whale watching from the air; **Kaikoura Helicopters** ☎ (03) 319 6609, **Whale Watch Air Ltd** Freephone 0800 655 121 or (03) 319 6580 and **Air Tours Kaikoura** ☎ (03) 319 5986. The flights last about half an hour.

Motueka

Sea Kayaking
Abel Tasman Kayaks
Marahau
☎ (03) 527 8022
Rentals & trips

Ocean River
Main Road
Marahau
☎ (03) 527 8266
Rentals & trips. Bookings essential.

Above: Traver's Saddle, Nelson Lakes National Park

Left: A pioneer cottage near Blenheim

Below: Inter-Island ferry, Marlborough Sounds

White Water Rafting
Ultimate Descents
PO Box 208
☎ (03) 528 6363
Offer trips on Buller, Karamea,
Motueka & other rivers.

Murchison

White Water Rafting
Go West Rafting
Chalgrave Street
☎ (03) 523 9315
On Lower Buller River.

Nelson Lakes
National Park

Tramping
Timetables for the following
services are subject to frequent
change, so always ring beforehand
or check with the relevant Visitor
Information Centre.

Nelson Lakes Transport has
a regular passenger service from
Nelson to the park. Departs
Mon-Sat. Departure point is
Nelson Visitor Information
Centre. Bookings essential
☎ (03) 548 6858.
   Nelson Lakes Shuttles
operate between St Arnaud,
Blenheim & Picton. Departs
Mon, Wed & Fri. Bookings
essential ☎ (03) 521 1887.

Picton

Boat Trips
The Magic Mail Run
Beachcomber Fun Cruises
8 London Quay
☎ (03) 573 6175
Departs: Picton, town wharf
Mon, Tues, Thurs & Fri at 11.15am.
Returns mid/late afternoon.
Free tea & coffee, bring your
own lunch. Bookings essential.

Cougar Line
The Waterfront
☎ (03) 573 7925
Offer three cruises in Queen
Charlotte Sound.
   Departs: Picton, town wharf
daily at 8.15am for 'Day Tripper'
(drops walkers off at Ship Cove,
start of Queen Charlotte Walkway);
11.15am for 'Luncheon Cruise'
($4^{1}/_{2}$ hrs); 2.15pm for 'Short Cruise'
(3 hrs).

*Swing bridges allow safe river
crossings on most national park
tracks*

Scenic Flights
Float Air Picton
☎ (03) 573 6433
Do scenic flights with their floatplanes as well as providing a transport link to the various farms and lodges on the Sounds. They also have a service to and from Wellington, landing at Porirua Harbour. This would be a very interesting alternative to the ferry trip.

Sea Kayaking
Marlborough Sounds Adventure Company
1 Russell St
☎ (03) 573 6078
Kayak rentals & trips.

ACCOMMODATION

See pages 288 and 300 in the FactFile for the accommodation and restaurant rating guide

Hanmer Springs
Amuri Backpackers $
41 Conical Hill Road
☎ (03) 315 7196
Central location.

Mountain View Holiday Park $
Main Road
☎/Fax (03) 315 7113
Tent sites, cabins, tourist flats.

Hanmer Lodge Hotel $$
☎ (03) 315 7021
Fax (03) 315 7071
Opened in 1932, this place has character.

Kaikoura
Top Spot Backpackers $
22 Deal Street
☎ (03) 319 5540
Non-smoking, good views, central.

Fyffe Gallery and Restaurant $$
(Bed & Breakfast)
3³/₄ miles (6km) south of Kaikoura
☎/Fax (03) 319 6869
Lovely garden and good restaurant.

Norfolk Pine Motor Inn $$
124 The Esplanade
☎ (03) 319 5120
Fax (03) 319 6405

Marlborough Sounds
For a comprehensive list of places to stay on the Queen Charlotte Walkway and elsewhere on the Sounds (including details on transportation possibilities) contact the Tourist Information Centre, **Picton**. A number of cheap hostels may be booked through The Villa (see Picton below).

Many of the hostels and lodges can be reached by water taxi or with Cougar Line and M.V. Beachcomber from Picton. Float Air Picton ☎ (03) 573 6433 operates floatplanes to any destination in the Sounds.

Hopewell $
Kenepuru Sound
☎ (03) 573 4341
Located in a remote part of Kenepuru Sound. Access by boat from Portage or floatplane from Picton.

Furneaux Lodge $/$$
Queen Charlotte Sound
☎/Fax (03) 579 8259
At this century-old house you can stay either in a private (self-contained) chalet, or bunkroom with communal kitchen. Activities include tennis, diving and kayaking. Access by boat from Picton.

St. Omer House $$/$$$
Kenepuru Sound
☎/Fax (03) 573 4086
Tent sites, cabins and cottages. Access by road or boat.

Craglee $$$
Queen Charlotte Sound
☎ (03) 579 9223
Beautifully situated.
All meals provided. Access by floatplane or water taxi.

Motueka

Twin Oaks Cottage $
(Backpackers)
25 Parker Street
☎ (03) 528 7882
Small cottage set in a nice garden. Closed June to August.

Equestrian Lodge Motel $$
Tudor Street
☎ (03) 528 9369
Fax (03) 528 6369
Swimming pool, quiet surroundings.

Nelson

Centre of NZ Hostel $
193 Milton Street
☎/Fax (03) 546 6667
Located in a historic mansion, built 1881.

Tasman Towers $
(Backpackers)
10 Weka Street
☎ (03) 548 7950
Fax (03) 548 7897
Spacious and clean.

Aloha Lodge $$
(Bed & Breakfast)
19 Beach Road
Tahunanui
☎ (03) 546 4000
Fax (03) 546 4420

California House Inn $$$
(Bed & Breakfast)
29 Collingwood Street
☎/Fax (03) 548 4173
Lovely old house, pretty garden, generous breakfast.

Picton

Baden's Picton Lodge $
(Backpackers)
3 Auckland Street
☎ (03) 573 7788
Fax (03) 573 8418
Close to ferry, good views over Harbour.

Marineland Guest House $
(Bed & Breakfast)
28 Waikawa Road
☎ (03) 573 6429
Fax (03) 573 7634
Swimming pool, friendly staff.

The Villa $
(Backpackers)
34 Auckland Street
☎/Fax (03) 573 6598
Popular place, good facilities.

Americano Motor Inn $$
32 High Street
☎ (03) 573 6398
Fax (03) 573 7892
Spa pool.

St Arnaud

The Yellow House $
(Backpackers)
☎/Fax (03) 521 1887
Spa pool, close to shop.

Alpine Lodge $$
☎ (03) 521 1869
Fax (03) 521 1868
The attached Alpine Chalet
offers cheaper rooms.

Tophouse $$
Shortly before St Arnaud
(signposted)
☎ (03) 521 1848
Unique cob cottage built
in the 1880's.

Takaka/Golden Bay

Golden Bay Holiday Park $
Tukurua Beach
☎ (03) 525 9742
Tent sites and cabins,
directly on beach.

Shady Rest Hostel $
141 Commercial Street
Takaka
☎ None
Nice old building,
friendly atmosphere.

Tukurua Beachfront Lodge $$
(Bed & Breakfast)
On SH60
Tukurua Beach
☎/Fax (03) 525 8644
Lovely garden, swimming
pool, private beach.

EATING OUT

Kaikoura

Act One $
(BYO/Licensed)
Main Highway
☎ (03) 319 6760
Good coffee, nachos, pizzas.

Why Not Café $
Westend
☎ (03) 319 6486
Good for a snack and a coffee.

White Morph $$
(BYO/Licensed)
94 The Esplanade
☎ (03) 319 5676
Good seafood meals.

Motueka

The Park Café $
Marahau
At entrance to National Park
☎ (03) 527 8270
Tasty home-made cakes.

Gothic Gourmet Restaurant $$
(BYO/Licensed)
208 High Street
☎ (03) 528 6699
Situated in an old church,
worth a visit.

Nelson

Land Of Pharoahs $
(BYO)
270 Hardy Street
☎ (03) 548 8404
Egyptian food, Egyptian chef.

Valeno's $
35 Bridge Street
☎ (03) 547 6724

Broccoli Row $$
(BYO)
5 Buxton Square
☎ (03) 548 9621
Vegetarian and seafood,
popular.

Picton

The Federal Hotel $
12 London Quay
☎ (03) 573 6077
Nothing fancy but okay.

Neptune's Seafood Restaurant $$
Waikawa Marina
Waikawa Bay
☎ (03) 573 7060
Good views, great seafood.

Marlborough Terranean $$$
31 High Street
☎ (03) 573 7122
Stylish interior,
good seafood.

PLACES TO VISIT

Collingwood

Te Anaroa Caves
Rockville (near Collingwood)
Open: guided tours daily during
summer (Dec 27 to Jan 23);
10.30am, 12.30pm, 2.30pm
& 4.30pm. Jan 24 to Dec 24
by appointment ☎ (03) 524 8131.

Blenheim

Brayshaw Museum Park
New Renwick Road
Open: During daylight hours.
Admission is free.

Carluke

Pioneer Cottage
(Near Rai Valley township)
Open: Daylight hours. No
admission charge.

Hanmer Springs

Molesworth Station
Open: for private vehicles
between Jan 1 & Feb 13.
Tours: Alpine Adventures,
Molesworth Station Safaris
(☎ (03) 315 7323), Hanmer
Springs and Back Country

Safaris (☎ (03) 578 9904),
Blenheim. Tours vary in length
from half a day to 2 days.
Both operators supply lunch &
refreshments. For more information
contact the tourist offices in either
Blenheim or Hanmer Springs.

Thermal Reserve
(hot pools)
Open: daily 10am-8pm.

Kaikoura

Maori Leap Cave
(A large stalactite cave)
2 miles (3km) south of Kaikoura
Open: Guided tours (45 mins) at
10.30am, 11.30am, 12.30pm,
1.45pm, 2.30pm and 3.30pm.

Lake Grassmere

Dominion Salt Ltd
Salt Works
Open: Guided tours Tues
1.30pm & Fri 1.30pm.

Nelson

Founders Park
Atawhai Drive
Open: daily 10am-4.30pm.

South Street Gallery
10 Nile Street
Open: Mon-Fri 10am-5pm,
weekends & public holidays
10am-4pm.

Suter Art Gallery
In Queens Gardens, Bridge Street
Open: daily 10.30am-4.30pm.

Picton

Edwin Fox Centre
Next to Ferry Terminal Complex
Open: daily 8.45am-5pm.

Smith Memorial Museum
London Quay
Open: daily 10am-4pm.

Stoke

Broadgreen House
276 Nayland Road
Open: 1 Nov-30 Apr.
Tues-Fri 10-30am-4.30pm,
weekends 1.30-4.30pm.
1 May-31 Oct Wed, Sat,
Sun 2-4.30pm.

Craft Habitat
SH6 (shortly after Stoke)
Open: daily.

Isel House
Isel Park
Open: During summer,
weekends 2-4pm.

Nelson Provincial Museum
In Isel Park, off Hilliard St
Open: Tues-Fri 10am-4pm,
weekends 2-5pm.

Takaka

Bencarri Farm Park
McCallum's Rd, Anatoki Valley
Open: daily 11am-4pm during
summer.

Rawhiti Cave
Open: For a guided walk to this
isolated cave contact Jane Baird
☎ (03) 525 9061.

Takaka Hill

Ngarua Caves
(20km from Motueka)
Open: daily Aug-mid June.
Guided tours from 10am.
Last tour 4pm.

REGIONAL TRANSPORT

Air

Picton to Wellington

Soundsair
☎ (03) 573 6184 or (04) 388 2594
in Wellington.
Offer a regular service to
Wellington.
See also Activities, Picton.

Bus

Collingwood to Nelson

Collingwood Bus Services
Tasman Street, Collingwood
☎ (03) 524 8188. Bus stops in
Takaka en route to Nelson

Nelson to Nelson Lakes National Park

Nelson Lakes Transport
Nelson
☎ (03) 548 6858

VISITOR INFORMATION & PARK VISITOR CENTRES

Abel Tasman National Park
DOC Office,
Cnr High & Edward Sts, Moutueka
☎ (03) 528 9117
Information on Abel Tasman N.P. can also be obtained from the DOC offices and Visitor Centres in Nelson and Takaka. The National Park Visitors Centre at Totaranui is open from late November to February.

Blenheim
The Forum Building,
Queen Street
☎ (03) 578 9904
Fax (03) 578 6084

Hanmer Springs
Hurunui Visitor Information
Cnr Amuri Avenue
& Jack's Pass Rd
PO Box 6
☎ (03) 315 7128

Kahurangi National Park
DOC Takaka Field Centre
1 Commercial Street
☎ (03) 525 8026
Information is also available from DOC offices in Motueka, Karamea and Nelson.

Kaikoura
The Esplanade, PO Box 6
Open: daily 8am-7pm (summer).
☎ (03) 319 5641
Fax (03) 319 6819

Motueka
236 High Street
Open: daily during summer
Mon-Fri 8.30am-7pm,
weekends 9.30am-7pm.
☎ (03) 528 6543
Fax (03) 528 6563

Nelson
Cnr Trafalgar & Halifax Street,
PO Box 194
Open: daily 7.30am-6pm.
☎ (03) 548 2304
Fax (03) 546 9008

Nelson Lakes National Park Visitor Centre
View Road, St Arnaud
☎ (03) 523 1806

Picton
Picton Information Centre,
Auckland Street,
PO Box 332
Open: daily 8.30am-8pm
(summer).
☎ (03) 573 8838
Fax (03) 573 8362

Picton Information Services
Picton Ferry Terminal Building
PO Box 309
☎ (03) 573 6855

Takaka
Golden Bay Information Centre
Commercial Street
☎ (03) 525 9136

THE WEST COAST (WESTLAND)

Oparara Basin

Karamea

Little Wanganui

67

Westport

Cape Foulwind

Buller River

6

Reefton

Charleston

69

Mitchell's Gully Goldmine

Reeftown

Pancake Rocks

Paparoa National Park

7

Punakaiki

6

Barrytown

7

Greymouth

Shanty Town

Lake Brunner

Hokitika

Arthur's Pass National Park

73

Ross

Lake Kaniere

Lake Ianthe

Arthur's Pass

6

N
W — E
S

0   30   60 miles

0   30   60 kms

Okarito Lagoon

Okarito

Whataroa

Westland National Park

Franz Josef

Lake Matheson

Mount Cook National Park

Fox Glacier

1

Tasman Sea

▲ Mount Cook

Lake Tekapo

Lake Paringa

6

Lake Paringa

Lake Pukaki

Lake Moeraki

Lake Moeraki

Lake Tekapo

79

Haast

Fairlie

8

Lake Ohau

Twizel

Timaru

Makarora

8

1

Mount Aspiring National Park

6

Omarama

South Pacific Ocean

Lake Wanaka

Lake Hawea

83

82

Lake Hawea

Fiordland National Park

Wanaka

8

83

Oamaru

THE WEST COAST (WESTLAND)

8

The West Coast is a thinly-populated sliver of land bounded on one side by the pounding waves of the Tasman Sea and on the other by the rainforest-clad slopes of the Southern Alps. Gold once brought a measure of prosperity to this wild, isolated coast and a touch of the old gold rush days can still be felt at Shantytown, near Greymouth and Mitchell's Gully Gold Mine. Other attractions include Franz Josef and Fox Glaciers, the sea-sculpted rocks at Punakaiki (Paparoa National Park) and Westland National Park. A useful booklet to pick up from one of the local tourist offices is *The Great West Coast Drive*. It is packed with tips on what to see and do.

• ROUTE 10 •
THE WEST COAST HIGHWAY

Westport

Established in 1861 after the discovery of gold in the **Buller Gorge**, Westport was the first European settlement on the West Coast. It is therefore perhaps appropriate that this journey begins here, even though the town is bypassed by SH6 from Nelson, as well as all those

Above: A typical West Coast landscape

tourists in a hurry to get down to the glaciers further south.

Once the gold rush was over, coal mining became the town's dominant industry. Though less glamorous, this black gold proved more dependable than its yellow counterpart and even today it ensures the town a measure of prosperity. A good insight into Westport's coal mining history can be gained by visiting 'Coaltown', an excellent little coal museum with a simulated coal mine and audio-visuals to help bring the past alive.

In recent years Westport has become increasingly well-known for its adventure tourism, which is no doubt at least partly the reason for the fresh paint on some pubs and a new-found interest in preserving the town's quaint old shop verandahs. Apart from white water rafting through the **Buller Gorge** it is possible to go 'underworld' rafting through fabulous glow-worm caverns and to abseil down sheer rock faces. The subterranean world can also be explored as part of a guided caving tour; one such tour is called simply **Te Tahi**, 'The One', and involves descending 100ft (30m) down a vertical hole. The tour operators claim you will experience 'rebirth' on this one — perhaps, but what most people will want to experience is a stiff drink beforehand. It is worth mentioning, however, that there are easier ways to enter the many cave systems in the area.

Less strenuous than an adventure tour is a visit to one of Westport's other main attractions — the seal colony at **Tauranga Bay**, only $7\frac{1}{2}$ miles (12km) away. Observation platforms atop the bluff behind the colony, allow good views of the seals below. A nice walk along the coast, which starts here, is the **Cape Foulwind Walkway** ($1\frac{1}{2}$ hours).

The road to **Karamea** follows the coast for much of its way, though at Mokihinui it weaves inland through a beautiful area of native forest, before touching the coast again at **Little Wanganui**. Close to Little Wanganui is the start of the **Wangapeka Track** (5 days).

Around Karamea

Karamea marks the end of SH67. The only way to get further north is to walk the **Heaphy Track** to Golden Bay. Even for those who do not want to walk the entire track, the beautiful coastal stretch of this walk to **Heaphy Hut** (5 hours) is well worth the effort. In any case, there are plenty of excellent day walks in the area such as the **Fenian, Mt Stormy** and **Karamea Gorge** tracks. The **Karamea Information & Resource Centre** has more information on these and other walks.

A must when in the area is a visit to the **Oparara Basin**, a $7\frac{1}{2}$ mile (12km) drive from the North Beach turn-off, north of Karamea. The main attractions here are the **Honeycomb Caves** and some spectacular limestone arches set in truly magnificent rainforest.

It is possible to walk to the Oparara Arch and Little Arch, but the caves can only be visited on a guided tour. This tour is worth the money however, as the caves serve as a repository for a remarkable collection of bones belonging to birds that have long since become extinct in this country. They include seven species of moa, a giant flightless goose and the giant New Zealand eagle (*Harpagornis*). Often referred to as Haast's eagle, after the man who first described it, this immense bird of prey had claws the size of a tiger's and a wing-span over 9 foot (up to 3m).

Carnivorous snails

Somewhat more modest in size, but still to be found in the surrounding bush, are snails of the genus *powelliphanta*. They are carnivorous, just under 3 inches (70mm) long and belong to a very ancient and primitive family of snails that is also present in Africa and Melanesia (division of of Oceania in the south-west Pacific Ocean. Powelliphanta and paryphanta snails (another genus of carnivorous land snails found in New Zealand) feed on earthworms and lay eggs similar to those laid by birds. All these snails are protected and should not be disturbed!

The road from Westport to Punakaiki and Greymouth is undoubtedly one of the loveliest coastal drives in New Zealand. Undisputed highlights of the drive are the **Pancake Rocks** and lush rainforests of **Paparoa National Park** but a visit to **Mitchell's Gully Gold Mine**, near Charleston, is also worthwhile as it provides an interesting glimpse into the Coast's lively goldmining past. Good views over the rugged coastal scenery can be had from **Irimahuwhero Point**.

Paparoa National Park

Punakaiki is the gateway to the national park and is situated right next to the famous **Pancake Rocks**.

Wind and waves have sculpted these stratified limestone rocks into a surreal landscape of bizarre columns and ridges that rise impressively above the coast. At high tide blowholes become active at those points where the sea has undermined the rocks and is squeezed up through narrow fissures to produce a spectacular spray of water. The rocks can be reached along a track that starts just opposite the Visitor Centre.

Weird limestone formations do not stop at the coast however, as the interior of the park is also a magnificent karst landscape of narrow rugged gorges, cliffs and cave systems. All these geological features are cloaked in a primeval rainforest, alive with native birds, that is just waiting to be explored on one of the park's well defined trails or perhaps on a canoe trip up the **Pororari Gorge**. In summer, when the rata trees are flowering red, the lowland forests are especially beautiful.

Apart from walking, the park and environs can also be explored by canoe, bicycle or on horseback. **Kiwa Sea Adventures** offer trips along the coast to see dolphins, fur seals and spotted shags. A real treat for bird-watchers is a visit to the world's only breeding colony of Westland black petrels (*Procellaria westlandica*). The best time to observe the birds is between June and October, but note that the colony can only be visited on a guided tour

Walks in Paparoa Park

Among the park's shorter walks are the Truman Track (30 minutes round trip) and Pororari River Track (3 hours). Both are located a few miles north of the Punakaiki Visitor Centre and serve as excellent introductions to the park's unique sub-tropical vegetation. Tree-ferns, nikau palms, yellow-flowering kowhai trees and native forest giants such as rimu, matai and kahikatea, are features of these tracks. An additional attraction of the Truman Track is the spectacular section of coastline where it ends.

Longer walks include the Inland Pack Track (2-3 days) and Croesus Track (2-3 days), although the latter is not actually within the park's boundaries. As flooding can make some of the inland tracks impassable, it is important to check at the Visitors Centre before setting out. Detailed information about all the tracks mentioned here, and others as well, can be obtained from the Centre.

with **Paparoa Nature Tours**. They also organise other bird-watching trips within the park.

Moving on

From Punakaiki the road continues south through **Barrytown,** near the start of the **Croesus Track,** and a couple of other small settlements before reaching **Greymouth** on the Grey River. For those who wish to spend the night along this wild and romantic stretch of coast, there is accommodation at Barrytown, at **Sandie's Vegetarian Bed & Break-fast** ☎ (03) 731 1889) a bit further south, and of course at Punakaiki itself.

Greymouth

Greymouth is the largest town on the West Coast and with a wide range of accommodation it serves as a good base for outdoor activities in

the area. Visitors can try their luck at gold-panning, go on a rafting adventure or join one of the scenic tours to old goldmining sites. There is plenty of good walking in the area and excellent trout fishing in the local rivers as well as at **Lake Brunner** further inland.

In spring people can be seen netting whitebait at the mouth of the Grey River. Whitebait are tiny fish (actually the young of the *Galaxiidae* family of fish) that are considered a real delicacy, not only on the Coast but all over New Zealand. They are usually cooked in batter and well worth trying if one has the chance.

Attractions

An interesting feature of town is the so-called **'Great Wall of Greymouth'**. This stone barrier was erected in recent years to protect the town from the sometimes

The Kea (Nestor notabilis)

To some a villain, to some a clown, the kea is the world's only alpine parrot and is only found in the high country and mountains of the South Island.

Its diet consists mainly of insects and berries, but it will eat carrion when the chance arises. There have been cases where the kea has actually attacked live sheep and with its powerful curved beak and strong claws it is well equipped for the purpose. However, this only happens very rarely and, though the kea was once shot due to exaggerated reports of such behaviour, it is now fully protected.

Most visitors to New Zealand are unaware of the kea's reputation as a killer among local farmers and tend to see this parrot in a completely different light: as the mischievous feathered clown of the mountains. Keas like sliding down the tin roofs of mountain huts (preferably in the early hours of the morning) and would not think twice about flying off with your watch or any other shiny object that you might leave lying about. Their natural curiosity and lack of natural enemies makes them quite unafraid of people and it is not difficult to get close to the birds.

Unfortunately, the kea's curiosity is developing into a bit of a problem in those areas where it has been fed by visitors who have been charmed by its antics. More and more notices are appearing at places like **Mount Cook National Park** advising people 'not to feed the keas'. Feeding keas attracts them to areas of human habitation and when they are not actually eating, the keas burn off their excess energy by ripping apart anything that their beaks can get hold of. This might be the rubber sealing on the windscreen of your car, your backpack or your expensive walking boots.

But more serious than the damage done to human property is the change in the kea's natural behaviour that feeding brings about. The kea's normal food has a much lower energy value than human food and a sandwich for the kea is like having breakfast, lunch and dinner all at once! Not that the conservation authorities are worried about lots of obese keas becoming yet another of New Zealand's flightless birds.

What really worries them is that the kea will stop foraging for its natural foods and become dependant on human leftovers. On top of all this, it is probable that human food is bad for the kea and that a kea that scavenges for scraps is living about as healthily as an adolescent on junk food. In other words: please don't feed the keas!

catastrophic flooding of the **Grey River**.

But probably the biggest single attraction in the vicinity of Greymouth is **Shantytown**, 5 miles (8km) further south. This replica of a typical West Coast gold mining town gives a good feeling for pioneering life at the turn of last century. It almost goes without saying that you can pan for gold here (they even guarantee that you will find some!) and a short ride on the quaint old steam train through native bush is also great fun.

For those who want to cross the Southern Alps to Christchurch there is a daily rail link from Greymouth with the **TranzAlpine Express**. There is also a bus link via Arthur's Pass (see Chapter 11) but in either case the trip over the Alps is quite spectacular. Otherwise this route along the coast continues to Hokitika.

Hokitika

In the 1860's, during the heady days of the West Coast gold rushes, Hokitika was known as the 'Capital of the Goldfields'. The best place for visitors to inform themselves about the town's gold mining past is at the **West Coast Historical Museum**. It features a large collection of gold mining equipment, historic photos and scale models of the various methods used to extract gold. A leaflet is available here (also at the information office) which describes a walk to places of historic interest such as the old wharf along **Gibson Quay** and the **Custom House**.

Like Greymouth, the town is also a good base for outdoor activities such as white water rafting and

Jade

Although some gold is still being mined in the Hokitika area, the town is now better known for the processing of greenstone (jade) or *pounamu* as the Maori call it. A major source of local greenstone is the **Arahura River** which enters the sea 5 miles (8km) north of town.

Greenstone jewelry and sculptures can be bought at a number of shops in town and it is also possible to see it being cut and polished at **Westland Greenstone** on Tancred Street. In the same street **The Gold Shop** specialises in jewelry made from locally mined gold.

kayaking. However, a nice lazy way to enjoy the local scenery is to take a paddle boat cruise along Mahinapua Creek to **Lake Mahinapua**. To get to the place where the paddle boat departs, take the Ruatapu Road a short distance south of Hokitika. If, however, a bit of exercise is called for, then one of the best walking areas in the vicinity is around the shores of picturesque **Lake Kaniere**, only some 11 miles (18kms) east of town.

Moving on

Continuing south from Hokitika the main road passes through **Ross**, yet another of those West Coast towns that can trace its history back to the goldrush days. It was near here that the largest gold nugget ever to be found in New Zealand was dug out in 1907. Two walkways, the **Water Race Walk** (1 hour) and **Jones Flat Walk** (1¹/₂ hours), lead through historic goldfields close to town.

Though the road winds inland after Ross the scenery loses nothing of its attractiveness and becomes, if anything, even more dramatic. On the northern shore of bush-clad **Lake Ianthe** a lovely picnic spot, with toilets provided, invites a break from driving. From here it is not much further to Whataroa and New Zealand's only breeding colony of white herons.

White Herons of Whataroa

Just as Kaikoura owes its popularity (and economic recovery) to the marine mammals in its coastal waters, so does **Whataroa** have reason to be grateful to the colony of white herons (the Maori name is *kotuku*) that enjoy refuge in a sanctuary on the banks of the Waitangitoana River. **White Heron Sanctuary Tours** conduct jet-boat tours to the colony during the November to February nesting season. One can also see a nesting colony of royal spoonbills (*Platalea regia*) here.

Okarito Lagoon

Another worthwhile excursion for bird-watchers and for anybody who loves beautiful natural scenery, is a kayak trip on Okarito Lagoon. **Okarito Nature Tours** operate guided boat tours, but it is also possible to just rent a kayak and paddle off on your own.

The turn-off to **Okarito** settlement is at The Forks, another 9 miles (15km) south of Whataroa. It was near Okarito, incidentally, that the Dutch explorer Abel Tasman first set eyes on New Zealand in 1642. A monument next to the Youth Hostel marks the event.

From The Forks turn-off it is no longer far, past the trout-rich waters of Lake Mapourika, to **Franz Josef Village** and the glaciers of Westland National Park.

Westland National Park

The glacial landscapes of this national park are so unique it has earned the title of '**World Heritage Park**' from UNESCO. Together with Mount Aspiring, Mount Cook and Fiordland National Parks it forms part of the South-West New Zealand World Heritage Area.

Nowhere else in the world do glaciers descend from alpine heights to end just short of luxuriant coastal rainforests. What is more, and contrary to world wide trends, the glaciers are advancing. At the moment they are roughly 9 miles (12km) from the sea, with **Franz Josef Glacier** moving forward at a rate of some 11¹/₂ inches (30cm) a day. How long this period of advance will continue is hard to say. Generally, the last century has shown a pattern of steady retreat; in the distant past the glaciers once reached right down to the sea and even in the 1930's the terminal face was much closer to the coast than it is now.

The Glaciers

Before setting out to explore **Franz Josef** and **Fox Glaciers** it is a very good idea to inform oneself about

Pancake Rocks at Punakaiki

The Sandfly: Scourge of the West Coast!

The adult sandfly measures only about 0.1 of an inch (2.5mm) long and has a hunch-back appearance. Various species of sandfly are found in many parts of the country, but the ones along the West Coast and in Fiordland are particularly voracious. They are especially numerous close to streams and lakes because this is where the insect lives during the larval stage of its life-cycle.

Only the adult female is a blood-sucker as she needs the hormonal stimulus that blood provides before she can lay her eggs. Normally sandflies would attack birds, but any warm-blooded animal will do and they seem to find humans especially delectable.

By way of consolation it might help to add that sandflies are mostly active during the day and, though their bite itches, it is not dangerous. Local repellants are quite effective at warding them off and should be used if you want to have a relaxing day by the sea or a lake.

This 'giant sandfly' hangs outside the Bushman's Centre close to Lake Ianthe

the park's natural history and geology at Westland National Park Headquarters in **Franz Josef Village**. Like all Park Visitor Centres they have leaflets describing many of the walks, both long and short, in the area.

Both glaciers look a little bit disappointing from a distance, so the only way to truly appreciate their dramatic beauty is to get as close as possible. The cheapest way to get close-up views of Franz Josef is to follow the unsealed access road a distance of $3^{1}/_{2}$ miles (6km) to the carpark where there is an information kiosk. From here the **Glacier Valley Walk** ($1^{1}/_{2}$ hours return) leads to a viewpoint close to the terminal ice. Admittedly it would be even better to actually walk onto the glacier, but this should only be done on a guided walk.

Most expensive, but certainly most spectacular of all, are flights over the glaciers. A 'Grand Circle' flight takes in not only **Fox** and **Franz Josef** but also the mighty **Tasman Glacier** in Mount Cook National Park. A snow landing on one of the glaciers allows visitors to experience a pristine world of snow and ice that is normally the exclusive preserve of experienced alpinists.

Fox Glacier Village

Fox Glacier Village is another $15^{1}/_{2}$ miles (25km) further south. Access to the glacier is provided by two unsealed roads a short distance to the south of the village.

The northern approach road (Fox Glacier Road) runs along the north bank of the **Fox River** and brings you closest to the glacier. From the carpark, a track leads over

rock debris to the impressive wall of ice that marks the terminal face. Once again visitors are warned not to venture onto the ice without a guide!

The southern approach road (Glacier View Road) runs along the other side of the Fox River. The **Chalet Lookout Walk** (1 hour return) starts from the carpark and allows panoramic views of the glacier's lower reaches. However, the views are even more spectacular if this track is combined with the **Cone Rock Walk**, a side track that branches off the Chalet route. The entire round trip would take about 3 hours. As at Franz Josef, it is also possible to take a spectacular helicopter or ski-plane flight over the glaciers.

Lake Matheson

The road to Gillespies Beach runs west of the village and allows a detour to Lake Matheson. In the very early morning, on windless days, the lake's dark waters reflect a perfect mirror image of the snow-capped alps — one of the most famous picture-postcard panoramas in New Zealand. A walk around the lake takes $1^{1}/_{2}$ hours.

Even if wind or a late breakfast has ruined the chances of a stunning lake photo, it is worth continuing the scenic drive to the coast as it provides plenty of other photographic opportunities. From **Gillespies Beach**, a 3 hour return walk leads to a large seal colony.

Lakes Paringa and Moeraki

The drive from Fox Glacier down to Haast is accompanied by magnificent

The Copland Track

The most challenging walk in Westland National Park is without doubt the Copland Track (4 days). It starts 15½ miles (25km) south of Fox Glacier near the Karangarua River Bridge. Here a signpost points the way to Copland Valley. This alpine traverse links Westland to Mount Cook National Park and should on no account be attempted by the inexperienced.

The **Copland Valley** section of the track is, however, quite easy walking. It is 6 hours from the road to **Welcome Flat** hut where there are hot springs. The springs, together with some magnificent alpine scenery, make the Copland Valley a very popular place in summer.

For those who want to attempt the alpine crossing, it is best to start from **The Hermitage** in Mount Cook National Park where a guide can be arranged (see Chapter 11).

A short walk through native forest leads from Lake Moeraki to the coast and Monroe's Beach, where there is a breeding colony of Fiordland crested penguins (July-November). The road itself soons reaches the coast just south of Lake Moeraki and follows it the rest of the way to Haast, passing several good viewpoints en route.

Haast region

Haast township is scattered over a wide area and comprises Haast (a small servicing settlement), Haast Junction on the main highway, and Haast Beach on the Haast Beach-Jackson Bay Road. Where exactly the middle of town might be is anybody's guess, but more importantly this loose collection of petrol stations, hotels and shop (there is only one general store) is the gateway to a beautiful, wild region known simply as 'Haast'.

Wilderness and Wildlife

The wilderness area of Haast is part of the South-West New Zealand World Heritage Area (Te Wahipounamu). Established in 1990, **Te Wahipounamu** encompasses Westland, Mount Cook, Mount Aspiring and Fiordland National Parks — roughly 10 per cent of New Zealand's total area.

The Haast region stretches along the coast south of Haast township to the Cascade River. This remote pocket of land between the sea and the Southern Alps preserves a unique natural environment composed of majestic kahikatea swamp forests, coastal lagoons, deserted driftwood-strewn beaches

scenery for the entire distance. After a brief interlude on the coast at Bruce Bay, the road winds inland again to pass Lakes Paringa and Moeraki.

Surrounded by dense forest, both offer good trout fishing but Moeraki is perhaps the more idyllic lake. Reasonably priced accommodation is provided by the **Lake Paringa Heritage Lodge** ☎ (03) 751 0894 and the **Lake Moeraki Wilderness Lodge** ☎ (03) 750 0881.

and beautiful rivers and lakes. At rocky points along the coast it is possible to view blue and Fiordland crested penguins and fur seals. Inland the lowland rainforests offer refuge to parakeets, kakas (bush parrots), kiwis and many other native birds.

> ## Useful information
>
> **A good base for activities in Haast would be the Haast Motor Camp at Okuru, but there is also hotel/motel accommodation at Haast Junction and Haast Beach. Information about walks and adventure activities in the Haast region can be obtained from the South Westland World Heritage Visitor Centre at Haast Junction. They also have a useful pamphlet describing short walks along the Haast Pass Highway.**

Haast Pass

Though Haast Pass (1,847ft/563m) is the lowest of the three road passes linking the West Coast to the east, the journey along the glacially formed **Haast River Valley** is nevertheless of great scenic beauty — but do not count on seeing snow-capped mountain peaks as they are often obscured by cloud.

The western side of the pass is characterised by the lush rainforests so typical of the West Coast, but once the pass is crossed the dense forest vegetation soon gives way to the golden tussock grasslands of Central Otago. Along the way there are several waterfalls that can be reached on short walks from the road. Especially picturesque are **Thunder Falls** and **Fantail Falls** (both are 5 minutes return).

Makarora

At Makarora on the far side of the pass there is a Visitor Centre for **Mount Aspiring National Park** (the road over Haast Pass actually cuts through the northern extremities of the park) and a tea room. The surrounding countryside offers some excellent walking, especially for those who prefer lesser known and less crowded tracks.

> ## Siberia adventure tour
>
> **A great way to get to know the area if you have limited time is the Siberia Experience. This adventure tour starts from Makarora and involves a 25 minute scenic flight to the remote Siberia Valley in Mount Aspiring National Park, a three hour bush walk (without a guide) and then a jet-boat ride back to Makarora. The Makarora Tourist Centre (☎ (03) 443 8372) offers the tour from mid-October to mid-April. People wishing to overnight in Makarora may choose between the motel or one of the simple DOC campsites to the north of town at Cameron Flat and Davis Flat.**

From Makarora the road continues south past the shores of lakes Wanaka and Hawea to **Wanaka** township, the first place of any size since Fox Glacier. The superb scenery of the West Coast has now been exchanged for a landscape that is perhaps even more spectacular: like sapphires adorning an emerald crown, the **Southern Lakes** fringe the vast untouched forests of **Fiordland**.

Left: Guided walks are the best way to appreciate Fox Glacier

Above right: Scenic flights with a snow landing are an unforgettable experience for visitors to Franz Josef and Fox Glaciers

203

ACTIVITIES

Fox Glacier

Glacier Walks
Alpine Guides Fox Glacier
Depart: daily 9.30am & 2pm.
Duration: 3 hrs.
☎ (03) 751 0825
They also organise various other
activities such as glacier skiing.

Scenic Flights
See under Franz Josef Glacier

Franz Josef Glacier

Glacier Walks
Franz Josef Glacier Guides
Depart: daily 9.15am & 2pm.
Duration: 3 hrs
☎ (03) 752 0763

Scenic Flights
All the following companies
offer snow landings.
Fox Glacier Helicopter Services
☎ (03) 7520 793 (Franz Josef)
or (03) 7510 0866 (Fox)

Glacier Helicopters
☎ (03) 752 0755 (Franz Josef) or
(03) 751 0803 (Fox)

Mount Cook Line Skiplanes
☎ (03) 752 0714 (Franz Josef)
(03) 751 0812 (Fox)
Grand circle flights (60mins).

Greymouth

White Water Rafting
Wild West Adventure Company
c/o Greymouth Information Centre
☎ (03) 768 6649
Also cave rafting.

Hokitika

Boat Trips
Scenic Waterways
Paddle Boat Cruises
Main South Road,
PO Box 290
☎ (03) 755 7239
Depart: 3 miles (5km) south
 of Hokitika. Daily 10.30am,
2pm & 6pm.

Scenic Flights
Westair
☎ (03) 755 7767
Flights over the glaciers,
Mt Cook and Milford Sound.

Wilderness Wings
c/o Information Centre
☎ (03) 755 8322 or 755 8118
To the glaciers and various
other destinations.

White Water Rafting
Alpine Rafts
Kawhaka Station
☎ (03) 755 8156
Exciting raft trips on the
Wanganui and Hokitika rivers.

Karamea

Adventure Caving
Adventures Unlimited
c/o Last Resort, PO Box 17
☎ (03) 782 6617 or 0800 505 042
Tours of Honeycomb cave system
and Oparara Basin.

Kayaking/Canoeing
Adventures Unlimited
c/o Last Resort
☎ (03) 782 6617
Kayak rentals and trips in
Oparara Basin.

Okarito

Nature Tours

Okarito Nature Tours
The Strand
☎ (03) 753 4014
Kayak trips on Okarito lagoon.

Punakaiki

Kayaking/Canoeing

Pororari Canoe & Cycle Hire
☎ (03) 731 1870

Nature Tours

Kiwa Sea Adventures
c/o Visitor Centre
☎ (03) 731 1893
Boat trips to the coastal fauna.

Paparoa Nature Tours
☎ (03) 731 1826
Bird-watching trips and canoe
excursions.

Westport

Adventure Caving

Norwest Adventures Ltd
41 Domett Street
☎ (03) 789 6686
This company offers the
Te Tahi cave tour and cave rafting.

White Water Rafting

Buller Adventure Tours
Buller Gorge Road
☎ (03) 789 7286
Buller, Karamea and other rivers.

Whataroa

Nature Tours

White Heron Sanctuary Tours Ltd
☎ (03) 753 4120
Tours of the White Heron
Sanctuary. Season is Nov-Feb.

ACCOMMODATION

*See pages 288 and 300 in the FactFile for the accommodation and
restaurant rating guide*

Fox Glacier

Fox Glacier Holiday Park $
Lake Matheson Road
☎ (03) 751 0821
Fax (03) 751 0813
Tent sites, cabins, tourist flats,
motel and 40 bed lodge.

Ivory Towers $
(Backpackers)
Sullivans Road
☎ (03) 751 0838

Fox Glacier Hotel $$
Cook Flat Road
☎ (03) 751 0839
Fax (03) 751 0868
Located in the middle
of the village.

Franz Josef

Chateau Franz $
(Backpackers)
8 Cron St
☎/Fax (03) 752 0738
Central location.

Above: *Shantytown near Greymouth*

Below: *One of the most beautiful drives in New Zealand;*
the West Coast Highway

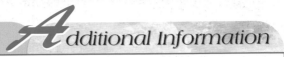
Franz Josef Glacier Hotel $$$
On SH6
☎ (03) 752 0719
Fax (03) 752 0709

Greymouth
Living Streams Hostel $
(Backpackers)
Cowper Street
☎ (03) 768 7272
Fax (03) 768 7276
Free use of kayaks.

Revington's Hotel $$
Tainui St
☎ (03) 768 7055
Fax (03) 768 7605
Oldest hotel in town.
Queen Elizabeth II stayed
here in 1954. The twin-bedded
rooms are budget priced.

Haast
**Haast Highway
Accommodation $**
Marks Road
☎ (03) 750 0703
Tent sites and units.

Wilderness Backpackers $
Pauareka Road
☎ 0800 750 029
Only 55 yards (50 metres)
from bus stop.

World Heritage Hotel $$
On SH6
☎ (03) 750 0828
Fax (03) 750 0827
Good restaurant.

Punakaiki
(Hostels, etc are often full
around here in summer).

**Punakaiki Backpackers
Beach Hostel $**
Cnr Webb St
& Dickenson Parade
☎ (03) 731 1852
Close to beach, facilities for
the disabled, tent sites.

Te Nikau Retreat $
2 miles (3km) north of
Pancake Rocks
☎ (03) 731 1111
Beautiful setting,
not easy to find.

Westport
Bazil's Hostel $
(Backpackers)
54 Russell Street
☎ (03) 789 6410
Popular, friendly and central.

Cosmopolitan Hotel $$
Palmerston Street
☎ (03) 789 6305

*Lake Matheson's still waters are famed
for their reflection of the Southern Alps*

EATING OUT

Barrytown

All Nations Tavern $
Main Highway
☎ (03) 731 1812
Typical pub food.
Also accommodation.

Fox Glacier

Cook Saddle Saloon & Cafe $$
On SH6
☎ (03) 751 0700
Tex-Mex style.

Franz Josef

Blue Ice Cafe $
(BYO/Licensed)
On SH6
☎ (03) 752 0707
Lamb and venison along with pizza and pasta.

D.A's Restaurant $$
(BYO/Licensed)
Main Road
☎ (03) 752 0721

Greymouth

Steamers Café Bar $
58 Mackay Street
☎ (03) 768 4193

Café Collage $$
(BYO)
115 Mackay Street
☎ (03) 768 5497
If available try the whitebait.

Hokitika

PR's Coffee Shop Bistro $
Tancred Street
☎ (03) 755 8379

Café de Paris $$
Sewell Street
☎ (03) 755 8933
Excellent food, whitebait available in season.

Tasman View $$
111 Revell Strewet
☎ (03) 885 5344
Good views over beach.

Punakaiki

Nikau Palms Café $
Main Road
☎ (03) 731 1841
Nice place to sit and relax.

Westport

Diego Restaurant & Bar $$
18 Wakefield Street
☎ (03) 789 7640
Best in town.

PLACES TO VISIT

Charleston

Mitchell's Gully Gold Mine
Open: daily 9am-4pm.

Greymouth

Shantytown
(5 miles/8km south of town)
Open: daily 8.30am-5pm.

Hokitika

West Coast Historical Museum
Tancred Street
Open: daily 9.30am-5pm.

Westland Greenstone
34 Tancred Street
Open: daily 8am-5pm.

Additional Information

Westport

Coaltown
Queen Street South
Open: daily.

Whataroa

White Heron Sanctuary
See Activities.

REGIONAL TRANSPORT

Picton/Christchurch – Greymouth
Coast to Coast Bus
☎ 0800 800 847 (toll free within New Zealand).

Christchurch to Hokitika and Greymouth via Arthur's Pass
Coast Shuttle
Blenheim Taxis
☎ (03) 578 0225
Picton to Greymouth.

VISITOR INFORMATION & PARK VISITOR CENTRES

Fox Glacier
Fox Glacier Visitor Centre
(Westland National Park)
State Highway 6
PO Box 9
☎ (03) 751 0807
Fax (03) 751 0858

Franz Josef Glacier
Franz Josef Visitor Centre
(Westland National Park)
State Highway 6, PO Box 14
☎ (03) 752 0796
Fax (03) 752 0797

Greymouth
Cnr Herbert & Mackay St
☎ (03) 768 5101
Fax (03) 768 0317

Haast
South Westland World Heritage Visitor Centre
State Highway 6
c/o Post Office Agency
Open: daily 8.30am-7pm
(Nov-April), otherwise
8.30am-4.30pm.
☎ (03) 750 0809
Fax (03) 750 0832

Hokitika
Westland Visitor Information Centre
Sewell Street
☎ (03) 755 8322
Fax (03) 755 8026

Karamea
Information & Resource Centre
PO Box 94
☎/Fax (03) 782 6652

Last Resort
PO Box 17
☎ (03) 782 6617
Fax (03) 782 6820

Paparoa National Park Visitor Centre
State Highway,
PO Box 1, Punakaiki
Open: daily 8.30am-6pm early
Nov to Easter. Otherwise
9am-4pm. ☎ (03) 731 1895
Fax (03) 731 1888

Westport
Buller Visitor & Information Centre
1 Brougham Street
☎ (03) 789 6658

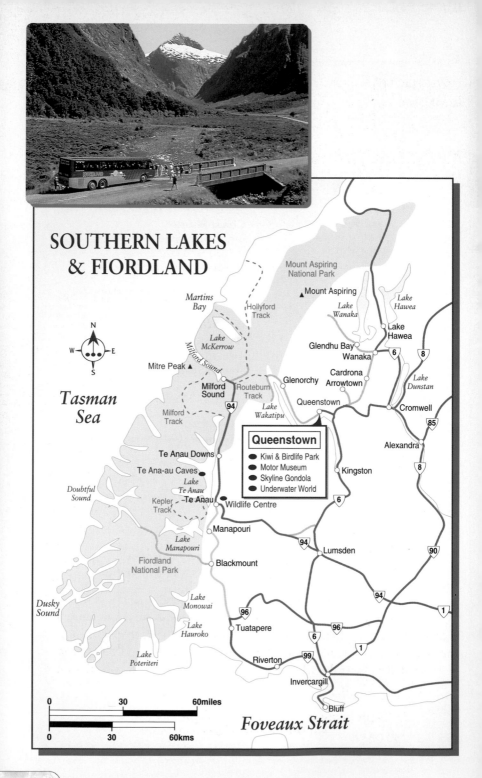

SOUTHERN LAKES & FIORDLAND

Mount Aspiring National Park

Martins Bay

Hollyford Track

▲ Mount Aspiring

Lake Wanaka

Lake Hawea

Lake McKerrow

Lake Hawea

Milford Sound

Glendhu Bay

Wanaka

Mitre Peak ▲

Glenorchy

Cardrona

Arrowtown

6

8

Milford Sound

Routeburn Track

94

Lake Wakatipu

Queenstown

Lake Dunstan

Cromwell

Tasman Sea

Milford Track

85

Queenstown

● Kiwi & Birdlife Park

● Motor Museum

● Skyline Gondola

● Underwater World

Alexandra

8

Te Anau Downs

Te Ana-au Caves

Lake Te Anau

Kingston

Doubtful Sound

Kepler Track

Te Anau

Wildlife Centre

6

Manapouri

Lake Manapouri

94

Lumsden

90

Fiordland National Park

Blackmount

94

Dusky Sound

Lake Monowai

96

1

Lake Hauroko

Tuatapere

96

6

99

Lake Poteriteri

Riverton

1

Invercargill

| 0 | | 30 | | 60miles |

| 0 | | 30 | | 60kms |

Foveaux Strait

Bluff

9 SOUTHERN LAKES & FIORDLAND

Carved by glaciers many thousands of years ago, lakes Wanaka, Hawea, Wakatipu, Te Anau and Manapouri are set in a landscape that is magnificent even by New Zealand standards. Hub of the region is Queenstown which not only enjoys a marvellous setting on the shores of Lake Wakatipu, but also offers superb skiing in winter and a dazzling array of outdoor activities in summer.

To the north and south-west of Queenstown are the untamed wilderness areas of Mount Aspiring and Fiordland National Parks. The former impresses with the splendour of its alpine scenery, whereas the latter is renowned for its spectacular fiords and evergreen rainforests. Even if time does not allow for the walk along Fiordland's famous Milford Track, no visitor should leave the region without taking a cruise on Milford Sound. The scenery is quite stunning and makes a visit to this fiord one of the absolute highlights of any trip to New Zealand.

Opposite page: Fiordland Travel Tour Coaches allow plenty of time for sightseeing

Above: Skiing, The Remarkables Skifield, Queenstown

• ROUTE 11 •
WANAKA TO MANAPOURI
AND BEYOND

Wanaka

So far, Wanaka has been spared the great flood of tourists that descend on Queenstown, the region's principal tourist resort further south. Situated directly on the shores of Lake Wanaka, the town serves as a relaxed base for a whole range of outdoor activities in the midst of splendid scenery. Kayaking, rafting, paragliding, horse trekking and tramping are just a few of the sports that can be enjoyed here.

In winter the town really comes alive as there is excellent downhill skiing at the Cardrona and Treble Cone fields. More experienced skiers have the chance to try some heli-skiing high up in the **Harris Mountains**, whereas the Waiorau ski area has been developed for cross-country skiing.

Gentler pursuits around Wanaka might include a round of golf at the **Wanaka Golf Club**, an aerial tour, a hovercraft trip on the lake or an attempt to solve the outdoor maze at the **Maze and Puzzle Centre**, a few kilometres out of town in the direction of Cromwell. But it might also be enough to simply go picnicking on the lake shore and to enjoy at leisure the unobstructed view of mountains and lake.

Like Lake Wanaka, nearby **Lake Hawea** is a popular place for trout and salmon fishing. However, this lake lacks Wanaka's beaches and gently sloping shoreline as they were drowned when the water level was raised in 1958 as part of a hydro-electric scheme. The lake is nevertheless still very picturesque and Lake Hawea township provides an even better place to get away from the tourist crowds than does Wanaka. But for those who want real solitude, the only solution is to pull on the hiking boots and to bid farewell to civilisation for two or three days among the mountains and valleys of Mount Aspiring National Park.

Mount Aspiring National Park

With a total area of 714,000 acres (289,000 hectares), New Zealand's third largest national park covers a large chunk of the Southern Alps — from the Haast River in the north, to where it joins Fiordland National Park in the south. At the heart of this park is **Mount Aspiring** (9,928ft/3,027m), a pyramid-like peak which has often been compared to the Matterhorn in the Swiss Alps. The Maori name for the region, *Titiraurangi* ('the land of many peaks piercing the clouds'), captures the essentially alpine character of a place that is as exhilarating for the tramper as it is for the mountaineer. Like Westland, Mount Cook and Fiordland National Parks, it belongs to the South-West New Zealand World Heritage Area.

From Wanaka it is a 33 miles (54km) drive along the Mount Aspiring Road to the park's boundaries.

Walking in Mt Aspiring Park

The track to **Aspiring Hut** (2-3 hours one way) starts from the car park at Raspberry Hut and follows the west branch of the **Matukituki River**. It would make a good day's walk for those who do not have the time to explore this valley more thoroughly. There are however, a number of side trips from this hut that would make a tour of two to four days very rewarding.

One such trip is the track to **Lucas Trotter Hut** which leads to the glaciers around Mount Aspiring and some stunning alpine scenery. The track between Aspiring Hut and **Dart Hut** via **Cascade Saddle** also guarantees magnificent alpine views but should only be attempted by the experienced.

Apart from the Matukituki Valley, other access points to the park are from the Haast Road, Makarora (see Chapter 8) and **Glenorchy** near Queenstown. Glenorchy is in fact the starting point for some of the best-known walks in the park such as the **Routeburn** and the **Rees-Dart** (see Queenstown). However walks in the central and northern regions of the park tend to be much less crowded and no less spectacular. A number of organised treks also start from Wanaka which enable trampers to reach areas of the park that are normally only accessible for the very experienced. Park headquarters in Wanaka can give advice on all the options available.

The road heads west along the lake to pretty **Glendhu Bay** from where it soon enters the Matukituki Valley, which is then followed to the road end at **Raspberry Hut**. On the way to Glendhu Bay, those with surplus energy could scale **Roy's Peak** (5,198ft/1,585m) for splendid views of Mount Aspiring (5 hours return, signposted from road).

Routes to Queenstown

The direct route from Wanaka to Queenstown would be along the Crown Range Road via Cardrona, which is the highest main road in the country. But as this scenic mountain road is partly unsealed, it does in fact take longer than the route via Cromwell on SH6.

In winter the **Crown Range Road** may be closed and anyway, it is an alternative that is best left for fine weather. However, if you do venture along this way it is well worth stopping in at the historic **Cardrona Hotel** restaurant. It was built in 1868 and is a popular eatery among skiers as it is close to the Cardrona skifield.

Cromwell and the Kawarau Gorge

The main road to Queenstown passes Cromwell before entering the scenic Kawarau Gorge. Around Cromwell there are a number of roadside stalls where you can replenish the picnic hamper with nectarines, apricots, peaches and a variety of other fruits at bargain prices. If time allows the local museum is worth visiting for its interesting displays on the region's gold-mining days.

What used to be 'Old Cromwell' is now covered by the waters of Lake Dunstan, an artificial lake that was created as part of a huge hydro-electric scheme. Some of the town's historic buildings were rescued however, and can now be seen in the Old Cromwell historic village on Melmore Terrace.

In the Kawarau Gorge, the Mining Centre is not only a place where visitors can have a look at genuine nineteenth century goldfield, but also where they can have a go at panning for gold themselves. Access to the site is across a footbridge over the gorge. Closer to Queenstown, it is worth stopping to have a look at the bungy jumping from the old Kawarau suspension bridge (143ft/ 432m). Bungy jumping as a spectator sport seems to be as popular here as actually doing it, and often tour buses will stop just to let people have a look.

At Arrow Junction a secondary road branches off the main road towards Arrowtown and then continues to Queenstown via Arthur's Point. For those who would rather save Arrowtown for later, the main road continues directly to Queenstown past Lake Hayes, a very pretty little lake that looks particularly attractive when the trees that surround it are aglow with the colours of autumn.

Arrowtown

With a main street lined by faithfully restored buildings from the nineteenth century, Arrowtown is probably the most atmospheric of all New Zealand's old gold-mining towns. On top of this, a good range of shops and accommodation makes the place a very pleasant alternative base for those who can do without Queenstown's nightlife. A good time to visit is definitely autumn when all the deciduous trees that have been planted around town are at their photogenic best.

The Lakes District Centennial Museum in Buckingham Street provides an excellent introduction to the town's gold-mining past. Once visitors have informed themselves here, it is worth walking to the site of the old Chinese miners' settlement at the western end of Buckingham Street, adjacent to the Arrow River.

The Chinese came to Otago in the 1860's to eek out a frugal existence searching for gold in the Shotover and Arrow Gorges. Unfortunately they had to suffer the prejudice of their European neighbours and were forced to live apart from the main settlement. A few simple dwellings as well as a Chinese store have been preserved at the site.

An interesting excursion from Arrowtown is to Macetown, an old gold-miners' settlement that is now a ghost town. It is a long slog on foot (6 hours round trip) but the trip can

Above: *Kelvin Heights Golf Course, Queenstown*

Right: *Arrowtown*

Below: *Bungy Jumping, Kawarau Suspension Bridge, Queenstown*

also be done on a mountain-bike, on horse-back or most comfortably on a four-wheel drive tour — ask at the museum for details. It is a good idea to check about river levels in Arrowtown before walking or biking the route, as there are 26 river crossings on the way!

Queenstown

Queenstown is set next to the shores of beautiful **Lake Wakatipu**, with **The Remarkables** mountain range providing a magnificent backdrop from across the lake's deep blue waters. In autumn or winter, when the surrounding peaks are capped with snow, like icing sugar on a cake, the setting is more than picturesque, it is absolutely stunning!

Inevitably, the South Island's premier holiday resort is as packed with tourists as it is with things to do, but no first time visitor to New Zealand can afford to miss it on their itinerary. Queenstown does, after all, cater to all pockets: Backpackers can find plenty of budget accommodation to offset the expensive hotels, and prices at many restaurants are surprisingly reasonable.

However, any visitor wishing to take part in organised activities in Queenstown should be warned that some of these can be expensive. Still, in Queenstown the rule of thumb is that if you can pay for it you can do it and the range of activities is enormous; ballooning, kayaking, jet-boating, parapenting, rafting, river surfing (shoot the rapids on a boogie board) and the list goes on.

Less of a test of courage but also very exhilarating are the jet-boat trips on the Shotover, Kawerau and Dart Rivers. In real demand

Bungy

Though bungy jumping is now offered elsewhere in New Zealand, it is still one of the most popular activities in Queenstown.

The majority of jumps are organised by bungy 'pioneer' A.J. Hackett, who brought the bungy craze to the world when he jumped off the Eiffel Tower in 1987. With a rubber cord tied securely around the ankles, the bungy jumper leaps into the void, reaching a top speed of around 93 miles (150km) an hour, before the cord checks the fall. As proof that the deed has been done, a video is taken of all jumpers as they plummet downwards.

Apart from the Kawarau Bridge already mentioned, it is also possible to jump off the more spectacular, and higher, **Skippers Canyon Bridge** (232ft/71m) on the upper reaches of the Shotover River. The latest

among many visitors is the ride with the famous **Shotover Jet** through the spectacular scenery of the Shotover River Canyons, but the trips offered by other companies such as **Kawerau Jet** and **Dart River Jetboat Safari** are certainly worth a try too.

White water rafting is also popular on the Kawarau and Shotover Rivers, though the trip on the Shotover

Jumping

additions to Queenstown's bungy repertoire are **The Ledge** and the **Pipeline Bridge** jumps. The Ledge is another brainchild of A.J. Hackett and takes place 1,312ft (400m) above Queenstown amidst breathtaking scenery on **Bob's Peak**.

At present the Pipeline Bridge bungy jump is the only one not organised by Hackett. In order to ensure that they could compete with the established jumps, the operators went to the extent of building the largest single-span suspension bridge in the southern hemisphere over Skippers Canyon. At 335ft (102m) it is even higher than the Skippers Canyon Bridge used by AJ Hackett. The Pipeline jump gets its name from an old water pipeline that was built for gold sluicing in 1864.

through the **Oxenbridge Tunnel** is meant to be the most exciting. Leisurely three-day rafting tours are organised on the **Landsborough River**.

Gold-mining history

Although the Shotover River is the realm of jet boaters and rafters today, its narrow gorges were once the scene of the country's largest gold rush. It had its beginnings in 1862 after two shearers discovered a large quantity of gold in the river. Before long, thousands of fortune hunters had arrived to stake their claims. The diggings around **Skippers Canyon** were particularly productive but the cost of extracting gold from this difficult area was so high that large scale operations were brought to an end in 1907.

Drivers who want to visit the area are warned that the road through the steep gorge of Skippers Canyon is narrow, unsealed and very windy. If a tour bus is encountered it can mean reversing considerable distances. Coaches make the trip regularly from Queenstown and this is probably the better alternative, even for those with their own transport. For more information about a bus trip to Skippers, contact **Mount Cook Line Travel Centre**, Rees Street (☎ (03) 442 7650).

Lake Wakatipu

Much more relaxing than jumping off bridges or shooting rapids is a lake cruise on the *TSS Earnslaw* (1912), a vintage steamer that once carried goods to and from isolated sheep stations scattered around the lake. In the mornings and afternoons, passengers are taken on a three-hour cruise to **Walter Peak** sheep station for a glimpse of life on a high-country farm. It is also possible to have lunch on board the boat during a short midday cruise and there are evening cruises with a meal at Walter Peak for the romantically minded.

Those who have missed a sailing can at least visit **Underwater World** on the pier at the end of the Mall — not far from the steamer wharf. An underwater-viewing gallery allows a close-up look at the lake's inhabitants; native eels, along with rainbow and brown trout are attracted by automatic feeders. Quite often small ducks known as scaup put in guest appearances as they dive in search of food.

Other attractions

Other places to visit in town include the **Queenstown Motor Museum** with its collection of vintage cars, and the **Kiwi and Birdlife Park**.

Both are located near the lower terminal of the **Skyline Gondola** in Brecon Street. The gondola is an attraction in itself and the spectacular ride up Bob's Peak is not to be missed. At the top one can enjoy a splendid panorama of lake and mountains from the comfort of a licensed restaurant.

Skiing

In winter Queenstown is no less active than in summer, the only difference being that activities have shifted to the surrounding ski fields. Closest to town are **Coronet Peak** and the

Walks around Glenorchy

A nice excursion, or break, from Queenstown is to follow the unsurfaced road along the Wakatipu shoreline to Glenorchy, at the head of the lake. Glenorchy is the starting point for the Routeburn, Rees-Dart, Greenstone and Caples tracks. Of these it is the Routeburn, a magnificent three to four day hike through Mount Aspiring and Fiordland National Parks, that is most famous. This route can be turned into a round trip by combining it with either the Caples or Greenstone Track.

Though not as spectacular, the Greenstone and Caples tracks have the advantage of being less crowded than the Routeburn and are usually done together as a loop walk in four or five days.

Least travelled of all these tracks is the Rees-Dart. This circular route through forest and dramatic alpine scenery can be walked in four days. An interesting option is to do the last section by inflatable canoe (known as a Fun Yak). The organisers bring trampers to the start of the track by van, from where they walk independently for three or more days through the Rees and Upper Dart Valleys. On the last day a guide meets trampers at Sandy Bluff in the Dart Valley for the canoe trip back to Glenorchy. This trip is advertised as the 'Fun Yak canoeing option'. For more information contact Danes in Queenstown, corner Shotover and Camp Streets ☎ (03) 442 7318. During the summer season, transport to the starting points of all three tracks can be arranged from either Queenstown or Glenorchy.

Above: Lake Hawea

Right: Continental cafe in the Mall at Queenstown

Below: View from Brunswick Lodge, Queenstown

Remarkables but daily shuttle buses also run to **Treble Cone** and **Cardrona** near Wanaka. The ski season lasts from about June to October.

Nightlife

Après-ski fans will appreciate that Queenstown's nightlife is somewhat more lively than in other New Zealand towns. There are a number of places where one can wine, dine and dance until late in the night. Live entertainment is offered at the **Skyline Restaurant**, **Chico's Restaurant and Bar**, the **Lone Star Saloon** and **Vilagrad**. A good cold beer can be enjoyed till the early hours at **McNeill's Brewery Café**, the **Pig & Whistle** or **Eichardt's**. **Solera Vino** is a wine bar which is meant to be good for a wild night on the town. All in all Queenstown has over 20 bars, four nightclubs and over 100 restaurants to choose from.

Day trips

Visitors who do not have their own transport, or want to save themselves the drive from Queenstown, can book a variety of day trips to **Milford** or **Doubtful Sound**. The trips include a cruise on the sounds and can be done with the bus, a combination of bus and plane or, quickest of all, by flying there and back.

The journey using only the bus is certainly the cheapest but it makes for a long day: the Doubtful Sound trip takes 14 hours and the Milford trip takes 12 hours. Day trips are offered by **Fiordland Travel, Mt Cook, Pacific Tourways** and a few others. Shop around for the best deals.

Moving on

The road south from Queenstown to Te Anau (109 miles/177km) is quite scenic with the first leg of the journey following the Wakatipu shoreline as far as **Kingston**, at the lake's southern tip.

The Kingston steam train

In the summer months an old steam train known as the *Kingston Flyer* runs along the track between Kingston and Fairlight. Passengers get to ride in old fashioned wooden carriages and can enjoy refreshments in a turn-of-the-century buffet carriage that has been fitted out with beautiful New Zealand native wood panelling.

At Five Rivers turn right off SH6 towards Mossburn. From here SH94 is followed to Te Anau and Fiordland.

Fiordland National Park

The largest of all New Zealand's national parks protects a vast, magnificent expanse of mountainous terrain covered by forests, penetrated by fiords and studded with glacially formed lakes. One of these lakes, **Lake Te Anau**, is surpassed in size only by Lake Taupo in the North Island. In view of all this, it is hardly surprising that Fiordland forms a vital part of the South-West New Zealand World

Heritage Area, one of the few places on earth that have survived the onslaught of civilisation in a virtually unspoiled state.

Survival of the takahe

That Fiordland has been able to escape the devastating effects of the axe and plough is largely due to its remoteness and rugged character. These factors have also been important in enabling the survival of one of the country's rarest birds. In 1948 the takahe (*Notornis mantelli*) was rediscovered in a secluded valley in the **Murchison Mountains**. This flightless bird had been presumed extinct for more than half a century and its rediscovery aroused worldwide interest. The area in which the birds were found is now closed to the general public in order to ensure that the colony remains undisturbed.

Te Anau

Te Anau, on the shores of the lake of the same name, is the springboard for trips to Milford Sound and walks in Fiordland National Park. There is not a great deal to do in town itself but those with time to spare can choose from a variety of lake cruises or perhaps indulge in a scenic flight on a floatplane.

About a ten minute walk from the Visitor Centre, in the direction of Manapouri, is the **Te Anau Wildlife Centre**. It is worth a look not only because it is free, but also because this is one of the few places where visitors can get a close-up look at the rare takahe. Other native birds to be seen here include kakas, keas, tuis and parakeets.

Te Ana-au Caves

A highlight of any Te Anau visit is the $2^1/_2$ hour excursion to Te Ana-au Caves, the 'Caves of Rushing Water'. Though the caves were referred to in Maori legends, their exact location had long been a mystery and it was not until 1948, after a search of several years, that they were rediscovered. Located on the lake shore, at the edge of the restricted takahe area, the cave system is accessible only by boat from Te Anau. A combination of footpaths and two short boat trips through spectacular limestone caverns, leads visitors past underground waterfalls and to a glow-worm grotto.

Walking in Fiordland Park

There are many short day walks that can be started from Te Anau but the goal of most enthusiastic trampers is one of the big walks: the **Kepler**, the **Hollyford**, the **Routeburn** (see Glenorchy) or the famous **Milford Track**. Vital equipment for all walkers on these tracks is good quality wet weather gear (Fiordland gets some of the highest rainfalls in New Zealand) and plenty of strong insect repellant to keep the sand-flies at bay. '**Dimp**' is a well known local brand of repellant but it also helps to wear long sleeve shirts and trousers.

Kepler Track

Of the tracks mentioned above it is only the Kepler that forms a circular route. The track starts at the Lake Te Anau outlet control gates, a 45 minute walk from the Te Anau park Visitor Centre. Those who wish can also catch a shuttle bus to the start of the track or take one of the boat services from Te Anau to **Brod Bay**, thus saving three hours walking. The tramp, which takes three to four days, features splendid views from alpine ridge tops, lovely beech forest and a U-shaped glacial valley. The huts along the way are quite comfortable but camping is also permitted at **Brod Bay** and **Iris Burn**.

Hollyford Track

The Hollyford Track is a very long walk (69 miles/112km total distance) from Hollyford Camp (formerly Gunn's Camp) on the Hollyford Road to the Tasman Sea at **Martins Bay**. The outward journey and return trip along the same route would take roughly eight days. However the time required to walk the track can be greatly reduced (4 days) by taking a pre-arranged jet-boat across **Lake McKerrow** (the stretch of track along the lake is rather dull and difficult) and then flying out from Martins Bay. This can all be arranged through **Hollyford Valley Walks** in Te Anau. They also conduct guided walks along the Hollyford Valley which include the jet-boat trip and the flight out as an optional extra. At remote Martins Bay there is a seal colony and Fiordland crested penguins may also be spotted.

Milford Track

Last but certainly not least is the **Milford Track**. Often described as 'the finest walk in the world' it is also New Zealand's most strictly controlled. The number of people who can walk the track in any one season is limited, it must be done within four days (31 miles/50km) and can only be walked in one direction. These controls, and others, are necessary to protect the track from overcrowding and to ensure that the natural environment remains intact.

In spite of all the limitations the walk is worth it. Waterfalls, lakes, mountain valleys carved by glaciers, luxuriant rainforest and stunning alpine views are all ingredients that combine to make the Milford Track so exceptional. One of the walk's most outstanding scenic highlights is the view of **Sutherland Falls**. With a drop of 1,900ft (580m) the falls are the highest in New Zealand and the fifth highest in the world. The only other way to see this spectacle is on one of the scenic flights from Te Anau or Queenstown — highly recommended if time is limited.

It is possible to do the Milford Track as an independent tramper or as part of a guided tour. Whereas the guided parties have everything provided, independent walkers must carry all the gear and supplies

Opposite page: — Main picture: A launch trip through Milford Sound is one of the highlights of any visit to New Zealand

Insert: Lake Wakatipu

they need themselves. The track starts at **Glade House** which is usually reached by boat from Te Anau or Te Anau Downs. A launch picks walkers up at the other end for the trip to **Milford Sound** township. Everybody who wants to walk the Milford should book well in advance; this also applies to independent walkers as they require a permit for the track. These permits or accommodation passes can only be booked through the Park Visitor Centre at Te Anau. Note that the track is only open from November to mid-April and that December, January and February are the months when demand is highest.

The road to Milford Sound

For those who have not been able to do the walk to Milford Sound, then the road is the next best thing. Visitors without private transport can take the bus from Te Anau but if you are driving yourself, try and pick up a copy of the free pamphlet describing the route which is available in Te Anau from either **Fiordland Travel** or the petrol station. As there are no petrol stations on the 73 miles (119km) stretch of road between Te Anau and Milford Sound (a 2 1/2 hour drive) it is wise to make sure the tank is filled before departing.

Leaving Te Anau the road first follows the lake shore before swinging inland to enter the national park. In fine weather, which is by no means guaranteed, this drive is one of the loveliest in New Zealand. Worthwhile stops on the way to the Homer Tunnel include the **Mirror Lakes, Cascade Creek** (refreshments) and **Lake Gunn**.

If time allows, the detour along the Hollyford Road to **Hollyford Camp** is also rewarding. Near the start of the road is a track leading up to **Lake Marian** (4 hours return) and some fine alpine views. At Hollyford Camp there are simple cabins with coal-range stoves, bunks and electric light (only a few hours in the evenings). The camp's small museum is worth a look and there is also a shop with basic supplies. Most people who stay here are going to do the Hollyford Track but it would also be an alternative to accommodation in Milford for those with cars.

From the Hollyford turn-off the Milford Road climbs towards the **Homer Tunnel**. Rough hewn and almost forbiddingly dark, the tunnel descends steeply for 3,998ft (1,219m) before it emerges dramatically into the magnificent upper reaches of the **Cleddau Valley**.

Continuing its steep descent the road winds past a signpost pointing the way to the **Chasm**. A short walk (15 minutes return) leads through beautiful native forest to where the **Cleddau River** has carved its way through the rock, sculpting it into bizarre shapes and forming a chasm, some 72ft (22m) deep. From here it is just over 6 miles (10km) to Milford Sound.

Milford Sound

Enclosed by walls of bare rock that rise vertically from the sea, the 9 mile (15km) long fiord known as Milford Sound was formed by glacial action during the last Ice Age, some 1.5 million years ago. One of the fiord's most picturesque features is the sheer rock pinnacle of **Mitre**

Peak which, rising as it does to a height of 5,556ft (1,694m), manages to stand out even in this landscape of superlatives.

Cruises

The only way to really appreciate the majesty of Milford Sound is, of course, on one of the boat cruises that depart regularly from the large wharf complex. Apart from the spectacular scenery, such a cruise also promises close-up views of seals and occasionally dolphins. Remember it can pay to book ahead in the summer season as these trips are very popular and furthermore, do not be put off by wet weather! When it rains, Milford's many waterfalls are at their most spectacular, especially the 505ft (154m)-high **Stirling Falls** which can only be seen from the boat.

An interesting variation on the day trips is the overnight cruise on the sailing boat *Milford Wanderer*. This trip, along with several others, can be booked through Fiordland Travel in Te Anau or Queenstown.

Walks

After the boat trip, which usually takes about 1 hour 45 minutes, it is worth making the short walk from the wharf to **Lady Bowen Falls**. The waterfall drops a spectacular 526ft (160m) from a hanging valley in the Darren Range. A large area at the foot of the falls is covered by a fine spray of water, including three old graves that must belong to the wettest in the world. The graves actually date back to the time of the early nineteenth century sealers and whalers who were sometimes marooned for many months on Fiordland's inhospitable shores. More information about other walks and the history of the area is available at the **Milford Sound Hotel.**

Around Manapouri

From Te Anau the way south continues via Manapouri, on the shores of beautiful **Lake Manapouri**.

In the 1970's this idyllic piece of New Zealand was the subject of an intense environmental controversy. The government wanted to raise the level of the lake by 39ft (12m) to generate electricity for the aluminium smelter at Bluff. Massive protests prevented the worst, and though the hydroelectric scheme went ahead, the lake was not raised to levels that would have dramatically altered the local environment.

Today it is possible to visit the hydro station, a trip that can be recommended even for environmentalists, if only because it is the most convenient way to visit isolated Doubtful Sound.

Doubtful Sound excursion

The trip to Doubtful Sound, dubbed 'Nature's Masterpiece', commences with a cruise on Manapouri to the underground power station at the end of the lake's West Arm. After leaving the launch, a bus descends the 1 mile (2km) spiral of the access tunnel, deep into the bowels of the earth, to the power station's machine hall. Here visitors can admire the ingenuity that was required to carve this huge cavern from the solid granite. After the tour of the machine hall the bus leaves the power station to climb over Wilmot Pass (2,197ft/670m) to **Deep Cove** in Doubtful Sound, which is then explored on a catamaran.

The Dusky Track

For the more energetic, Manapouri also serves as a base for the challenging but uncrowded walk to **Dusky Sound** (10 days). The Dusky Track offers trampers an insight into the more remote reaches of Fiordland National Park as it threads its way through wild, rain-drenched forests and over alpine passes to reach isolated **Supper Cove Hut** on Dusky Sound. Because of the very rough nature of the terrain, this

track is only suitable for experienced parties but it can be shortened to 4 or 5 days by flying in or out of Dusky Sound.

Instead of starting at Manapouri it is also possible to start from **Lake Hauroko** further south. Both variations of the tramp can be linked for a trip taking from 8 to 10 days.

The Southern Scenic Route

The way south from Manapouri continues along the Southern Scenic Route, which has its 'official' starting point in Te Anau. It skirts the eastern borders of Fiordland National Park to the coast, which it then follows part of the way to Invercargill.

As the road nears the coast it is bordered by huge hedges of native flax that function as wind-breaks. Macrocarpa trees have also been planted along the road for the same purpose and many of them have been bent into incredible shapes by the prevailing wind.

Just over 54 miles (88km) from Invercargill, the small town of Tuatapere serves as a base for those who want to explore **Lake Hauroko** and the southern reaches of Fiordland National Park. **Colac Bay** and **The Rocks** near **Riverton** are safe areas for swimming.

From Invercargill, the Southern Scenic Route follows SH92 through the Catlins to where it ends at **Balclutha**. The section from Invercargill is described in the following chapter. A pamphlet with a map of the route is available from the tourist offices in Te Anau, Invercargill and Dunedin.

Authors' Tip

Rather than fly over the fiords (the sheer number of sightseeing flights over Milford Sound has caused a noise pollution problem), an environmentally friendly alternative is to try the Fiordland Ecology Holiday offered by Lance and Ruth Shaw at 1 Home Street, Manapouri. These natural history tours are especially devised for small groups and include a trip on a yacht through the lesser known regions of Fiordland.

For more information ☎ (03)249 6600.

ACTIVITIES

Fiordland National Park

Tramping

Dusky Track: Waterwings Airways, Te Anau fly trampers to Supper Cove, thus saving the walk in.
☎ (03) 249 7405
Fax (03) 249 7939

Hollyford Track: Hollyford Valley Walks, Queenstown & Te Anau, arrange transport and also offer guided walks.
☎ (03)249 8012 (Te Anau) or (03) 442 3760 (Queenstown).

Kepler Track: Te Anau Motor Park operates a shuttle bus to the track ☎ (03) 249 7457. The yacht *Manuska* (☎ (03) 249 7106) and **Lakeland Boat Hire** (☎ (03) 249 8364) bring trampers to Brod Bay from Te Anau Wharf.

Mitre Peak, Milford Sound

Milford Track Guided Walk: Bookings can be made through **Te Anau Travelodge**, 'Milford Track Guided Walk', PO Box 185, Te Anau
☎ (03) 249 7411
Fax (03) 249 7050.

Milford Track Independent Walk: Bookings are made through **Fiordland National Park Visitor Centre**, PO Box 29, Te Anau.
☎ (03) 249 8514 or
Fax (03) 249 8515

Bookings for both walks should be made several months or even a year in advance.

For independent trampers, transport connections to and from the track can be booked with the application form for an accommodation pass that is available from the **National Park Visitor Centre**, Te Anau.

Trampers must have transport arranged before they can pick up their accommodation passes.

Kingston

Steam Train

Kingston Flyer

Steam locomotive between Kingston and Fairlight. Return trip takes 1 hour. Departs Kingston twice daily during the summer months. For more information contact the Travel and Visitor Centre, Queenstown.

Queenstown

Adventure Packages

There are many packages to choose from. What follows is a selection.

'**Awesome Foursome**' involves a helicopter ride, white water rafting, jet boat trip and bungy jump ☎ (03) 442 7318 or AJ Hackett ☎ 442 7100. A similar combination is the *Shotover Assault* which includes the Pipeline Bungy Jump ☎ (03) 442 9792.

Big Bay Wilderness Adventure starts with a flight to Big Bay on the West Coast. From here you walk through native forest, paddle in a canoe and finally return by plane to the starting point. ☎ (03) 442 6228

Dane's Trio Grand includes a jet boat trip, helicopter flight and raft trip ☎ (03) 442 7318.

Boat Trips

TSS Earnslaw

Departs the: Steamer wharf daily for the cruise to Walter Peak Sheep Station. Here visitors can watch demonstrations of sheep shearing and sheep dogs at work.

Bungy Jumping

AJ Hackett's Action Culture

Queenstown Bungy Centre (situated in The Station), Shotover Street
Open: office is open daily 7.30am-7.30pm. Bungy jumps take place daily, except Christmas Day. Bookings essential ☎ (03) 442 7100.

This company also offers a 1000ft (300m) jump from a helicopter.

Pipeline Bungy

Pipeline Iglu, Shotover Street ☎ (03) 442 5455
At 335 feet (102m) the Pipeline is at present the highest bridge jump around Queenstown. There are daily departures to the jump site in Skippers Canyon.

Jet Boating

Further details at the Information Centre, Cnr Camp & Shotover Sts.

Dart River Jet Boat Safari ☎ (03) 442 9992
This trip lasts 5½ hrs.

Kawarau Jet ☎ (03) 442 6142

Shotover Jet ☎ (03) 42 8570

Twin Rivers Jet ☎ (03) 442 3257

Scenic Flights

Scenic flights are popular and there are plenty to choose from. An interesting possibility is to take a fly/cruise/coach trip. This involves a scenic flight, a cruise on Milford Sound and a bus trip either to or from Queenstown. Companies offering such trips include **Fiordland Travel** ☎ (03) 442 7500 and **Amazing Tours** ☎ (03) 442 9437.

White Water Rafting

Danes
Information Centre
Cnr Shotover & Camp Streets
☎ (03) 442 7318

Kiwi Discovery Tours
Camp Street
☎ (03) 442 7340

Landsborough River Expeditions
PO Box 410
☎/Fax (03) 442 3630
A 3 day tour or contact Danes for a 2 day trip on the Landsborough.

Manapouri

Boat Trips

DOUBTFUL SOUND TRIP

Fiordland Travel
Pearl Harbour
☎ (03) 249 6602
Long trip: daily 10.30am
(23 Oct-31 March).
Short Trip: daily 8.30am
(1 Oct-31 March) & daily
10.30am (1 April-30 Sept.)
   Fiordland Travel arranges connecting coaches from Queenstown and Te Anau.

Milford Sound

Boat Trips

Fiordland Travel
Steamer Wharf, Queenstown
☎ (03) 442 7500 or
0800 656 501 (Te Anau)
This company offers a variety of cruises on Milford Sound. The standard launch cruise departs 11am & 1pm daily (all year round) and also 3pm daily from 1 Oct-20 April. Overnight cruises take place on the Milford Wanderer,

a motorised sailing vessel. The season for these cruises is 1 Oct-30 April. Day cruises are also offered on this boat at 10.45am (2¹/₂ hrs) & 1.30pm (1 hr 50 mins) daily from 1 Oct-30 April.

Red Boat Cruises
☎ (03) 249 7926
Bookings can also be made at various tour agencies in Queenstown.
Departures: 11am & 1.30pm (all year round) and 10.30am, 1pm & 3pm from 1 Oct-30 April.

Fiordland Fish 'n' Dive
☎/Fax (03) 249 8833
This company does not offer a normal cruise but, instead swimming trips to the seals and dolphins as well as scuba diving expeditions to the Sound's famous red and black corals. They also offer fishing trips outside Milford Sound.

Sea Kayaking

Roscoe's Milford Sound Sea Kayaks
☎ (03) 249 8840
An interesting alternative to the usual cruises. Transport is arranged to and from Te Anau.

Mt Aspiring National Park

Tramping

Routeburn Track: Glenorchy Holiday Park can arrange transport to this track and also Dart-Rees and Greenstone-Caples tracks. They operate the Backpacker Express which also runs from Queenstown ☎ (03) 442 9939.

Matukituki Valley: Matuki Services provide a regular mini-bus service between Wanaka and the Matukituki Valley ☎ (03) 443 7980. A similar service is offered by **Mt Aspiring Express** ☎ (03) 443 7414.

Te Anau

Boat Trips

Te Ana-au Caves Trip
Fiordland Travel
Lakefront Drive
☎ (03) 249 8900 or 0800 656 501
Departures: daily 2pm & 8.15pm.
The trip to the caves takes 2¹/₂ hrs.

Sinbad Cruises
15 Fergus Square
☎ (03) 249 7106
Offer a variety of cruises on Lake Te Anau on board their yacht Manuska.

Sea Kayaking

Fiordland Wilderness Experiences
66 Quintin Drive
☎ (03) 249 7700
Kayak trips and hire. A fascinating way to explore Milford or Doubtful Sounds.

Scenic Flights

Air Fiordland
☎ (03) 249 7505
The flight over Sutherland Falls is well worth it if you cannot do the Milford Track. The flights from Milford (where they have a plane based in summer) are cheaper.

Southern Lakes Helicopters
☎ (03) 249 7167

Waterwings Airways Ltd
☎ (03) 249 7405
Their short flight over the Kepler Track is worthwhile. Also flights to Milford, Dusky and Doubtful Sounds.

Wanaka

Boat Trips

Hovercraft Cruise
Wanaka Lake Services
The Wharf
Departs: regularly for 15-45 min cruises.

Jet Boating

Clutha River Jet
Wanaka Lake Services
The Lakefront
☎ (03) 443 7495

Kayaking

Alpine River Guides
99 Ardmore Street
☎ (03) 443 9023
Kayak trips and hire.

Scenic Flights

Aspiring Air
☎ (03) 443 7943

Wanaka Aviation
☎ (03) 443 1385

White Water Rafting

Edgewater Adventures
☎ (03) 443 8311
Also various other outdoor activities.

ACCOMMODATION

See pages 288 and 300 in the FactFile for the accommodation and restaurant rating guide

Arrowtown

New Orleans Hotel-Motel $
27 Buckingham Street
☎ (03) 442 1745
Small hotel with 7 bedrooms
and a bunkhouse.

Glenorchy

Glenorchy Holiday Park $
2 Oban Street
☎ (03) 442 9939
Fax (03) 442 9940
Cabins, tourist flats and tent sites.
Transport to all the tracks.

Milford

Milford Sound Hotel $$$
☎ (03) 249 7926
Fax (03) 249 8094
Beautifully situated.

Queenstown

Bumbles $
(Backpackers)
2 Brunswick St
☎ (03) 442 6298
Close to middle of town.

McFee's Waterfront Hotel $
Shotover Street
☎ (03) 442 7400
Fax (03) 442 7403
Rooms with en suite bathrooms.

Adelaide Street Guest House $$
(Bed & Breakfast)
15 Adelaide Street
☎/Fax (03) 442 6207
Cosy atmosphere, good
views, 5 minutes to town.

Queenstown Parkroyal $$$
Beach Street
☎ (03) 442 7800
Fax (03) 442 8895
Large hotel with views of
the lake and the Remarkables.

Te Anau

**Lake Te Anau
Backpackers Lodge $**
48 Lakefront Drive
☎ (03) 249 7713
Fax (03) 249 8319
Friendly place, central location.

Anchorage Motel $$
47 Quintin Drive
☎ (03)249 7256
Fax (03) 249 7102

Shakespeare House $$
(Bed & Breakfast)
10 Dusky St
☎ (03) 249 7349
Fax (03) 249 7629
Hearty breakfasts served here.

Wanaka

Matterhorn South Lodge $
(Backpackers)
56 Brownston St
☎ (03) 443 1119
Fax (03) 443 8379
Small, cosy and central.

Te Wanaka Lodge $$
(Bed & Breakfast)
23 Brownston St
☎ (03) 443 9224
Fax (03) 443 9246
Non-smoking, wood fires,
pleasant atmosphere.

EATING OUT

Queenstown

Eichardts Tavern $
(Licensed)
The Mall
☎ (03) 442 8369
Light meals and snacks.

Avanti Restaurant $$
20 The Mall
(Licensed)
☎ (03) 442 8503
Italian cuisine.

Gourmet Express $$
(BYO/Licensed)
62 Shotover Street
☎ (03) 442 9619
Good place for breakfast.

Lagos Bar & Cafe $$
(Licensed)
Steamer Wharf
☎ (03) 442 5969
Mediterranean-style food.

Roaring Meg's $$$
(Licensed)
57 Shotover St
☎ (03) 442 9676
A New Zealand specialty offered here is mutton bird.

Saguaro's Mexican Restaurant $$$
(BYO/Licensed)
Trust Bank Arcade,
Beach Street
☎ (03) 442 8240
Tasty Tex-Mex food.

Te Anau

La Toscana $
(BYO/Licensed)
108 Town Centre
☎ (03) 249 7756
Good pasta and pizza.

Wanaka

Relishes $$
(BYO/Licensed)
99 Ardmore Road
☎ (03) 443 9018
One of the better cafes in town.

Ripples Restaurant $$
(BYO)
Pembroke Mall
☎ (03) 443 7413
Specialities include venison, lamb and seafood.

PLACES TO VISIT

Arrowtown

Lakes District Centennial Museum
Buckingham Street
Open: daily 9am-5pm.

Cromwell

Cromwell Museum
44 The Mall
Open: daily 10am-4pm.

Kawarau Gorge Mining Centre
In the Kawarau Gorge, 8km west, on SH6
Open: daily .

Queenstown

Kiwi & Birdlife Park
Base of the Gondola, Brecon Street
Open: daily 9am-5pm, during summer until 9pm.

Queenstown Motor Museum
Base of the Gondola. Brecon Street
Open: daily 9am-5.30pm.

Underwater World
On the pier, end of The Mall
Open: daily.

Te Anau

Te Anau Wildlife Centre
On road to Manapouri
Open: daily. Admission is free.

Underground Trout Observatory
Lakefront Drive
Open: daily. Entrance is through
a coin-operated turnstile.

Wanaka

The Puzzling Place & Great Maze
On main highway,
just south of Wanaka.
Open: daily 8.30am-5.30pm.
Entry to Hologram Exhibition
is free.

VISITOR INFORMATION & PARK VISITOR CENTRES

Fiordland National Park Visitor Centre
Lakefront Drive, Te Anau
Open: daily.
☎ (03) 249 7921 or
(03) 249 8514
Fax (03) 249 8515
(Bookings for independent
Milford Track walkers).

Mount Aspiring National Park
Visitor Centre
Ardmore St, Wanaka
Open: Mon-Fri 8am-5pm.
☎ (03) 443 7660

Queenstown
Travel & Visitor Centre Ltd
Clocktower Centre, Cnr Shotover
& Camp Streets, PO Box 253
Open: daily from 7am-7pm
(summer).
☎ (03) 442 4100
Fax (03) 442 8907
They also offer complete internet
services and will pass on e-mails
sent to visitors at their e-mail
address: **qvc@xtra.co.nz**.
There are several other places
in Queenstown which offer

information and take bookings.
They include: **The Station**
☎ 442 5252 opposite the Travel
& Visitor Centre; **The
Backpacking Specialists**
☎ 442 8178 at 35 Shotover Street;
**Dane's Queenstown Information
Centre** ☎ 442 7318 on the
corner of Shotover and Camp
Streets and the **Information
& Track Walking Centre**
☎ 442 9708 on Shotover Street.

Te Anau
Fiordland Travel Ltd,
Te Anau Terrace, PO Box 1
☎ (03) 249 8900 7419
Fax (03) 249 7022
Located in same building as
Fiordland Travel which arranges
a variety of excursions in the
area ☎ (03) 249 7419 or
Freephone 0800 656 501.

Wanaka
Ardmore Street, PO Box 147
☎ (03) 443 1233
Fax (03) 443 9238
Shares premises with Mount
Aspiring National Park Visitor
Centre.

10 THE DEEP SOUTH & OTAGO

This chapter covers the region of Southland, including Stewart Island, in the far south of the South Island, and all of Otago except for the lakes district around Queenstown. A natural border to the west is Fiordland National Park, and to the north the Waitaki River. For those coming from Queenstown, the quickest route to Invercargill is on SH6 but a much more interesting alternative is the Southern Scenic Route which starts at Te Anau (see Chapter 9). The section between Invercargill and Dunedin is described in the following pages.

Climate and character

Southland and **South-East Otago** are both areas that are relatively neglected by most visitors to New Zealand, many of whom get no further south than Queenstown or Milford Sound. Admittedly the weather is not as attractive as it is around Marlborough or Nelson (lots of rainy days and the country's lowest mean average temperatures) but the trip is still worth it, especially for those visitors who are interested in New Zealand's unique flora and fauna.

East of Invercargill, the beautiful **Catlin's Forest Park** shelters many different species of native birds as well as a variety of sea mammals along its rocky coastline. On **Stewart Island,** nature still seems to reign supreme; there are hardly any roads, only a tiny resident population and

Above: The famous Moeraki boulders at Moeraki

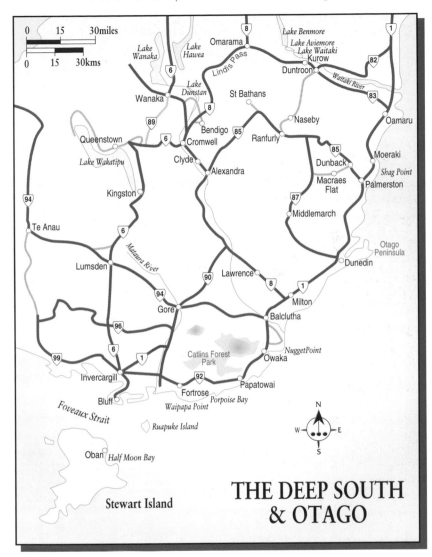

THE DEEP SOUTH & OTAGO

most of the island is covered by dense forest. If you want to see a kiwi in the wild, Stewart Island may be your best chance.

Otago is wedged in between Southland and Canterbury and is separated from the former by the Mataura River which enters the sea east of **Invercargill**. In general the climate is drier and sunnier than Southland's, especially in the area of **Central Otago** which lies in the rain shadow of the Southern Alps. In places like Dunback, St Bathans and Clyde, the romance of the Otago gold rushes still lingers on, whereas the **Otago Peninsula** awaits visitors with a rich diversity of wildlife and a Scottish baronial hall. Largest city is Dunedin, as proud of its Scottishness as Christchurch is of its Englishness.

• ROUTE 12 •
THE SOUTHERN SCENIC ROUTE TO DUNEDIN

Invercargill

Invercargill is a flat, sprawling city (population 52,000) in the far south of the South Island. It is the southernmost city in New Zealand and one of the southernmost settlements of any size in the world. The city's prosperity is based on the fact that it is situated in the midst of some of New Zealand's richest pasture lands, where a high but evenly spread annual rainfall allows the year round growth of grass. But to Frederick Tuckett, who came to the South Island in 1844 to survey land for a proposed Scottish settlement, the area seemed distinctly lacking in potential. He described the present city site as *'a mere bog, and quite unfit for human habitation'*. The Scots came anyway and today Invercargill's Scottish heritage is reflected in the fact that many of its streets are named after Scottish rivers.

The main place of interest is the **Southland Museum and Art Gallery** in Gala Street, near the main entrance to Queens Park. Housed in a building shaped like a large white pyramid, the museum focuses on Southland's history and natural history. A main attraction is the **Tuatara House**, where it is possible to see these rare and ancient reptiles in a setting that attempts to reproduce their natural environment as accurately as possible. Also of great interest is the *'Roaring Forties Experience'*, an audio-visual that vividly portrays the flora and fauna of New Zealand's remote subantartic islands.

After visiting the museum a pleasant place to stroll is through the manicured lawns and gardens of **Queens Park**. Within its spacious confines there are duck ponds, a play ground, a swimming pool and even an 18 hole golf course. Snacks and light lunches are provided by the tea kiosk which is open daily.

Bluff

Invercargill's port is Bluff, 16 miles (27km) further south. The port's main claim to fame is the delicious oysters that are harvested during a

Bluff oysters

Oysters fresh from the sea can be sampled from March 1 until August 31, but the highlight of the season is undoubtedly the week-long **Bluff Seafood Festival** in mid-April. Those who wish can visit the oyster sheds during the season to watch skilled workers scooping the delectable molluscs from their shells. Although purists will prefer them raw, the oysters are commonly disguised in a (hopefully) crisp batter and sold by the local take-aways as oysters and chips.

limited season from **Foveaux Strait** and which send New Zealand's seafood gourmets into raptures of delight.

The pleasures of seafood aside there is not a great deal more to Bluff to distract the attention of visitors eagerly awaiting the departure of the Stewart Island ferry. One 'sight' that is impossible to miss is the rather unattractive industrial complex of the **Tiwai Point Aluminium Smelter**, just across the water. The smelter is one of the largest in the world and Southland's largest single employer. A free tour of the complex takes about two hours.

Another place of interest is the unique **Paua Shell House**, a private home decorated with thousands of brightly polished paua (abalone) shells.

At **Stirling Point** (follow SH1 through Bluff, along the coast) there is a restaurant with sea views and the start of a coastal walkway (2 hours). For the best views around, either walk or drive to the top of **Bluff Hill** (869ft/265m).

Stewart Island

Separated from the South Island by Foveaux Strait, Stewart Island is New Zealand as it once was: a thickly forested island where the sound of birds dominates over the sounds of human activity, where roads are less significant than forest tracks and where the light of stars on a clear summer night shine brighter than the modest lights of **Oban**, the island's only real concession to civilisation. On some clear nights, visitors might even witness the *aurora australis*, the 'southern lights',

a natural spectacle that perhaps explains the Maori name for Stewart Island which is Rakiura (heavenly glow). If one does not have the luck to see the fantastic shimmering of the southern lights, then a brilliant blood-red Stewart Island sunset should be compensation enough.

Roughly the size of Singapore, Stewart Island can only be appreciated in the course of a visit of several days and because there is not much more than 12 miles (20km) of road, the best way to explore the island is on foot, along one of the island's many forest tracks. Day tours from Bluff or Invercargill are possible, but can only be recommended for people who really are in a hurry.

Oban

The tiny settlement of Oban on the shores of **Halfmoon Bay** is the base for all activities on the island. Near the ferry wharf the **Visitors Information Centre** can provide a list of all the accommodation possibilities as well as information on various walks. Of interest in Oban is the **Rakiura Museum** with its displays on the Maori and European history of the island and **The Fernery**, a craft shop and gallery set in a pleasant bush setting at the edge of town.

Stewart Island walks

The two main walks on Stewart Island are the **Rakiura Track** (2-3 days) and the **North-West Circuit** (8-10 days).

The Rakiura is by far the easier of the two and provides a gentle introduction to the island's virgin forests and isolated beaches. Though there are nice beaches along the circuit

Above: *No matter what the weather, South Island landscapes can be dramatic*

track as well, it can often mean crossing some very rugged and muddy terrain to get to them.

Because the first stretch of the track is fairly easy and runs quite close to the coast, many people only go as far as **Christmas Village Hut** (2-3 days one way) and then return the same way to Oban. Unfortunately, the first few huts along the trail can get very crowded in summer so it might pay to bring a (mosquito-proof) tent.

Trampers who want to save themselves some walking on the North-West Circuit can get dropped off at certain points along the coast by water taxi. However, those who have endured the hardships of the entire 74 miles (120km) long track will no doubt feel justified in toasting their effort at Oban's only pub with a cold, locally brewed beer.

Those who are not so keen on walking could content themselves with some of the shorter tracks around Halfmoon Bay, for instance the 15 minute stroll to **Observation Rock**, or perhaps take a tour by bus or launch. The scenic minibus tour (☎ (03) 219 1269) lasts about an hour and there are daily launch trips to **Ulva Island Bird Sanctuary** (a paradise for bird-watchers) and the salmon farms in **Big Glory Bay**. It is also possible to explore Stewart Island's fascinating coastline by sea kayak.

Kiwi spotting

One activity that nobody should miss is kiwi spotting. Stewart Island is probably the best place in New Zealand to see kiwis in the wild. The local variety is known as the Stewart

Island brown kiwi (*Apteryx australis lawryi*), which is unusual in that it is active during the day as well as at night. Because it is not purely nocturnal and likes to forage on the beaches instead of just in dense bush, it is much easier to see than its North and South Island cousins. Phillip Smith of **Bravo Adventure Cruises** offers a guided kiwi-spotting tour that includes a twilight boat trip and a short walk through native forest to where kiwi can be seen. Numbers are limited and the trip only takes place on alternate nights, so it is probably necessary to book ahead. Trampers doing either the Rakiura or North-West Circuit tracks also have a good chance of seeing kiwi, as well as penguins and fur seals on the more remote beaches.

Below: Land's End, Bluff

Relax and Enjoy

But one does not have to go bird-watching, tramping, fishing or swimming to enjoy Stewart Island. It is a place where one can sit down and do nothing at all — and not feel guilty about it! A quiet evening on the beach enjoying the sunset, a beer and a yarn in the pub with the locals, that might be enough for frayed urban souls desperately seeking to 'get away from it all'.

Back to the Mainland

From Invercargill the **Southern Scenic Route** continues east along SH92 through the Catlins Forest Park to Balclutha and then Dunedin. The more direct route to Dunedin is along SH1, but SH92 is definitely the more picturesque alternative. However, those who like fishing might consider a detour along SH1

to **Gore** as the area is famed for its brown trout. Anglers come from around the world to fish the waters of the **Mataura River** which is claimed to have the highest trout populations and catch rates of any river in New Zealand.

The Catlins

Described in tourist brochures as one of 'New Zealand's best kept secrets', the shaggy bush-covered hills of the Catlins region stretch from **Nugget Point** in Otago to **Waipapa Point** in Southland.

Protected within the boundaries of the **Catlins Forest Park** is the largest remaining area of native forest on the east coast of the South Island. Here the southern beech forests reach their southernmost extremity and impressive stands of tall podocarps like totara, rimu, kahikatea and miro fringe the wild, rocky shores of the Catlins coast. Native birds abound (once the ancient Maori hunted the now extinct moa in this region) and ornithologists have registered around 60 different species within the forest park alone.

On the coastal rocks it is possible to see fur seals, elephant seals, Hookers sea lion and the rare yellow-eyed penguin (*Megadyptes antipodes*). A trip through the Catlins gives a good idea of what the once densely forested east coast must have looked like before the timber-millers and farmers arrived.

After leaving Invercargill along SH92, the countryside is at first very flat and pastoral but it gradually takes on a hillier, more untamed aspect as the Catlins are approached. At **Fortrose** one has the choice of either following the partly unsealed coastal road to **Curio Bay** (21 miles/ 35km) or of continuing along SH92 (27 miles/44km).

Curio & Porpoise Bays

Curio Bay is a beautiful, isolated little spot where the remains of a petrified forest are visible on a rocky platform at low tide. About 160 million years ago the fossilised tree stumps and fallen logs were part of a sub-tropical Jurassic forest.

In neighbouring Porpoise Bay it is often possible to see Hector's dolphins playing in the surf. As the beach is safe for swimming there is nothing to stop visitors from joining them. For those who want to spend more time in the area there is a camping ground with basic facilities on the Porpoise Bay headland, just above the beach.

Catlins State Forest Park

State Highway 92 enters Catlins State Forest Park shortly after the turn-off to Curio Bay. Though the road is now unsealed until near Owaka, it should present no difficulty to motorists if appropriate care is taken. The first worthwhile detour along the way is to **Cathedral Caves**. This impressive cave system is only accessible at low tide but tide-tables are posted at the start of the dirt access road. From the car park at the end of the road (1 mile/ 2km) it is a 10 minute walk through lovely native forest and then another 10 minute stroll along the beach to the caves.

Scenic walks

Between Cathedral Caves and Papatowai are a few interesting

scenic walks all of which are signposted from the main road. One track (15 minutes) leads to the splendid sandy beach at **Tautuku Bay** whereas another nearby leads to the forested shores of **Lake Wilkie**. The latter walk is really no more than a 10 minute stroll from the road and is especially worthwhile in summer when the rata trees flower red around the small lake.

Papatowai

At Papatowai there is a small service station with connected tea-room. Those who stop here for a snack will probably have noticed the large framed photograph on the wall depicting **Purakaunui Falls**. As the photo suggests, the falls are one of the area's scenic highlights. A few kilometres out of town a signpost points out the 6 mile (10km) detour necessary to get to them. Near the falls, which are reached along a forest path, is a pleasant picnic area with toilet facilities. There are other waterfalls in the vicinity but these ones are certainly the most photogenic. **A tip: the best photos are taken in the late morning.**

Jacks Bay Blowhole

Further north another detour can be made to Jacks Bay Blowhole by following the road along **Catlins Lake** (actually an extension of the Catlins River) towards the coast. The blowhole lies in the middle of farmland and is connected to the sea by a 656ft (200m) long subterranean tunnel. The plume of sea-water that spurts out of the 196ft (60m) deep hole is at its most impressive at high tide and in stormy weather.

However, if the weather is fine there is no need to feel disappointed as the beach at Jacks Bay is one of the finest around.

Owaka

Continuing along the main road it is not long before the small settlement of Owaka is reached. This is the main town of the Catlins district and it has all the essential facilities, including a Department of Conservation (DOC) Visitor Centre. This is the place to go for information about walks in the area.

Among the more interesting walks is the **Catlins River Walk** (5 hours), which passes through pretty silver beech forest and can be started from the Tawanui camping area west of Owaka. Another good walk for those interested in the local flora is the **Pounawea Nature Walk** (45 minutes). It starts from the Pounawea Motor Camp just to the south-east of Owaka. There is a good chance of spotting white-faced herons, pied shags, paradise ducks and other aquatic birds along this loop track.

Nugget Point Wildlife

Before finally leaving the Catlins it is well worth making the detour to Nugget Point. Here visitors may see fur seals, elephant seals and the rare Hooker's sea lion. Shortly before the car park at the road end is another parking spot from where a track leads down a steep bank to the yellow-eyed penguin viewing platform. As it is not permitted to go beyond the platform when the penguins are ashore, it is a good idea to bring a pair of binoculars. Photographers

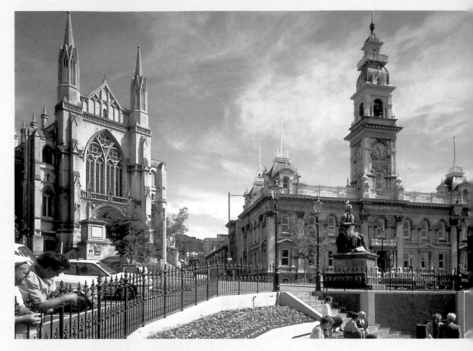

Above: *St Paul's Cathedral and Town Hall, Dunedin*

Left and below: *Larnach Castle, Dunedin*

will need at least a 500mm telephoto lens for a close-up shot of these small birds. Yellow-eyed penguins can usually be observed on-shore after about 3pm. Other sea-birds that may be spotted include little blue penguins, gannets, sooty shearwaters and spotted shags. At the end of the point is a stone lighthouse that was built in 1870.

From Nugget Point it is possible to follow the road via Kaka Point and Port Molyneux to **Balclutha**. This town on the banks of the Clutha River marks the 'official' end of the Southern Scenic Route but the remaining distance to Dunedin are not without interest.

State Highway 1 continues on from Balclutha via Milton to Dunedin. To the north-west of Milton, near the town of Lawrence, is Gabriel's Gully.

Gabriel's Gully

In 1861 Gabriel Read discovered a rich deposit of gold here and in so doing sparked off the Central Otago gold rushes. Within a couple of months there were over 11,000 prospectors in the district, searching feverishly for a quick fortune in the ground. Today there is still some evidence of the old workings around Gabriel's Gully and those wishing to know more about the gold rush can visit the small museum in Lawrence which also doubles as the local Information Centre .

Dunedin

Dunedin (pop. 120, 000), the South Island's second largest city after Christchurch, was originally a mainly Scottish settlement and is still often referred to as the 'Edinburgh of the South'. Today the city's Scottish roots are most obviously reflected in its name (Dun Edin was the old Gaelic name for Edinburgh), the country's only kilt shop, the large statue of the Scottish bard Robert Burns and, almost inevitably, the only whiskey distillery in New Zealand. A slight rolling or at least burr of the 'r', that may be heard throughout Southland and Otago, also hints at an ancestry reaching back to the 'bonny hills of Scotland'.

History

The first boatload of Scots arrived at **Port Chalmers**, Dunedin's port, in 1848 to take up land that had been bought from the local Maori for about a penny an acre. Though the first settlers were mainly Scottish and Presbyterian by faith, there were also enough Englishmen around to allow some scope for traditional frictions to come to the fore. Job advertisements sometimes carried the line 'Englishmen need not apply' and the early settlement's leader, Captain William Cargill, once directed an English gentleman to go back to Canterbury (a predominantly English settlement) 'where he belonged'.

In the 1860's the Otago gold rushes brought sudden prosperity to the town. They stimulated not only a dramatic increase in population, but also provided a firm economic basis for the rapid development of industry and agriculture. For many years Dunedin was the most important manufacturing and commercial city in the country.

Legacies of this early wealth are the city's many fine old Victorian buildings and the country's first university and medical school. Though still an important industrial area (heavy engineering), it is in the role of a university town that Dunedin now commands most recognition. The 14,000 or so students have a pervasive influence on the city's day-to-day life, as is reflected in the many student pubs, the cheap cafés and the vibrant local arts and entertainments scene.

Attractions

The best place to start exploring is from the Octagon, an eight-sided garden area in the heart of the city. As proud of its Scottish heritage as Dunedin is, it is not surprising to find that the Octagon is presided over by the statue (1887) of Robert Burns, Scotland's national poet.

Behind the statue rises **St Paul's Anglican Cathedral**, which was built of Oamaru stone in 1915. It is worth a look inside because of the impressive stone vaulted ceiling, some fine interior woodwork and the stained-glass windows.

Located within the recently refurbished Municipal Chambers (1880) nearby is the excellent **Dunedin Visitor Centre**. Also close is the **Dunedin Public Art Gallery** with a fine collection of contemporary New Zealand art. In Stuart Street, just above the Octagon, and not far from the cathedral, are a number of decorative terrace houses from the Victorian period.

Edwardian architecture

At the lower end of Stuart Street, in the direction of the bay, is Dunedin's **Edwardian railway station** (1904). Decorated with stained-glass windows and a magnificent mosaic floor, the station foyer vividly reflects the city's early wealth and optimistic belief in a prosperous future. A few of the old steam locomotives that once puffed their way into the station are on display at the **Otago Early Settlers Museum** in Cumberland Street, a short distance away.

The **Presbyterian First Church** is situated to the north-west of the museum in Moray Place. Dedicated in 1873 it has been described as 'a masterpiece of Gothic revival'.

To the north-west of the Octagon, at 42 Royal Terrace, is **Olveston**. Built in 1904-06 as a home for the wealthy businessman David Theomin, its beautifully furnished rooms can be visited in the course of an hour-long guided tour. Crammed as it is with valuable antiques and early New Zealand paintings, Olveston provides a fascinating insight into the lifestyle of a cultivated turn-of-the-century family.

The Museum

The **Otago Museum** can be reached from the Octagon along Great King Street. Especially worth seeing here are the excellent southern Maori and Pacific Island exhibits and the natural history displays. Of note among the other exhibits is a surprisingly good collection of art and sculpture from classical Greece, Rome and the Middle East. A recent addition to the museum is 'Discovery World', where working exhibits introduce children and adults alike to the world of science.

The University

A little further east of the museum is the **University of Otago** campus. Founded in 1869, New Zealand's oldest university began its life with a roll of only 81 students and a staff of three professors. The original nineteenth century building complex has been retained and is worth taking a stroll around. Particularly photogenic is the turreted clock tower. Guided walking tours are available for those who want to know more about the university and its history.

Taste tours

As change from history and architecture, visitors with a penchant for the local beer or whiskey might enjoy taking part in tours of either **Wilson's Whiskey Distillery or Speights Brewery**. Both tours last about $1\frac{1}{2}$ hours and, most importantly, include a sampling of the wares.

On a sweeter note are tours of the **Cadbury** chocolate factory. Children in particular will enjoy the free samples offered at the end of this one hour tour.

Otago Peninsula

When in Dunedin do not leave without making the side trip to Otago Peninsula. Though within easy reach of the city, the peninsula is unique in that it provides a breeding habitat for such rare or seldom seen birds as the royal albatross and yellow-eyed penguin. There is enough to see and do here to keep most visitors occupied for a full day, but at least a half day is necessary for the main attractions. A pleasant circular tour of the peninsula can be made by first following the coast road (Portobello Road) and then Highcliff Road back to Dunedin. Those without private transport can join a bus tour from Dunedin. Contact **Newtons Coach Tours** ☎ (03) 477 5577.

Royal Albatross

As far as the peninsula's natural attractions are concerned, it is the famous royal albatross colony at **Taiaroa Head** that draws most attention. With a wing-span of over 9ft (3m) the royal albatross (*Diomedea epomophora*) is the world's largest sea-bird. Nowhere else on the globe do they breed so close to human habitation. In fact except for here and a few remote subantarctic islands, they are rarely seen on land as they spend the greater part of their solitary lives gliding over the oceans of the Southern Hemisphere. When they do come ashore it is only to breed.

The single egg laid in November hatches in January and by September the young birds are ready to depart the colony. It will be eight to ten years before these birds are ready to breed themselves, but with a life-span of well over 60 years, plenty of time remains to produce offspring.

Albatross tour

The albatross colony can only be visited as part of a one hour guided tour which needs to booked in advance at the **Dunedin Visitor Centre**. A slightly longer tour ($1\frac{1}{2}$ hours) also includes a visit to **Fort**

KAKAPO (STRIGOPS HABROPTILUS)

This nocturnal, flightless parrot is one of the world's rarest birds. When in danger, the kakapo simply stands still and hopes that it will not be noticed. Unfortunately, behaviour of this kind is of no help against introduced predators such as cats and weasels. Today the kakapo is virtually extinct on the mainland and only a few breeding pairs are found in Fiordland and on Stewart Island. Attempts are being made to resettle the bird on small off-shore islands that are free of predators. The current population of kakapos stands at around 50.

KIWI (APTERYGIDAE)

New Zealand's national bird is nocturnal and rarely seen in the wild. To say that it is unique is something of an understatement. Its feathers resemble hair, it lays an egg that in relation to its size is disproportionately large (it weighs 1lb, 450g) and has, for a bird, an excellent sense of smell. The kiwi's nostrils are situated at the tip of its long bill (also unusual for a bird) and this no doubt helps it in its search for insects and worms on the forest floor. There are three species of kiwi: the brown kiwi (*Apteryx australis*), the great spotted kiwi (*A. haasti*) and the little spotted kiwi (*A. oweni*). The kiwi is found only in New Zealand.

Kiwi Bird

The flightless Weka has a penchant for shiny objects and will steal anything left lying about

MOA (DINORNITHIFORMES)

There were many different species of moa, ranging in size from relatively small forest-dwelling birds to huge ostrich-like giants around 10ft (3m) tall and weighing up to 507 pounds (230kg). Though known to the early Maori, the giant moa (*Euryapteryx gravis*) became extinct long before the arrival of the first Europeans. However, it is believed that at least a few of the smaller species survived into the early nineteenth century.

TAKAHE (NOTORNIS MANTELLI)

The takahe was believed to be extinct for many years until its rediscovery in 1948. It is a member of the rail family and is powerfully built with bright blue and green plumage. The introduction of deer, which eat the same plants as the takahe, are thought to be the main reason for the birds declining numbers. Today the takahe is only found in the Murchison Mountains of Fiordland National Park. The present population consists of around 200 birds.

WEKA (GALLIRALLUS AUSTRALIS)

Wekas are neither shy nor endangered and are often seen by trampers in New Zealand's national and forest parks. The birds, which are about the same size as a chicken, have a predominantly brown colouring and are omnivorous. Like the kea parrot, the weka has a weakness for shiny objects and will run off with anything that is left lying around.

Taiaroa where the main attraction is a historic Armstrong 'disappearing gun'. Placed on the headland in 1888 to counter a feared Russian invasion (which did not eventuate), the gun was only raised above ground when it was ready to fire.

Penguins

From the albatross colony follow the signs to get to **Penguin Place**, a privately run conservation reserve. The best chance of viewing the yellow-eyed penguins that breed here is during the last few hours of daylight when the birds come ashore to their nests. Apart from the penguins it is also possible to see a fur seal colony.

Penguin tour

Tours of the penguin colony start from **McGrouther's Farm**, at Penguin Place, on a daily basis throughout the season (October to August). A longer tour (8 hours) also includes a visit to the ornithological section of **Otago Museum**, the albatross colony and other points of related interest around the peninsula. It starts from and can be booked through, the Dunedin Visitor Centre. Participants may be interested to know that the penguin reserve is funded entirely through profits gained from these tours.

Lanarch Castle

On the way back to Dunedin it is well worth making the short detour off Highcliff Road to see Lanarch Castle. New Zealand's only 'castle' was built by William Lanarch, a wealthy financier and politician, for what was then the immense sum of £125,000. Construction began in

1871, but in spite of the fact that 200 labourers were working on the house, it took five years before the family could move in. The entire building was constructed using only the very best materials available and Lanarch did not even shy from the expense of importing European craftsmen to do some of the interior work. Outstanding features of the house include the hanging staircase with a handrail carved from solid kauri, the beautifully carved foyer ceiling and the huge ballroom.

Other attractions

Other attractions on the peninsula include **Glenfalloch Gardens**, which are at their most attractive from

The Taieri Gorge Railway

Of Dunedin's many attractions, the trip on the Taieri Gorge Railway is something quite special. One of New Zealand's great train journeys, this 4 hour return trip from Dunedin to Pukerangi goes through rugged, spectacular scenery that cannot be seen from the road. There are two or three photo stops along the way and refreshments are available on board.

At certain times of the year, a longer version of this trip (5¹/₂ hours) is offered to **Middlemarch**, 51 miles (83kms) north-west of Dunedin on SH87.

September to October, and the **Trust Bank Aquarium** which features local marine life as well as a tuatara. Saturday is feeding day at the aquarium and visitors are welcome to help feed the fish. Both attractions are clearly signposted from Portobello Road.

Moving on

From Dunedin SH1 continues north to **Palmerston** where the visitor is presented with two alternatives: either follow SH1 further north to Oamaru and then turn inland along the **Waitaki River** to Omarama or follow SH85 north-west through Central Otago and then continue north over the Lindis Pass to Omarama. Both routes have their scenic attractions but the drive through the **Lindis Valley** is particularly beautiful. From Omarama it is not far to Mount Cook National Park and the lakes of southern Canterbury.

• ROUTE 13 •
OAMARU AND THE WAITAKI VALLEY

The Coast Section

Shag Point

Like Taiaroa Head and Penguin Place on the Otago Peninsula, Shag Point, just over 5 miles (8km) north of Palmerston, is a great place for anybody interested in wildlife. Though aptly named for the hundreds of shags that perch on the rocky islets off-shore, it is the large colony of fur seals and a small yellow-eyed penguin colony that attract most visitors here. It is possible to venture quite close to the fur seals while they bask on the rocks but visitors should not attempt to get close views of the penguins as they are easily disturbed.

Moeraki boulders

Further up the coast, near the fishing village of **Moeraki**, are the famous Moeraki boulders. Strewn like giant marbles across the sand of **Hampden Beach**, the spherical boulders are not in fact the product of erosion but of a natural chemical process. They were formed some 60 million years ago by the gradual accumulation of lime salts around a central lime crystal core. These septarian concretions, as geologists prefer to call them, gradually appear from the cliffs behind the beach as the soft mudstone in which they are embedded is eroded away by the sea. Some of the concretions are over 13ft (4m) in circumference and weigh several tons. In a strategic position near the boulders is a large, reasonably priced restaurant with excellent views over the sea.

Oamaru

Next stop on the coast is Oamaru. Though the town lacks the Mediterranean flair of art deco Napier, it too can boast some of the country's most interesting architecture. Oamaru's historic buildings generally reflect the classical styles favoured throughout New Zealand during the nineteenth century. What makes them distinctive however, is the widespread use of local limestone; a material that is soft enough to be quarried with a circular saw but which gradually hardens when exposed to air.

Many of these old limestone buildings are to be found in the **Tyne-Harbour Street Historic Precinct**, the only complete example of a nineteenth century commercial area in New Zealand. Some of the noble old premises are at present a bit dilapidated, but a restoration scheme is under way that will hopefully return them to their former grandeur in the not-too-distant future. On holiday weekends a steam train runs through the Historic Precinct to provide that extra touch of nostalgia (check at the Information Centre for details).

Within walking distance of the Historic Precinct and downtown Oamaru is, surprisingly enough, a blue penguin colony. The world's smallest penguins have built their nests around the Harbour area and a section of foreshore has been set aside as a refuge for them. From the viewing platforms at the end of **Waterfront Road**, the dapper little birds can be seen just after dusk as they return from a day's fishing at sea. The yellow-eyed penguin site at Bushey Beach can be reached by following **Graves Walkway** (2 hours return) from the blue penguin colony.

Inland

Those in a hurry to get north might prefer to travel directly from Oamaru to **Christchurch** on SH1, but a much more scenic alternative is to follow SH83 inland along the Waitaki Valley to Omarama.

En route the road passes lakes **Waitaki**, **Aviemore** and **Benmore**, all of which were created as part of a major hydro-electric scheme on the Waitaki River. Well stocked with trout and salmon, the lakes are as popular with anglers as they are with water sport enthusiasts.

Worth a brief stop is the small settlement of **Duntroon**. In town the historic blacksmith shop can be visited whereas a short distance outside town, in the direction of Kurow, there are some Maori rock drawings to be seen. Signposted from the main road the **Takiroa Rock Drawings** were probably executed by pre-European Maori between 1000 and 1500 AD.

Another 12 miles (20km) away, **Kurow** is the starting point for jet boat trips on the Waitaki River.

Omarama

Omarama, on the fringe of the Mackenzie country, has a wide reputation for gliding due to favourable thermal air currents in the locality. There is plenty of accommodation in town and a reason for visitors to stay longer is the rare opportunity of going on a scenic flight with a glider ☎ (03) 438 9621.

Not to be missed if the weather is right are the beautiful **Clay Cliffs**. In certain light-conditions, the bizarrely eroded cliffs can display a remarkable range of colours, giving them an almost surreal atmosphere. The Clay Cliffs are signposted from SH8 on the way to Lindis Pass but an organised tour ☎ (03) 438 9428 can be arranged for those without transport.

Above: *A fur seal at Shag Point*

Right: *Fossilised tree trunk at Curio Bay, Catlins*

Below: *High rainfall in parts of South Island has enabled the growth of dense rainforests and, with the advent of man, lush pasturelands*

• ROUTE 13A •
THE GOLDFIELDS ROUTE (PIGROOT) TO LINDIS PASS & OMARAMA

The Pigroot was the route to the goldfields of Central Otago, a route now followed by SH85 as it winds its way from Palmerston towards Ranfurly on the Maniototo Plains.

Some claim that the name for the route described the early road's bad condition, whereas others claim that it derives from the name given to a hill by a certain John Thomson who was surveying the locality in the 1850's. Thompson, a man with a marked fondness for naming geographical locations after farm-yard animals, is supposed to have chanced upon a tame wild boar and commemorated the event by naming the hill on which he found it 'Pigroot Hill'.

The tiny settlement of **Dunback** is situated just over 6 miles (10kms) north-west of Palmerston. To the north of town a turn-off to the left leads to **Macraes Flat**, the site of a modern gold mine as well as the historic **Golden Point Mining Battery**. Tours of the gold mine can be arranged from **Stanley's Hotel** ☎/Fax (03) 465 2400, a century-old pub at Macraes Flat. This small hotel offers inexpensive lodgings and, in summer, guests have access to tennis courts, a swimming pool and gymnastic equipment.

Ranfurly

From Dunstan the road continues over the Horse Range before eventually descending to the Maniototo Plains and Ranfurly, the largest town

(pop. 994) in the area. There is not a lot to Ranfurly other than a railway station and of course a pub. For tourists the most interesting fact about the place is that it is centrally located and makes a useful base for visits to the gold-mining towns of Naseby and St Bathans.

Naseby

Naseby lies to the north of Ranfurly. Once the largest gold-mining town on the Maniototo, it is now a sleepy little place with only a few old buildings left to conjure up an impression of the wild gold rush days. Worth visiting is the **Maniototo Early Settlers Museum** as well as the old watchmaker's shop to which it is connected. In winter the local ice rink is popular among followers of the sport of curling.

The unsealed road that heads north-west from town leads past the **Kyeburn Diggings**, where miners gouged away the cliffs in a fevered search for gold, to the historic **Dansey Pass Hotel**. Built in the 1880's to serve the goldminers, the hotel still offers food and accommodation in the remotest of surroundings. Continuing on from Dansey Pass, it is another 29 miles (48km) to **Duntroon** and the Waitaki Valley (see Route 13).

St Bathans

About 24 miles (40km) further west of Naseby, on a loop road off SH85, is the former gold-mining township of St Bathans. Strung along the main street are a number of buildings that date from the nineteenth century gold rushes. In those days the town had a loud, hard-drinking community of 2000 miners who were catered for by no less than thirteen pubs. Of these only the **Vulcan Hotel** (1869) has survived but it has no trouble catering to the needs of St Bathan's present population of around twenty. **Blue Lake**, a popular picnic spot close to town, was formed by miners sluicing for gold.

Alexandra

Continuing along SH85 from Ranfurly it is another 54 miles (88km) to Alexandra. Located in what is now a rich fruit growing region, Alexandra was also a mecca for those smitten by gold fever. Thousands of diggers flocked to work the nearby **Dunstan Fields** but this rush proved short lived and it was not until the gold dredging boom of the 1890's that the town was really able to prosper. More information on gold dredging is available at the **Sir William Bodkin Museum** on the corner of Thompson and Walton streets.

An excellent viewpoint over Alexandra, from where the old dredge tailings are clearly visible, can be reached by turning off Tarbert Street at the north-east end of town and then following Little Valley Road to the top of **Tucker Hill**. It is also worth stopping in at the Information Centre as they have plenty of tips on other things to see and do in the region. They take bookings for four-wheel-drive safaris into the Dunstan Mountains

and Old Man Range, trips definitely worth considering if you want see the more remote areas of Central Otago. They also have an excellent collection of brochures detailing walks or cycle tours for those who prefer to explore under their own steam.

Clyde

Only a short distance up the road from Alexandra is Clyde. The many stone buildings that still line Clyde's streets are reminders of the days when the town was in the middle of the Dunstan Gold-rush (1863). Located in the stone courthouse of 1864 is the **Courthouse Museum**. It mainly concentrates on the history of the early goldfields whereas the **Briar Herb Factory** nearby displays historic herb processing machinery and has exhibits illustrating the pioneering days in general. Those who want to enjoy a good meal in historical surroundings should try **Oliver's Restaurant**. It is housed in what used to be a general store that served the gold miners.

From Clyde, SH8 follows the shores of Lake Dunstan, by-passing Cromwell (see Chapter 9) on its journey northwards to Lindis Pass and the lakes of South Canterbury. Near the northern end of Lake Dunstan a loop road leaves the main highway and leads to the ghost town of **Bendigo**. All that remains of this old quartz-mining town are a few ruined stone dwellings and the vague sense of melancholy that clings to such places. **Logantown** and **Welshtown**, also ghost towns, are in the near vicinity. Take extreme care when exploring as there are many unmarked mine shafts in the area.

The Lindis Pass

The Lindis Pass links Central Otago to the Mackenzie Country and Mount Cook, and provides a magnificent exit from the region. The drive over the pass to **Omarama** is especially beautiful in the late afternoon when the tussock-covered hills glow in subtle hues of gold and bronze. The effect can be overwhelming; on some clear days it is as though the entire landscape is bathed in an enchanted, almost otherworldly light, so intense are the colours. Painters and photographers will love this route. From Omarama it is less than 62 miles (100km) to the start of Route 14 at **Mount Cook**.

Right: An historic watchmaker's shop, Naseby

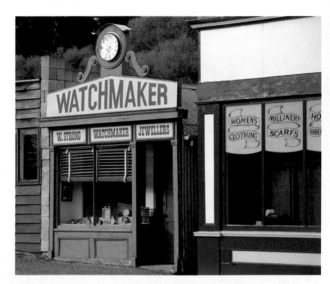

Below: Pub at Naseby

ACTIVITIES

Alexandra

Jet Boating
Riverside Hostel
☎ (03) 448 8152

Kayaking/Canoeing
Central Outdoor Adventures
☎ (03) 448 6360
Rentals, guided trips and also mountain bike hire.

Catlins

Nature Tours
Catlins Wildlife Trackers
PO Box 2192, Dunedin
(or c/o Dunedin Visitor Centre)
☎ (03) 455 2681
Depart Dunedin for 2 day safaris through the Catlins.

Dunedin

Boat Trips
Monarch Cruises
Cnr Wharf & Fryatt Streets,
PO Box 102
☎ (03) 477 4276
Otago Harbour cruises and wildlife cruises.

Train Trips
Taieri Gorge Railway
Dunedin Railway Station
PO Box 140
☎ (03) 477 4449
A memorable 4 hour journey. Timetables are available from Dunedin Visitor Centre.

Kurow

Jet Boating
Waitaki Jets & Tours
Liverpool Street
☎ (03) 436 0778

Otago Peninsula

Nature Tours
Penguin Place
Yellow-Eyed Penguin Colony
Off Portobello Road
There is a short $1\frac{1}{2}$ hour tour and a very informative 7 hour tour. For more details and times contact the **Dunedin Visitor Centre** or the **Yellow-Eyed Penguin Conservation Reserve**
☎ (03) 478 0286.

Royal Albatross Colony
Taiaroa Head
Open: guided tours daily of one hour's duration (Closed 16 September to 24 November). Prior bookings necessary. Contact **Dunedin Visitor Centre**.

Stewart Island

Boat Trips
Moana Charters
☎ (03) 219 1202
Offer half-day cruises to Ulva Island and salmon farms as do several other operators (contact DOC office for more addresses).

Kayaking/Canoeing
Inne's Backpackers
Argyle Street, PO Box 32
☎/Fax (03) 219 1080
Rentals and guided tours. Also accommodation. For other kayaking possibilities contact the Visitor Centre.

Nature Tours
Bravo Adventure Cruises
PO Box 104, ☎ (03) 219 1144
Offer guided kiwi spotting. Includes boat cruise. Bookings recommended.

Thorfinn Charters
PO Box 43, Halfmoon Bay
☎ (03) 219 1210
Guided bird watching and
nature walks.

Tramping
Stewart Island Water Taxi
☎ (03) 219 1394
Drops trampers off at various
points along coast. Several other
operators offer the same service.
Contact DOC office.

ACCOMMODATION

*See pages 288 and 300 in the FactFile for the accommodation and
restaurant rating guide*

Alexandra
Alexandra Holiday Park $
Manuherikia Road
☎ (03) 448 8297
Fax (03) 448 8294
Tent sites and cabins. Near a river.

The Willows $$
(Bed & Breakfast)
3 Young Lane
☎ (03) 449 2231

Clyde
Dunstan Hotel $
35 Sunderland Street
☎ (03) 449 2817
In the middle of town.

Oliver's Lodge $$$
34 Sunderland Street
☎ (03) 449 2860
Fax (03) 449 2862
This complex of buildings from the
gold mining era has been restored
with great originality.

Dunedin
Elm Lodge $
(Backpackers)
74 Elm Row
☎ (03) 474 1872
Central location, non-smoking,
good views.

Law Courts Hotel $$
Cnr Stuart & Cumberland Sts
☎/Fax (03) 477 8036
Art Deco building with Cobb & Co.
restaurant. Central location.

Sahara Guest House $$
(Bed & Breakfast)
619 George Street
☎ (03) 477 6662
Fax (03) 479 2551
Gabled brick house built in
1906. Central location.

Quality Inn $$$
Upper Moray Place
☎ (03) 477 6784
Fax (03) 474 0115

Invercargill
Southern Comfort Backpackers $
30 Thomson Street
☎ (03) 218 3838
Housed in a wonderful old villa
this is one of the best backpackers
in the South Island. Non-smoking,
free use of bikes around town.

Coachman's Inn $$
705 Tay Street
☎ (03) 217 6046
Fax (03) 217 6045
Also cheap cabins.

Montecillo Lodge $$
(Bed & Breakfast)
240 Spey Street
☎ (03) 218 2503
Fax (03) 218 2506
Quiet location close to City Centre.
Some non-smoking rooms.

Oamaru

Anne Mieke Guest House $
(Bed & Breakfast)
47 Tees Street
☎/Fax (03) 434 8051
Non-smoking, sea views,
close to penguin colony.

Swaggers Backpackers $
25 Wansbeck Street
☎ (03) 434 9999
Cosy hostel with a central location.
Sea views from most rooms.

Oban (Stewart Island)

Ann's Place $
(Backpackers)
Halfmoon Bay
PO Box 103
☎ (03) 219 1065

South Sea Hotel $$
Elgin Terrace
☎ (03) 219 1059
Fax (03)219 1120

Omarama

Buscot Station $
SH8, 5 miles (8km)
north of Omarama
☎ (03) 438 9646
Fax (03) 438 9427
Stay in an original homestead on
a merino sheep and cattle station.
Closed 15 May to 15 August.

Killermont Station $
SH8, 8 miles (13km)
west of Omarama
☎ (03) 438 9864
Fax (03) 438 9866
A 12,000 acre (5,000 hectares)
high country station running
merino sheep and deer. Close
to Ahuriri River, famous for
its trout fishing. Closed June,
July, August.

Omarama Hotel $
Main Road
☎ (03) 438 9713
Comfortable rooms.

Owaka

(Catlins)
Pounawea Motor Camp $
On Catlins Estuary
☎ (03) 415 8483

Tokanui

Pope's Place $
(Catlins)
Slope Point Road
Haldene
☎/Fax (03) 246 8420
This farmstay (sheep farm)
also provides room for tents
and campervans.

Waikawa

(Catlins)
Waikawa Holiday Lodge $
Waikawa-Niagra Road
☎ (03) 246 8552
Fax (03) 246 8895

Cathedral Caves, Catlins

EATING OUT

Alexandra

Dandelion Wine Bar $
12 Limerick Street
☎ (03) 448 8704
Light meals, live entertainment
Sundays.

Fruitlands Gallery $
SH8 8 miles (13km) south of
Alexandra
☎ (03) 449 2192
Light lunches.

Clyde

Oliver's Restaurant $$$
34 Sunderland Street
☎ (03) 449 2860
Great food, stylish surroundings.

Dunedin

Mega Bite $
388 George Street
☎ (03) 477 7343
Light meals.

Stewart's Coffee House $
12 Lower Octagon
☎ (03) 477 6687
Best coffee in town.

The Terrace Café $$
118 Moray Place
☎ (03) 474 0686
Casual dining in pleasant
surroundings.

Bell Pepper Blues $$$
474 Princes Street
☎ (03) 474 0973
The venison dishes are
recommended.

Invercargill

Zookeepers Café $
50 Tay Street
☎ (03) 218 3373
Open until late.

Gerrard's $$$
3 Leven Street
☎ (03) 218 3406
One of the best in town.

Oamaru

The Last Post $$
12 Thames Street
☎ (03) 434 8080
Located in an old post office.

PLACES TO VISIT

Alexandra

Alexandra Museum
(Sir William Bodkin Museum)
Walton Street
Open: by arrangement, contact
Visitor Information.

Bluff

Paua House
Cnr Marine Parade
& Henderson St
Open: 9am-5pm daily.

Tiwai Point Aluminium Smelter
Open: guided tours Mon-Fri at
10am. Bookings essential.
Minimum age is 12.
☎ (03) 218 5999

Clyde

The Clyde Historical Museums
(Dunstan Courthouse
& Briar Herb Factory)
Open: Tue-Sun 2-4pm.

Dunedin

Cadbury Confectionery Ltd
(chocolate factory)
280 Cumberland Street
Open: guided tours.
Bookings essential.
☎ (03) 474 1126

Dunedin Public Art Gallery
Octagon
Open: daily 10am-4.30pm.

Lanarch Castle
(Otago Peninsula)
Open: daily 9am-5pm.

Olveston
42 Royal Terrace
Open: Guided tours (1 hr)
daily at 9.30am, 10.45am,
12pm, 1.30pm, 2.45pm & 4pm.

Otago Early Settlers Museum
220 Cumberland Street
Open: Mon-Fri 10am-5pm,
weekends 1-5pm.

Otago Museum
419 Great King Street
Open: Mon-Fri 10am-5pm,
weekends 1-5pm.

Penguin Place
Off Portobello Road
Otago Peninsula

Royal Albatross Colony
Taiaroa Head
Otago Peninsula

Speights Brewery
Rattray Street
Open: guided tours (1hr 45min)
at 10.30am Mon-Thurs.
Bookings essential
☎ (03) 477 9480

Trust Bank Aquarium
Portobello
(Otago Peninsula)
Open: daily 1 Dec-1 March
12noon-4.30pm.

University of Otago
Open: for guided walking tours
contact Dunedin Visitor Centre.

Wilson Distillers
(whiskey distillery)
Open: guided tours, book
at Dunedin Visitor Centre.

Invercargill

Southland Museum & Art Gallery
Gala Street, Queens Park
Open: Mon-Fri 9am-5pm,
weekends 1-5pm.

Lawrence

Goldfields Museum
Ross Place
Open: daily 10am-4pm.

Macraes Flat

Macraes Gold Mine
Open: guided tours weekends
and public holidays at 1.30pm
(May-Aug, first weekend in
month only). Contact **Stanleys
Hotel**, Macraes Flat
☎ (03) 465 2400

Naseby

Maniototo Early Settlers Museum
Open: Nov-April daily (except
Mon) 1.30-3.30pm.

Oamaru

Blue Penguin Colony
Oamaru Harbour
Open: Sept-March, evenings.

**Tyne-Harbour Street
Historic Precinct**
Open: Guided tours of Oamaru's
historic buildings can be arranged
by contacting the Visitor
Information Centre.

Oban (Stewart Island)

Rakiura Museum
Ayr Street
Open: Tues & Thurs 10am-noon;
Mon, Wed & Fri 10am-2pm; Sat
11am-noon and Sun 1-2.30pm.

Roaring Forties Brewery
Open: tours on request
☎ (03) 219 1269.
Southernmost brewery
in the world.

The Fernery
440yds (400m) from Post Office
Open: ☎ (03) 219 1453

REGIONAL TRANSPORT

Stewart Island

Air

There are daily flights to Stewart
Island from Invercargill with
Southern Air ☎ (03) 218 9129.
Flying standby could be cheaper
than the ferry — check current
rates beforehand!

Boat

The *Foveaux Express* (catamaran)
departs Bluff (summer season)
Mon-Fri 9.30am & 5pm, Sun 5pm.
Winter sailings (21 May-23 Aug)
Mon, Wed, Fri & Sun. Trip takes
60 minutes but please note that
the crossing can be very rough
☎ (03) 212 7660.

VISITOR INFORMATION & PARK VISITOR CENTRES

Alexandra
**Central Otago Visitor
Information Centre**
22 Centennial Ave, PO Box 56
☎ (03) 448 9515
Fax (03) 448 9516

Catlins
DOC Visitor Centre
Cnr Ryley & Campbell Sts, Owaka
☎ (03) 415 8341

Dunedin
48 The Octagon, PO Box 5457
Open: Mon-Fri 8.30am-5pm,
weekends 9am-5pm.
☎ (03) 474 3300
Fax (03) 474 3311

Invercargill
Victoria Avenue, PO Box 1012
Open: Mon-Fri 9am-5pm,
weekends 1-5pm.
☎/Fax (03) 218 9753

Lawrence
17 Ross Place
☎ (03) 485 9222

Oamaru
Cnr Thames & Itchen Sts,
Private Bag 50058
Open: Mon-Fri 9am-5pm,
weekends 10am-5pm.
☎ (03) 434 1656
Fax (03) 434 1657

Omarama
On SH83
☎ (03) 438 9808

Stewart Island
DOC Visitor Centre
Main Road, Half Moon Bay,
PO Box 3
☎ (03) 219 1218
Fax (03) 219 1555

11 CANTERBURY

This region features two dramatically different landscapes: the broad flat expanse of the Canterbury Plains and the alpine majesty of the Southern Alps. The main city is Christchurch, which has a distinctly English flavour; and to the south-east is lovely Banks Peninsula and the old French settlement of Akaroa. Here baguette and wine hold a slight edge over tea and scones. The Alps form the region's western boundary and are best explored in the vicinity of Mount Cook and Arthur's Pass National Parks, both areas of stunning natural beauty.

• ROUTE 14 •
MOUNT COOK TO CHRISTCHURCH

Mount Cook Village can be reached by bus or plane from Christchurch or Queenstown. For those driving from Christchurch, the quickest route (around 5 hours) is to follow SH1 south via Ashburton and then turn off onto SH79 via Fairlie

and lakes Tekapo and Pukaki. More scenic however, is the route along state highways 79 and 72 as described here from Mount Cook. From Omarama at the end of Route 13 it is not much more than an hour's drive.

Above: Mount Cook, Southern Alps

Mount Cook National Park

Mount Cook National Park is part of the World Heritage Area (see also Westland National Park, Chapter 8 and Mount Aspiring and Fiordland National Parks, Chapter 9) and protects some of the most spectacular alpine scenery in the Southern Alps. Within the park's boundaries are five major glaciers and more than 140 peaks over 6,560ft (2000m). But rising above them all, at a height of 12,313ft (3,753m) is **Mt Cook**, the highest mountain not only in New Zealand, but in all of Australasia.

Only a few years ago Mt Cook was even higher, but in December 1991 a gigantic landslide removed more than 32ft (10m) from the peak. The mountain acquired its European name in 1851, when the captain of a survey ship named it after the explorer Captain James Cook. However, to the Maori it has long been known as **Aoraki**, after a figure in Maori mythology whose name translates as 'cloud in the sky'.

Walks from Mt Cook Village

In spite of the rugged alpine character of the park there are a number of short walks in the vicinity of Mount Cook Village that can be undertaken by most people. Starting from the **Hermitage Hotel** are the **Hooker Valley** (4 hours), **Kea Point** (3 hours) and **Sealy Tarns** (4 hours) walks.

The popular Hooker Valley walk leads to a lake at the terminal face of Hooker Glacier whereas both the Kea Point and Sealy Tarns walks

impress with dramatic views of glaciers and mountain peaks. An added attraction of the Sealy Tarns track is the abundance of alpine flowers in summer. The most famous of these flowers is the Mount Cook lily, the world's largest buttercup. Keep an eye out also for keas, New Zealand's mountain parrot.

Longer excursions

Full day or overnight trips in the park are generally restricted to those with mountaineering experience, but the tracks to Mueller and Hooker huts can be attempted by the fit and properly equipped. Anybody doing an overnight trip should inquire first at the Visitor Centre as to the degree of difficulty and make sure they sign the park intentions book. Note that the Copland Pass Track over the Alps is definitely not for the inexperienced.

Glaciers

From the end of the Tasman Valley Road there is a track along the side of the mighty Tasman Glacier to Ball Shelter. With a length of 16 miles (27km) this glacier is the longest in New Zealand and one of the largest anywhere in the world outside the polar regions.

Though walking the track allows some excellent views of the glacier's lower reaches, it is only by taking a scenic flight that one can appreciate its beauty to the fullest. Some of these flights include a landing on the glacier whereas others also take in

Fox and Franz Josef glaciers in neighbouring Westland National Park. Those who want to combine a scenic flight with a bit of adventure can ski the Tasman. This all-day tour is an unforgettable experience and one does not need to be a champion skier to take part.

However the more sedentary among us need not fear: it is neither necessary to walk, climb or fly to get a wonderful view of mountain scenery. All one needs is a seat in the air-conditioned comfort of the Hermitage Hotel's Panorama Room.

The vista of snow-capped peaks, including Mt Cook, that greets the eye through generously proportioned windows, is perhaps compensation enough for the rather expensive menu they set before you.

Where to stay

Accommodation within Mount Cook Village is provided by the luxury Hermitage Hotel, the slightly cheaper Mount Cook Travelodge, Mount Cook Chalets and the Mount Cook Youth Hostel. Cabins, camping and caravan sites are provided at the Glentanner Park motor camp, about 12 miles (20km) from the village on the shores of Lake Pukaki. Heliskiing trips also start from here.

Cheapest of all is the White Horse Hill camping area, to the north of the village, where the facilities are accordingly basic; running water and toilets but no electricity or showers.

Twizel

Twizel is located about 35 miles (58km) south of Mount Cook Village and offers itself as an alter-native place to stay. Built in 1968 as a base town for the Upper Waitaki Hydro-electric Power Development Scheme, Twizel would have been bulldozed once work was completed were it not for the tourist potential of the area and the tenacity of the residents who wanted to remain.

Close to town are lakes Pukaki, Ohau, Ruataniwha and Benmore. Apart from the fishing and water sport activities that these lakes provide, there is also a unique attraction in the form of a black stilt breeding farm $5^{1}/_{2}$ miles (3km) south of town.

Black stilts

The black stilt has the unfortunate reputation of being the world's rarest wading bird — there are only around 70 of them living in the wild. Visitors can observe stilts in the rearing aviaries from a specially constructed viewing hide.

Mackenzie Country

The tussock-covered plains of which Twizel marks the heart, are popularly known as the Mackenzie Country. The region is named after the legendary sheep thief James McKenzie, who was caught with a large flock of stolen sheep on the fringes of the basin that now bears his name. McKenzie was accused of stealing the sheep from a run near Timaru in March 1855, a charge which he denied. Though convicted of the crime he always proclaimed his innocence and he was eventually pardoned in 1856. The current theory is that McKenzie may really have been innocent but, whatever the truth may be, the mystique of this man (about whom little is known) continues to live on as part of the country's folklore.

Lake Tekapo

Still within the Mackenzie Country and just over 31 miles (50km) northeast of Twizel, is beautiful **Lake Tekapo**. The waters of this glacial lake have an exquisite turquoise colouring that contrasts magnificently with the bronzed, almost treeless, surroundings. This unique colouring is produced by rocks that have been ground to a fine powder by glacial action and which now hang suspended, as 'rock flour', in the water. Though the water looks inviting, the lake is as chilly as the glaciers that feed it, so a swim is something only the bold should attempt.

The township of **Lake Tekapo** is located at the lake's southern end. On the lake shore a short distance from town is the **Church of the Good Shepherd**, a simple stone building that was erected as a memorial to the pioneer runholders of the Mackenzie. Not far away is the bronze statue of a sheepdog, a fitting tribute to an animal which played, and continues to play, an indispensable role in the grazing of the high-country.

Although the desolate beauty of the scenery which surrounds the lake can be enjoyed for free, it is nevertheless worth considering spending a dollar or two on the scenic flights which start from here. The 'Grand Traverse' offered by **Air Safaris** is a 50 minute scenic flight around Mount Cook and Westland National Parks which takes in Franz Josef, Fox and Tasman Glaciers. The same company also offers roughly the same tour from Glentanner Park, near Mount Cook. In any case, these flights are great value for money and a bit cheaper than those offered by other airlines at Mount Cook.

From Tekapo, SH8 curves its way eastwards through vast tussock grasslands until, at **Burke Pass**, the wide-open spaces of the Mackenzie are abruptly left behind for an altogether gentler landscape. The rolling downs on which towns like Fairlie and Geraldine are situated are a first hint of the Canterbury Plains, one of the most prosperous farming regions in New Zealand.

Moving on

Fairlie, the 'Gateway to the Mackenzie' for those coming from Timaru or Christchurch, is noted for its pretty tree-lined avenues and makes a good base in winter for those skiing at either **Fox Peak** or **Mount Dobson** in the Two Thumb Range. If time is pressing it is probably best to leave Fairlie on SH8 for Timaru and then follow SH1 directly to Christchurch through the middle of the **Canterbury Plains**. However a more scenic and leisurely alternative is to follow state highways 79 and 72 via Geraldine and Mount Hutt.

Geraldine

Geraldine is a nice little town with a few interesting things to see and do in the vicinity. About 12 miles (20km) north of town is **Peel Forest Park**, one of the few remaining stands of native forest in the area.

Snowboarding, Mount Hutt, Canterbury

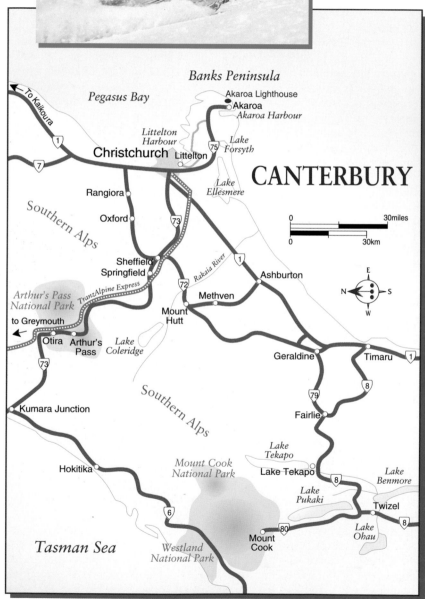

Banks Peninsula

Pegasus Bay

Akaroa Lighthouse
Akaroa
Akaroa Harbour

To Kaikoura
1

Littelton Harbour
Christchurch Littelton
75
Lake Forsyth

7

CANTERBURY

Rangiora

Lake Ellesmere

Oxford
73

Southern Alps

0   30miles
0   30km

Sheffield
Springfield
72
Rakaia River
1
Ashburton

TranzAlpine Express

Arthur's Pass National Park

Methven

to Greymouth

Mount Hutt

Otira Arthur's Pass
Lake Coleridge

E
N   S
W

73

Southern Alps

Geraldine   Timaru
1

Kumara Junction
79

Fairlie
8

Hokitika

Mount Cook National Park

Lake Tekapo
Lake Tekapo

Lake Benmore

Lake Pukaki
8

6

Twizel

Tasman Sea

Westland National Park

Mount Cook
80
Lake Ohau
8

Above: Several spectacular train journeys start from Christchurch

Below: St Patrick's, Akaroa

There is a good camping ground here for those who enjoy a secluded setting, as well as some lovely picnic spots in the forest.

Some of the park's well-marked trails lead to waterfalls but the **Big Tree Walk** (1 hour) leads, appropriately enough, to a huge totara tree with a circumference of over 29ft (9m). At the end of the road that leads on from the forest park is **Mesopotamia**, a sheep run once owned by the great English writer Samuel Butler, who briefly tried his luck as a sheep farmer back in the 1860's.

In Geraldine itself, the **Vintage Car and Machinery Museum** is worth a look for those interested in things technical and just out of town, in the direction of Fairlie, visitors can enjoy the taste of elderberry wine at **Barker's Wines**.

Timaru

Probably the best time to visit the port of Timaru, south of Geraldine, is when the **Christmas Carnival** is held at **Caroline Bay**. The carnival starts on 26 December and lasts about 10 days. In town, the **Aigantighe Art Gallery** is of interest along with the **South Canterbury Museum**. The museum has among its exhibits a replica of the plane designed by pioneer aviator Richard Pearse, who may have been airborne a few months before the Wright brothers.

Mount Hutt skiing

The main route continues north of Geraldine towards Mount Hutt. The **Mount Hutt** ski field is regarded as one of the best in the Southern Hemisphere. Reliable snowfall means that the season here can last for as long as six months. There are slopes suitable for beginners but the experienced can go higher up to enjoy the challenges of off-piste heli-skiing. All the necessary amenities are available, including a large ski school. Other ski fields within reasonable driving distance are Mount Dobson, Craigieburn and Porter Heights.

Methven

The base for winter activities at Mount Hutt is Methven, a short distance from SH72. Obviously this town is at its liveliest during the winter months when tourists with sun-tanned faces strut down the main street looking for the best place to enjoy their apres-ski. However, there are things to do in summer too when trendy ski clothes are exchanged for the gumboots and check-shirts of a small farming town. Apart from a beautiful 18-hole golf course there is good walking (Mt Hutt Forest) and fishing in the vicinity, as well as the possibility of jet boat rides through the dramatic **Rakaia Gorge**. A walkway allows a more leisurely look at the gorge (3-4 hours return).

At the intersection of state highways 72 and 73 the visitor can either choose to go left for a last close look at the Alps in the vicinity of Arthur's Pass, or turn right on the road to Christchurch. For those who are starting their exploration of the South Island from Christchurch, the Arthur's Pass Road can be highly recommended as a very scenic route to the 'Wild West Coast' (see Chapter 8).

Arthur's Pass National Park

Arthur's Pass township is the gateway to the national park and only 2 miles (4km) from the 3,030ft (924m) pass itself. There is accommodation as well as a Park Visitor Centre. It has detailed information about all the tracks and inexperienced trampers should seek advice from the staff as to the difficulty of the walks they intend to do. The weather here can change very rapidly, making many normally 'safe' walks quite dangerous.

Flora and fauna

The national park spreads over both sides of the **Southern Alps**, covering an area of 243,000 acres (98,408 hectares). Dry tussock grasslands and mountain beech forest dominate in the east, whereas the park's western slopes, where rainfall is much higher, are characterised by dense, tangled rainforests of podocarp, beech and broadleaved trees. The alpine regions are also rich in flora; in fact more than fifty per cent of the alpine species found in New Zealand occur within the boundaries of this national park.

Such a diversity of vegetational zones also supports a wide range of native birds. Most common are wood pigeons, riflemen, bellbirds and silver-eyes. In the alpine regions, keas amuse trampers with their antics. Less commonly seen are parakeets, yellowheads and blue ducks. Great spotted kiwis are also found throughout the park, but due to their nocturnal habits they are more often heard than seen.

Walks

The walks within this mountainous park vary from easy strolls to demanding tours of four or five days. Short walks close to the township include the **Dobson Nature Walk** (1½ hours return), **Devil's Punchbowl Falls Walk** (1 hour return) and **Bridal Veil Track** (1½ hours return).

An excellent two day tramp which crosses from the eastern beech forests to the rainforests of the West Coast is the **Mingha-Deception Track**. It starts only 3 miles (5km) south of the village at **Greyneys Shelter**. Also within easy reach, the **Temple Basin Track** (3 hours return) is hard to beat for magnificent views of alpine peaks, some of which exceed 6,500ft (2,000m). In winter a ski field operates here.

CHRISTCHURCH

Christchurch is frequently described as 'the most English city outside England' which, however true the statement may or may not be, is at least partly reflected in its **Cathedral Square**, punting on the willow-lined **Avon River**, some noble old stone buildings and the very English traditions of Christ's College secondary school for boys.

The first settlers in the area (organised settlement took place in the 1850's) were certainly English to the core and brought with them not only their Anglican faith but also their cricket bats. Christchurch has been the headquarters for New Zealand cricket ever since. The city was named, after Christ Church College at Oxford, where one of the early settler leaders had studied.

Above: Christchurch Gondola, Mount Cavendish, Christchurch

Left: Christchurch Cathedral

Below: New Regent Street, Christchurch

Above: *Sheepfarmers, Canterbury*

Right: *Black swans can be seen in their hundreds on Lake Ellesmere (Banks Peninsula)*

The City Centre

Cathedral Square, in the middle of town, is a good place to start a walk around the inner city. For those who are driving (and who have successfully negotiated the one-way street system) there is parking at the corner of Gloucester and Manchester Streets.

Cathedral Square

Dominating the square is the neo-Gothic **Christ Church Cathedral.** For an elevated view of the surroundings, the energetic can climb halfway up the 206ft (63m) tower to the observation balconies. During the week at 1pm, weather permitting, the city's most eloquent eccentric comes to harangue crowds in the square with his view of the world. Famed throughout the country as 'the Wizard', and dressed in flowing robes, he is an 'official' attraction with his postcards and upside-down maps of the world, available from the Tourist Information Centre.

Canterbury Museum

At the end of Worcester Boulevard, on Rolleston Avenue, is the Canterbury Museum. Among the most interesting displays is the reconstruction of a Christchurch street from the pioneer days, and the **Hall of Antarctic Discovery** where exhibits chart the trials and tribulations of antarctic exploration. The recently opened gallery **Iwi Tawhito — Whenua Hou** (Ancient People — New Land) takes visitors far back into New Zealand's pre-European past, to a time when the now extinct giant moas were hunted by the early Polynesian ancestors of today's modern Maori.

Directly behind the museum, the **Robert McDougall Art Gallery** has large permanent collections of New Zealand and international art.

The Hagley Parks

Access to the art gallery is through the **Botanic Gardens** which, combined with the adjacent South and North Hagely Parks, spread out

Canterbury Information Centre

From the square, continue west along Worcester Boulevard towards Rolleston Avenue. Just before crossing a bridge over the Avon River it is worth stopping at the Canterbury Information Centre which is housed in an attractive old red brick building. Here visitors can get all the information they need on the many things to do in and around Christchurch. Apart from town plans they also have a pamphlet describing various walks around the central city.

Opposite the Information Centre is a statue of the Antarctic explorer Robert Falcon Scott, who set off from here on his ill-fated expedition to the South Pole.

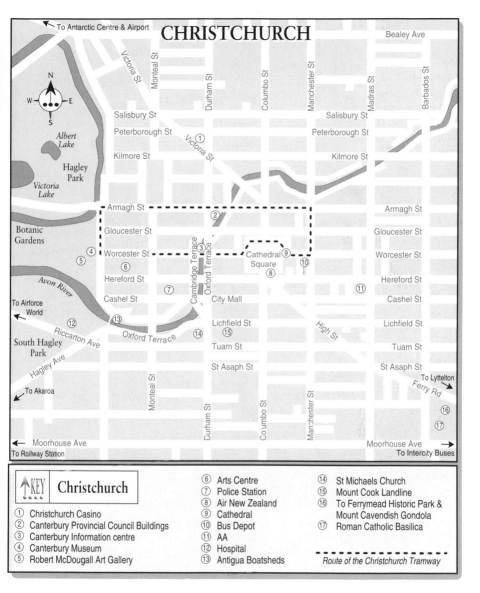

CHRISTCHURCH

To Antarctic Centre & Airport

Bealey Ave

Victoria St
Monteal St
Durham St
Columbo St
Manchester St
Madras St
Barbados St

Albert
Lake

Hagley
Park

Victoria
Lake

Salisbury St
Peterborough St
Victoria St
Kilmore St

Salisbury St
Peterborough St
Kilmore St

Botanic
Gardens

Armagh St
Gloucester St
Worcester St

Cambridge Terrace
Oxford Terrace

Cathedral
Square

Armagh St
Gloucester St
Worcester St

Avon River

Hereford St
Cashel St

City Mall

Hereford St
Cashel St

To Airforce
World

Lichfield St
Tuam St
St Asaph St

High St

Lichfield St
Tuam St
St Asaph St

Riccarton Ave

Oxford Terrace

South Hagley
Park

Hagley Ave

To Akaroa

To Lyttelton
Ferry Rd

Moorhouse Ave
To Railway Station

Monteal St
Durham St
Columbo St
Manchester St

Moorhouse Ave
To Intercity Buses

KEY — Christchurch

① Christchurch Casino
② Canterbury Provincial Council Buildings
③ Canterbury Information centre
④ Canterbury Museum
⑤ Robert McDougall Art Gallery

⑥ Arts Centre
⑦ Police Station
⑧ Air New Zealand
⑨ Cathedral
⑩ Bus Depot
⑪ AA
⑫ Hospital
⑬ Antigua Boatsheds

⑭ St Michaels Church
⑮ Mount Cook Landline
⑯ To Ferrymead Historic Park & Mount Cavendish Gondola
⑰ Roman Catholic Basilica

- - - - - - - - - -
Route of the Christchurch Tramway

behind the museum like a green oasis in the middle of the city. Bordered by the gently flowing **Avon River**, with magnificent old trees providing shade and luxuriant flower beds adding a splash of colour, the gardens make a very pleasant setting for a relaxing stroll. A tea kiosk offers light refreshments.

The Arts Centre

Just across the road from the Botanic Gardens and museum, in the former Canterbury University buildings, is the Arts Centre. Once cloaked in the sober mantle of academia, the dignified stone buildings are now a gathering place for artists, musicians and craftspeople. Live entertainment, craft shops, galleries and good restaurants ensure that there is plenty to see and do here. Especially popular is the weekend market where a colourful melange of stalls sell everything from handicrafts to exotic foods.

The River Avon

The **Antigua Boatsheds** at the southern end of Rolleston Avenue, hire out single and double canoes for those who want to paddle themselves along the Avon. If you prefer someone to do the work for you, punts complete with a boatman wearing his boater, depart from the Canterbury Information Centre, the Town Hall Restaurant and the Thomas Edmonds Restaurant; all of which are within walking distance of Cathedral Square.

From the boatsheds follow Cambridge Terrace back to Worcester Boulevard and Cathedral Square. This part of the walk is particularly attractive as it follows the tree-lined banks of the River Avon. On the way, the very impressive wooden structure of **St Michael's Church** (1872) can be seen across the river.

The Casino

A relatively new addition to the city's entertainment scene is the casino. **Christchurch Casino** is situated north of the Council Buildings on Victoria and Kilmore Streets. Dress standards are quite strict, so do not attempt to turn up in jeans.

Around Christchurch

Some of the city's other attractions are best reached with either the bus or car.

The **International Antarctic Centre** is located out near the airport. It offers an insight into the Antarctic

Architecture

The **Canterbury Provincial Council Buildings** (1859-65), which are considered to be the best examples of neo-Gothic architecture in the country, can be reached from Cathedral Square by going north along Colombo Street and then turning left into Armagh Street. The most interesting feature of the complex is the magnificent high Victorian Gothic interior of the **Stone Council Chamber**.

Further afield but also of great interest to architecture buffs is the **Roman Catholic Basilica** (1901-05) in Barbados Street. The Irish playwright George Bernard Shaw (1856-1950) was greatly impressed by this cathedral; it is generally regarded as New Zealand's finest neo-Renaissance church.

research schemes that are being carried out by American and New Zealand scientists. Christchurch is in fact, the US headquarters for 'Operation Deep Freeze', as the aerial supply link to their main Antarctic research station at McMurdo Sound is known. Multimedia special effects and the fascinating *Great White South* audio-visual presentation make the trip here a memorable experience.

Around 4 miles (6km) north-east of the City Centre is the **National Marae — Nga Hau E Wha** (The Meeting Place of the Four Winds of the Earth). The largest marae in New Zealand features the traditional art of New Zealand's main tribal groups. Entrance to the marae is through a finely carved gateway that symbolises the Maori settlement of New Zealand and later European colonisation. The *whare nui* (meeting house) is decorated with traditional carvings and painting (*kowhaiwhai*) whereas the *whare wananga* (house of learning) recounts ancient Maori myths and legends using contemporary styles and colours.

Air Force World is an imaginatively arranged museum, only a 15 minute drive from the City Centre. Pride of place is taken by 16 vintage aircraft that have seen service in the New Zealand Air Force over the years. A special attraction is the chance to fly in a Tiger Moth biplane.

Roughly the same distance away, but this time to the south-east of the City Centre, the **Ferrymead Historic Park** focuses on transport and technology. Visitors who passed on the role (and expense) of being a World War One flying ace at the previous museum, can at least ride on a steam train or tram here.

Only a few minutes away, the **Mount Cavendish Gondola** offers spectacular views of the Southern Alps and Banks Peninsula on its way up to the top of the **Port Hills**.

Banks Peninsula

The rugged hills of Banks Peninsula stand in dramatic contrast to the flat plains surrounding Christchurch. These hills are, in fact, the heavily-eroded flanks of two offshore volcanoes that formed millions of years ago and were eventually linked to the mainland by an accumulation of shingle that was washed down from the Alps. Around 15,000 years ago, the huge twin craters filled with sea-water to form the natural bays at Lyttelton and **Akaroa**.

Getting there

The quickest way to get to the peninsula, as well as Christchurch's port at Lyttelton, is to take Ferry and then Tunnel Road through the road tunnel. An alternative is to go south on Colombo Street and over Dyers Pass. This route offers excellent views and allows the possibility of a stop at the **Sign of the Takahe**, an impressive medieval-looking stone building that houses a good restaurant. Those without their own transport can take advantage of the **Akaroa Shuttle**, a minibus that runs between Akaroa and Christchurch ☎ (03) 304 8600 or 0800 500 929.

Probably the most interesting thing to do in **Lyttelton** is to take one of the cruises that start from here. Apart from that there is not much else to engage one's interest except for a small museum and the **Timeball Station**. For many years, the lowering of a timeball at precisely 1pm enabled mariners in the bay to adjust their chronometers.

The road from Lyttelton to Akaroa is narrow, winding and very picturesque. After passing Governors Bay and Allandale you can choose between two routes for the onward journey. The easiest to drive is the one over Gebbies Pass Road which then links with SH75 to Akaroa. The other road is less busy but partly unsealed and goes via Port Levy and Pigeon Bay.

Akaroa

Akaroa was originally intended as a French colony but, to the dismay of the colonists who arrived from France in 1840, the Treaty of Waitangi had already been signed and New Zealand was now under British sovereignty. The French stayed on, nevertheless, and the Gallic influence persists in many of Akaroa's street names (Rue Jolie, Rue Benoit) and the French-flavoured menus of some local restaurants.

The town itself is quite charming; it stretches along a palm-fringed waterfront with quaint little cottages dotted here and there. The oldest house in town, and possibly Canterbury, is **Langlois-Eteveneaux Cottage** (1841-45). Behind the cottage is a museum that deals with Akaroa's colourful history. Other places of interest are the picture-postcard **Church of St Patrick** (1864) and the historic **Akaroa Lighthouse** (1878).

But apart from viewing any specific sights, it is also nice to just

wander about town and enjoy the relaxed atmosphere of the place. For those who linger, a perfect way to end the day would be with a bottle of (New Zealand) wine and a seafood meal at the **Pier Café**, or any of the other restaurants in town for that matter. Akaroa is, all in all, a great place to while away a few days.

Walks and beaches

Many of the little bays and inlets on Banks Peninsula can be reached by car, including lovely **Okains Bay** where there is an excellent **Maori and Colonial Museum**. However, the really secluded places are only accessible on foot. One of the peninsula's most interesting walks is the four day **Banks Peninsula Track**. It begins and ends in Akaroa and covers $18^{1}/_{2}$ miles (30km) of remote coastline. The track offers spectacular coastal scenery, safe swimming beaches and the chance to see penguins, seals and rare Hector's

The TranzAlpine

Before finally leaving the South Island's largest city, it is worth mentioning the TranzAlpine Express. The route this train takes over the Southern Alps via Arthur's Pass is quite spectacular and some consider it to be one of the world's finest train journeys. The train departs daily from

dolphins. For more information about the track and hut bookings ☎ (03) 304-7612. The tourist office in Akaroa should also have a few useful pamphlets about this and other walks.

From Akaroa, SH75 winds its way back to Christchurch past **Lake Forsyth** and **Lake Ellesmere**. Both lakes serve as breeding grounds for hundreds of black swans and provide a habitat for around 150 other species of bird as well.

Back to Auckland

State Highway 1, on which this long exploration of New Zealand began, is the road now followed for all those who are returning to Auckland for the flight home. The main place of interest on the way to Picton is **Kaikoura** and those who took the direct route to the West Coast as described at the end of Route 9 in Chapter 7 have the chance of stopping here now.

Express

either Christchurch or Greymouth (on the West Coast). The trip can also be done as part of a package tour that combines a ride on the TranzAlpine Express with a jet-boat ride and a visit to a high country sheep farm.

Contact **Pacific Tourways** ☎ (03) 359-9133).

THE CHATHAM ISLANDS

As a footnote it is worth mentioning one final place: 533 miles (860km) east of Christchurch is a remote group of islands known as the Chathams.

Windswept and about as far off the beaten track as most tourists are likely to get, the Chathams are home to a small community of fishermen and farmers. Most of the thousand or so islanders live on Chatham Island's 222,000 acres (90,000 hectares), the largest of the 10 islands in the group. The only other island that is inhabited is tiny **Pitt Island** where the population stands at around 50. A feature of the main island is the large central lagoon which, together with many shallow lakes, covers almost a quarter of its entire area.

History

The European discoverer of the islands was the British naval officer Lieutenant William Broughton, who landed in 1791 at **Kaingaroa**, near the north-eastern tip of Chatham. His encounter with the island's original inhabitants, the Moriori, was less than satisfactory and resulted in one of the Moriori being shot during a dispute. After him the islands were visited periodically by sealers and whalers but a serious attempt at European settlement did not begin before the 1840's.

The Moriori

When and from exactly where the Moriori came is not known for certain. Some theories maintain that these Polynesians arrived here before the Maori settlement of New Zealand, whereas others suggest that the Moriori migrated here from the South Island. Whatever the case may be, the Moriori evolved, isolated as they were, a culture which differed in many respects from that of the mainland Maori.

At the time of European discovery there were about 2,000 Morioris living on the Chathams. However, in the early nineteenth century an invasion by mainland Maoris, along with diseases introduced by sealers and whalers, decimated the population. The last supposedly full-blooded Moriori died in 1933 but many islanders still claim to be of Moriori descent.

Not much remains as a reminder of early Moriori culture, but those who are interested in the Moriori can visit the small museum at **Waitangi**, on Chatham, where there are a few Moriori artefacts and early photos of the islands. Also of interest are the Moriori tree carvings (dendroglyphs) near the old **Te Hapupu** airfield.

Bird-watching and activities

But as fascinating as the mysteries of Moriori culture may be, the reason more and more people are beginning to visit the Chathams is to go bird-watching.

The rarest of the eighteen species of bird that are unique to the islands is the black robin. Once there were only five of these birds in the world, but successful breeding techniques have rescued them, for the moment, from the brink of extinction. On the other hand, introduced birds like black swans and wekas are so common that they feature in the local cuisine along with freshly caught seafood such as crayfish.

Other activities on the islands include horse-riding, diving and tramping. It is also possible to hire four-wheel drive vehicles on Chatham Island which, apart from walking, are the only way to get around as there is no public transport.

Getting there

Those who want to visit this tiny insular world of lagoons, peat bogs, rugged coastlines and deserted beaches should plan well ahead. Though there are weekly flights from Wellington and Christchurch, demand is high and seats are very limited.

From Napier, two shipping lines service the islands. Both these cargo ships carry a small number of passengers and require 36 to 40 hours for the voyage. There is also a ship that sails from Auckland. Otherwise another possibility is to join one of the cruises organised by **Southern Heritage Expeditions**. This company also specialises in trips to New Zealand's sub-antarctic islands.

Useful background reading for visitors to the Chathams is *Moriori — A People Rediscovered* by Michael King and *A Land Apart* by Michael King and Robin Morrison. As **Napier** is a sister city to the Chathams, their tourist information will also be able to provide further details about the islands and how to get there.

ACTIVITIES

Akaroa

Harbour Cruises

MV Canterbury Cat
Office opposite wharf
☎ (03) 304 7641
These cruises have an accent on natural history. Take binoculars. Daily at 11am & 1.30pm.

Kayaking/Canoeing

Banks Peninsula Sea Kayaks
114 Rue Jolie
☎ (03) 304 8776
Rentals and guided tours.

Chatham Islands

Boat Trips

Southern Heritage Expeditions
offers a cruise to the Chathams and New Zealand's subantarctic islands. The trip takes 14 days. Contact:
New Zealand
PO Box 22, Waikari
☎ (03) 314 4393
Fax (03) 314 4137

UK
Naturetrek Chautara
Bighton, Hants. SO24 9RB
☎ (01962) 733 051
Fax (01962) 733 368

USA
NZCRO,
6033 West Century Blvd,
Suite 1270, Los Angeles , CA 90045
☎ (310) 395 7480

Christchurch

Jet Boating

Jet Stream Tours
☎ (03) 352 2961
On Waimakariri River.

Punting/Canoeing

Antigua Boatsheds
Rolleston Ave
Open: daily 9.30am-6pm
☎ 366 5885
Single and double canoes for boating on the Avon. Punts depart daily 9am-6pm, in winter 10am-4pm.
   Departure points: Canterbury-Christchurch Information Centre, corner Worcester Street & Oxford Terrace, the Town Hall Restaurant (cnr Colombo St & Kilmore St) and Thomas Edmonds Restaurant (Cambridge Terrace).

Lake Tekapo

Guided Walks

Alpine Recreation Canterbury Ltd
PO Box 75, Lake Tekapo
☎ (03) 680 6736 Fax (03) 680 6765
Offer the Mackenzie High Country Walk, an easy 3 day alpine walk.

Kayaking/Canoeing

Lake Tekapo Motels & Motor Camp
PO Box 43
☎ (03)680 6825

Scenic Flights

Air Safaris
☎ (03) 680 6880
Offer Grand Traverse flight around Mt Cook and Westland National Parks. Cheaper than comparable flights at Mt Cook.

Lyttelton

Harbour Cruises

☎ (03) 328 8368
To Ripapa Island Historic Reserve.
Daily 2.45pm

Methven

Jet Boating

Rakaia Gorge Scenic Jet
☎ (03) 318 6515
Through Rakaia River Gorge.

Mount Cook

Boat Trips

Glacier Explorers
Contact Hermitage booking desk.
Glacial lake tours (2¹/₂ hrs).

Guided Walks

Alpine Guides Ltd
Mount Cook
☎ (03) 435 1834 Fax (03) 435 1898
Can provide a guide for the
Copland Pass Track.

Alpine Recreation Canterbury Ltd
(see Lake Tekapo above)
Offer a 2-3 day alpine crossing over
Ball Pass in the national park. A good

standard of fitness is required. No
mountaineering experience necessary.

Heliskiing

Heliskiing is offered by the **Helicopter
Line** (see Scenic Flights) in association
with Alpine Guides and Glentanner
Park. Bookings are essential for
heliskiing and the Tasman Glacier
ski trip ☎ (03) 435 1834.

Another possibility is **Southern Alps
Guiding**, PO Box 32, Mount Cook
☎ (03) 435 1890.

Scenic Flights

Mount Cook Airline
☎ (03) 435 1848
Offer snow landings on Tasman,
Fox & Franz Josef Glaciers.

The Helicopter Line
Glentanner Park
☎ (03) 435 1855 or (03) 435 1801
Similar trips to Mount Cook Airline.

ACCOMMODATION

*See page 288 and page 300 for accommodation and restaurant
rating guides in the FactFile*

Akaroa

Chez La Mer $
(Backpackers)
Rue Lavaud
☎ (03) 304 7024
Pleasant lodge with a
secluded garden.

Lavaud House $$
(Bed & Breakfast)
83 Rue Lavaud
☎ (03) 304 7121
An old colonial house set in
a pretty garden.

Arthur's Pass

Mountain House $
(Backpackers)
PO Box 12
☎ (03) 318 9258
From May to September stay
three nights for the price of two.

Chalet Hotel & Restaurant $$
Main Road (Bed & Breakfast)
☎/Fax (03) 318 9236
No smoking in rooms.
Swiss-style accommodation.

Christchurch

Christchurch has a wide range of accommodation to suit all budgets. Camping grounds that are not too far from the City Centre (2 to 3 miles/3 to 5km) include the **Showground Motor Camp** ☎ (03) 338 9770 at 47-51 Whiteleigh Rd, **Meadow Park Holiday Park** ☎ (03) 352 9176 at 39 Meadow St and **Amber Park Motel & Caravan Park** ☎ (03) 348 3327 at 308 Blenheim Rd. Most of the city's motels are to be found along either Bealey Avenue or Papanui Road. The **Christchurch Motel Guide** has a map showing their locations.

Dreamland $
(Backpackers)
21/23 Packe Street
☎ (03) 366 3519
Small hostel with gardens.
15 minutes to City Centre.

Vagabond Backpackers $
232 Worcester Street
☎ (03) 379 9677
Small hostel with modern facilities.
Middle of town. Non-smoking.

Adelphi Motel $$
49 Papanui Road
☎ (03) 355 6037 Fax (03) 355 6036
About 5 minutes by car to the city.
Several restaurants nearby.

Ambassador's Hotel $$
(Bed & Breakfast)
19 Manchester Street
☎/Fax (03) 366 7808
Also has cheaper
'backpackers' rooms.

Eliza's Manor House $$
(Bed & Breakfast)
82 Bealey Avenue
☎ (03) 366 8584 Fax (03) 366 4946
Impressive old Victorian house built in 1856. Elegantly decorated bedrooms.

Tudor Court Motel $$
57 Bealey Avenue
☎ (03) 379 1465 Fax (03) 379 1490
Only a 15 minute walk to City Centre.
Plenty of restaurants nearby.

Windsor Hotel $$
(Bed & Breakfast)
52 Armagh Street
☎ (03) 366 1503 Fax (03) 366 9796
Colonial style building,
central location. No smoking.

Cashmere House $$$
(Bed & Breakfast)
141 Hackthorne Road, Cashmere
☎ (03) 332 7864
Luxurious villa, beautifully restored.

Parkroyal $$$
Cnr Kilmore and Durham Sts
☎ (03) 365 7799
Fax (03) 365 0082
Luxury class hotel.

Mount Cook

Glentanner Park $
SH 80 (at head of Lake Pukaki)
☎ (03) 435 1855 Fax (03) 435 1854
Tent sites and cabins. $12^{1}/_{2}$ miles (20km) from Mt Cook Village.

Mount Cook YHA Hostel $
Cnr Bowen & Kitchener Drives
☎ (03) 435 1820 Fax (03) 435 1821
Reservations are advisable from December to April.

The Hermitage Hotel $$$
☎ (03) 435 1809 Fax (03) 435 1879
The Travelodge and Mount Cook Chalets can also be booked with the above numbers.

Lake Tekapo

Tailor-Made Tekapo Backpackers $
9-11 Aorangi Crescent
☎ (03) 680 6700
Set in a large garden.
Plenty of books for rainy days.

Lake Tekapo Motels & Motor Camp $$
Lake Side Drive
☎ (03) 680 6825
Fax(03) 680 6824
Also cheap cabins,
tent sites and tourist flats.

Methven

Blue Pub $
Barkers Road
☎ (03) 302 8046
Fax (03) 302 8048
Centre of town.

Pudding Hill Chalets $$
SH72 (3 miles/5km from town)
☎/Fax (03) 302 8416
Also tent sites. Base for tandem
parachuting.

Twizel

Glenbrook Station $$/$$$
On SH8, 5 miles (8km)
south of Twizel
☎ (03) 438 9704
Fax (03) 438 9443
This high-country sheep station
offers a variety of accommodation.
Most expensive are the rooms in
the farmhouse with dinner, bed and
breakfast. The three cottages are
quite modestly priced and cheapest
of all are the backpacker beds in
the shearers' quarters.

Mountain Chalets $$
Wairepo Road
☎ (03) 435 0785
Fax (03) 435 0551
Cheaper than the motel units are
twin rooms in the attached lodge.

Waitangi

(Chatham Islands)
Hotel Chathams $$
Waterfront Road
☎ (03) 305 0048
Fax (03) 305 0097

EATING OUT

Akaroa

Bruce Restaurant $$
Akaroa Village Inn, Beach Road
☎ (03) 304 7421
Fresh seafood is a specialty. In the
same building is Jacques Cafe & Bar.

La Rue $$
6 Rue Balguerie
☎ (03) 304 7658
Seafood including crayfish
(lobster) in season.

Port of Call Cafe $$
Main Wharf
☎ (03) 304 7272
Good seafood, nice setting.

Arthur's Pass

The Chalet $$
Main Road
☎ (03) 318 9236

Christchurch

Dux de Lux $
(BYO/Licensed)
Cnr Hereford & Montreal Sts
☎ (03) 366 6919
They brew their own beer here,
mainly vegetarian.
Some nights live music.

Bardelli's $$
98 Cashel Mall
☎ (03) 353 0000
Popular place, quite stylish inside.

Il Felice $$
(BYO/Licensed)
Lichfield St
☎ (03) 366 7535
Excellent Italian cuisine.

Thomas Edmonds Restaurant $$
(BYO/Licensed)
Cnr Cambridge Terrace
& Manchester Street
☎ (03) 365 2888
Nicely situated by the river.

Canterbury Tales $$$
Parkroyal Hotel
Kilmore & Durham Sts
☎ (03) 365 7799
Excellent food with full silver service.

Tiffany's $$$
(BYO/Licensed)
95 Oxford St
☎ (03) 379 1350
Good food in a lovely old house
near the Avon River.

Timaru

Casa Italia $$
2 Strathallan St
☎ (03) 684 5528
One of the best restaurants in town.

The "Bold As" Brasserie $$
335 Stafford Street
☎ (03) 688 3981
Good views, casual dining.
A bit cheaper than Casa Italia.

GENERAL INFORMATION

Christchurch, Area Code: (03)

Consulates
UK: ☎ 365 5440
USA: ☎ 379 004
Post Office
Chief Post Office is on Cathedral Square.

Important Telephone Numbers

Emergency Chemist	☎ 366 4439
Emergency Medical	☎ 365 7777
Taxis	☎ 379 9799

Transport

Airport Transport
Bus from city to airport leaves from Tower Building, Cathedral Square.
They depart half-hourly from 6am-6pm, then less frequently until 9.45pm.
For exact times: ☎ 366 8855
   Super Shuttle offers a door to door service to airport ☎ 365 5655.

Bus Services & City Tours

For local bus timetables enquire at **Bus Kiosk**, Cathedral Square ☎ 366 8855. Those travelling further afield will find the **Mt Cook Landline Coach Terminal** at 40 Lichfield Street (Reservations: ☎ 379 0690. The **Intercity Coachlines Terminal** is at 471 Moorhouse Avenue, by old railway station ☎ 379 9020.

Alternatively bookings for long distance buses can also be made through **Christchurch Information Centre**. They can also advise about the various shuttle services from Christchurch to Akaroa and other destinations in the South Island.

The **City Circuit Bus** departs the Information Centre hourly from 9am-6pm. You can get on and off whenever you like along the route ☎ 385 5386.

The **Double Decker Bus Company** offers a 90 minute circuit of the city covering many of the main sights ☎ 377 1644.

More details on the above mentioned bus tours and others are available from the **Information Centre**. Tours can also be booked there.

Christchurch Tramway

Trams have been recently reintroduced to the city's streets. They run along a 1¹⁄₂ mile (2¹⁄₂ km) inner city loop which includes some of the city's more interesting attractions and shopping areas. The trams run daily between 8am and 11pm.

Mount Cavendish Gondola
10 Bridle Path Road
Open: Mon-Thur 10am-11pm; Fri & Sat 10am-midnight;
Sun 10am-9.30pm.

Trains

Railway Station is off Clarence Street, a longish walk from the City Centre. Reservations freephone 0800 802 802 or contact **Visitor Information Centre** Worcester Street. The latter also have information about the morning bus service to the railway station.

Nightlife & Entertainment

Christchurch

The Town Hall ☎ 366 8899 on Kilmore Street provides a venue for performances of classical music. Live theatre can be seen at the **James Hay Theatre** (part of town hall complex) and the **Theatre Royal**, Gloucester Street. Movie-goers will find a large cinema complex in the former railway station.

On the weekends there are a number of pubs where you can listen or dance to rock and folk music. Quite popular are **Bush Inn** at 364 Riccarton Road, **Dux de Lux** and **His Lordships Hotel** at 106 Litchfield Street. Nightclubs include **Warners** in Cathedral Square and **Caesars** in Chancery Arcade.

PLACES TO VISIT

Akaroa
(Banks Peninsula)
Akaroa Lighthouse
Beach Road
Open: Sun 1-4pm (daily during Jan).

Akaroa Museum & Langlois-Eteveneaux Cottage
Cnr Rue Lavaud & Rue Balguerie
Open: daily 10.30am-4.30pm.

Christchurch
Air Force World
Main South Road
Bus: No. 25 or 8. A courtesy bus leaves Christchurch Information Centre 3 times daily.
Open: daily 10am-4pm.

Arts Centre
2 Worcester Boulevard
Open: daily Mon-Fri 8.30am-5pm, weekends 10am-4pm.

Canterbury Museum
Rolleston Avenue
Open: daily 9am-4.30pm. Free guided tours 10.15am, 11.30am, 1.15pm & 2.30pm. Admission is free (donations welcome).

Canterbury Provincial Council Buildings
Durham Street
Open: Mon-Fri 10am-4pm. Guided tours Sun 2-4pm. Admission is free except for guided tours.

Cathedral of the Blessed Sacrament
(Roman Catholic Basilica)
Barbados Street
Open: daily 8am-4pm.
A 15 min walk from the Square.

Christ Church Cathedral
Cathedral Square
Open: tower is open Mon-Sat from 8.30am, Sun 11.30am. Free guided tours Mon-Fri at 11am & 2pm, Sat 11am & Sun 11.30am.

Christchurch Casino
Victoria & Kilmore Sts
Open: Mon-Wed 11am-3am, then without a break from 11am Thurs-3am Mon.
Suitable attire required (no jeans, t-shirts etc).

Ferrymead Historic Park
269 Bridle Path Road, Heathcote
Bus: No. 3
Open: daily 10am-4.30pm.

International Antarctic Centre
Orchard Road
Bus: Airport bus
Open: daily 9.30am-8.30pm (1 Oct-31 Mar), 9.30am-5.30pm (1 Apr-30 Sep).

Nga Hau E Wha National Marae
250 Pages Road
Bus: No. 5
Open: Tours take place at 9am and 11am and 1pm and 3pm Mon-Fri.

Robert McDougall Art Gallery
Rolleston Avenue
(Access via Botanic Gardens)
Open: daily 10am-4.30pm.
Guides available 11am-3pm daily.

Geraldine
Barker's Wines
Off SH79
(5 miles/8km from Geraldine)
Open: Mon-Sat until 6pm.

Vintage Car & Machinery Museum
174 Talbot Street
Open: daily 10am-12noon, 1.30-4pm
(Labour Weekend to Queen's Birthday
Weekend).

Lyttelton
Lyttelton Museum
Gladstone Quay
Open: 2-4pm Tues, Thurs &
weekends (Dec-Feb), otherwise
only weekends 2-4pm.

Timeball Station
Reserve Terrace
Open: Mon-Fri 10am-4pm,
weekends 10am-5pm.

Okains Bay
(Banks Peninsula)
Maori & Colonial Museum
Open: daily 10am-5pm.

Timaru
Aigantighe Art Gallery
49 Waiiti Road
Open: Tues-Fri 11am-4.30pm,
weekends 2-4.30pm.

South Canterbury Museum
Perth Street
Open: Tues-Sun 1.30-4.30pm.
Admission is free.

Twizel
Black Stilt Breeding Centre
Off SH8
Open: guided tours Mon-Fri at
10.30am & 2pm, weekends 3pm.
Bookings must be made beforehand
at Visitor Information Centre,
Wairepo Rd, Twizel.

Waitangi
(Chatham Islands)
Chatham Islands Museum
South Road
Open: daily.

REGIONAL TRANSPORT

Chatham Islands
Air
Flights to the Chatham Islands depart from Wellington and Christchurch. For
details contact **Air New Zealand** Fax (64) 9 388 075, **Air Chathams**
Fax (64) 3 3050 208 or your local travel agent. The flight takes 3 hours.
Book well ahead.

Boat
It is possible to get to the Chathams by ship from Auckland or Napier. Contact
Cook Islands National Line Agency Ltd, PO Box 37-009, Parnell, Auckland
Fax (64) 9 309 7604 or **Napier Visitor Information** for details. For natural
history cruises to the Chathams, see under Chatham Islands in the section
Activities above.

VISITOR INFORMATION & PARK VISITOR CENTRES

Akaroa
80 Rue Lavaud
PO Box 80
Open: daily.
☎ (03) 304 8600

Arthur's Pass National Park
Main Road, PO Box 8
☎ (03) 318 9211
Fax (03) 318 9271

Christchurch
Christchurch/Canterbury Information Centre
Cnr Worcester St & Oxford Tce,
PO Box 2600
Open: Mon-Fri 8.30am-5pm,
weekends 8.30am-4pm.
☎ (03) 379 9629
Fax (03) 377 2424

Visitors' Information Centre
Christchurch International Airport
PO Box 14-001
Open: times coincide with arrival
of international flights.
☎ (03) 353 7783/4

Visitors' Information Centre
Domestic Terminal
Harewood,
PO Box 14-001
Open: 6.30am-10.30pm.
Saturdays 6.30am-8pm.
☎ (03) 353 7774/5

Fairlie
The Sunflower Centre
31 Main Street
☎ (03) 685 8258

Geraldine
Talbot Street
☎ (03) 693 8597

Methven
Mt Hutt Road
☎/Fax (03) 302 8955

Mount Cook National Park
Visitor Centre,
Bowen Drive
PO Box 5
Open: daily 8am-5pm.
☎ (03) 435 1818
Fax (03)4 35 1895

Twizel
Wairepo Road, Private Bag
Open: daily.
☎ (03) 435 0802
Fax (03) 435 0852

ACCOMMODATION

There is a wide range of accommodation from the cheap motor camps and backpacker hostels to modern motels and luxury hotels. The *Where to Stay Guide* published by the NZTB lists many of New Zealand's motels, hotels, guest houses and motor camps and is available from New Zealand's overseas tourist offices.

There are also a number of publications available locally which list the various forms of accommodation. Some of these are available free of charge at Tourist Information Centres, motor camps, motels or at railway stations and airports. *AA Accommodation Guides* published by the Automobile Association (AA) are free to overseas visitors who belong to an affiliated automobile club. These guides are available from AA offices throughout the country. Jason's accommodation guides are available in bookshops but some are also distributed free, as for instance *Jason's Budget Accommodation* which can be picked up at many motor camps.

It is possible to get a double room in cheap hotel for less than $60. The moderately priced places might cost up to $130 for two people.

In the Additional Information section at the end of each chapter, the various forms of accommodation are graded as follows (for double rooms):

$ = *inexpensive* $$ = *moderate* $$$ = *expensive*

Camping

New Zealand has some of the best camping facilities in the world. Camping grounds are well spread around the country and are often called 'motor camps', though some of the larger ones are called 'holiday parks'. Most camping grounds have not only tent sites but also powered sites for campervans and caravans, and cabins. There are a number of free booklets available in New Zealand which list camping grounds, for instance the *Holiday Accommodation Parks Directory*, published by the Camp & Cabin Association of N.Z.

The kitchens at camping grounds are usually very well equipped with stoves or microwave ovens, toasters, electric jugs and hot water for washing up. All you need to supply is your own crockery and pots, etc. Hot water showers and laundry facilities are also available.

Many camping grounds offer cabins. The simplest are the standard cabins which are not much more than a bunk, a mattress and a roof over the head. There are a few better grades of cabin but the best of the lot are the tourist flats which may be equipped with tv, shower and cooking facilities. Usually you have to bring your own sleeping bag or blankets, though they can sometimes be hired.

Cabins are excellent value for the budget visitor and can cost as little as NZ$20 for two persons. Tourist flats hover around the NZ$45-$50 mark.

There are also camping sites run by the Department of Conservation (DOC) which are situated in national, maritime or forest parks as well as in various forest reserves. Some of these sites are serviced (hot showers, etc) but others are very simple and might only have a toilet and water supply. The brochure *Conservation Campsites* lists these sites and is available from DOC offices or by writing to DOC, PO Box 10420, Wellington, New Zealand.

Hostels

YHA hostels and private or backpacker hostels are found throughout New Zealand and cater to budget conscious visitors. Many have single or double rooms as well as dormitory-style accommodation. Fully equipped communal kitchens and laundry facilities are generally available. Many hire out bicycles and will also help organise outdoor activities. Some hostels offer a pick-up service if they are located outside town. Reservations are recommended for all hostels in the summer season. Average price for a double room is about NZ$15 per person.

YHA Hostels (Hostelling International)

In New Zealand there is no age limit, no curfew, no duties and 24 hour access for guests. Bedding is supplied. YHA members are also entitled to discounts on travel in N.Z. with Air New Zealand, Ansett New Zealand, certain bus services and long-distance trains. You can join the YHA in N.Z. For more information contact:

YHA New Zealand,
National Office
PO Box 436
Christchurch
☎ (03) 379 9970
Fax (03) 365 4476

National Reservation Centre
PO Box 68-149
Auckland
☎ (09) 309 2802
Fax (09) 373 5083

Backpackers Hostels

Have similar services and facilities to YHA hostels but are more likely to have private or double rooms, at least at the moment. Premises are open all day and there are no membership fees. The optional VIP Backpackers Discount Card entitles holders to discounts similar to those available to YHA members.

Booklets listing backpacker accommodation are available at Information Centres or the hostels themselves. For more information contact:

A.T.A
PO Box 8
Kaikoura
☎/Fax (03) 319 5916

Backpackers Resorts of
New Zealand Ltd
PO Box 991
Taupo
☎/Fax (07) 377 1157

Budget Backpackers
Hostels NZ Ltd
99 Titiraupenga St
Taupo
☎/Fax (07) 377 1568

Guesthouses and Bed & Breakfasts

These vary a lot in price and in the standard of accommodation offered. In the cheaper guesthouses you may have to share bathroom facilities but the more expensive places have private facilities. The breakfasts at the B&B's can be very good value and they generally provide a more personal touch than motels or hotels. Lists of B&B accommodation are available at the guesthouses themselves or from the Tourist Information Centres.

Hotels, Motels & Motor Inns

Hotels can be quite cheap and basic or offer all the luxury one could ever wish (to pay) for. They are usually centrally located, often have an attached café or restaurant, guest lounge and laundry facilities. New Zealand's traditional 'pub' hotels are licensed to sell alcohol and may have both lounge and public bars. Many of the smaller hotels also offer budget or backpacker rooms. These budget rooms are normally without private bathrooms and tv's, etc.

Motel units are equipped with bathrooms and always provide tea or coffee-making facilities. Bedding is usually provided. Many have very well equipped kitchens with everything necessary to prepare a proper meal. Other facilities include television, radio, heating and electric blankets. Sauna, spa and swimming pool may also be available.

Motor Inns are a cross between a motel and hotel. They usually have a bar and a public restaurant. All rooms have attached bathrooms and tea or coffee making facilities are usually provided. A few rooms might also have kitchens. As is the case with a motel it is possible to park very close to your room.

Farmstays and Homestays

These places offer foreigners a chance to get to know a New Zealand family in either a rural, town or city environment. On the farmstays it is possible to participate in such typical farming activities as milking or rounding up sheep. Rooms may be in the family's house or in a separate cottage. Costs for this type of accommodation vary greatly. Some farm and homestays are listed at the back of the *Where to Stay Guide* mentioned earlier, otherwise contact one of the Tourist Information Centres or:

Homestay Ltd	**Rural Holidays New Zealand Ltd**
PO Box 25 115	PO Box 2155
Auckland	Christchurch
☎ (09) 575 5980	☎ (03) 366 1919
Fax (09) 575 9977	Fax (03) 379 3087

WWOOF

A cheaper way to stay on a farm than a farmstay is to join Willing Workers on Organic Farms (WWOOF). Members receive a list with organic farms throughout New Zealand. In exchange for your work the farmer provides food and accommodation. The best time of the year to take advantage of WWOOF is from October to March/May. To join contact: Janet & Andrew Strange, PO Box 1172, Nelson, New Zealand ☎ 025 345711 (mobile phone).

ARRIVAL AND CUSTOMS

All visitors to New Zealand need to have valid passports to enter the country and the passport must be valid for at least three months beyond the time of your intended stay. Holders of British, Canadian, USA or Australian passports do not require a visa. British passport holders are permitted to stay for up to six months, Canadian and USA passport holders are given a permit on arrival that enables a stay of three months and Australian citizens can stay in New Zealand indefinitely.

Apart from a passport it is necessary to be able to produce a return or onward ticket to a country that you are permitted to enter and evidence that you have sufficient funds to support yourself during the time of your stay. This is usually NZ$1000 per month; often it is enough to produce one of the major credit cards (Visa, Amex, MasterCard, Diners Club, Bankcard).

Vaccination certificates are not required.

As entry requirements are subject to change it is always wise to check the current situation with your airline, travel agent or a New Zealand embassy or consulate before departing.

CUSTOMS REGULATIONS

New Zealand has, so far, managed to remain relatively free of many of the animal and plant diseases that affect other countries. The accidental introduction of such diseases could have disastrous effects on the nation's economy which still relies heavily on agriculture. Because of this the interiors of all planes arriving from overseas are sprayed with an insecticide (harmless to humans) before passengers can alight. Furthermore all arriving passengers must fill out a form declaring whether or not they are carrying any plants, animal products or foodstuffs.

All personal belongings (clothing, cameras etc) needed for a visit are duty-free. The following goods are duty free for persons over 17 years of age: 200 cigarettes or 250g tobacco or 50 cigars (or a mixture of all three that does not exceed 250g); 4.5 litres of wine (e.g. 6,750ml bottles) or 4.5 litres of beer and one bottle of spirits of no more than 1,125ml.

If you are not carrying goods exceeding a total combined value of $NZ700 (your duty and tax free passenger concession), you can import two extra bottles (1,125ml each) of duty free spirits. Note that Auckland International Airport is one of the few airports in the world where it is possible to buy duty free goods on arrival.

Visitors are warned against bringing illegal drugs into the country.

BANKS

Are open Monday to Friday 9am-4.30pm. Overseas exchange services are available at international airports for all incoming and outgoing flights.

BUSINESS HOURS

Shops are generally open Monday to Friday 9am-5.30pm, Saturdays 9am-12.30pm and some shops (especially in the cities) may be open all day Sunday. On late shopping nights (Thursdays or Fridays) the hours are 9am-9pm.

CHEMISTS

Chemist shops are found in all towns and cities. They keep normal business hours but in larger towns and cities there is also an after-hours emergency service. Telephone numbers of Emergency Chemists are given in the General Information sections for Auckland and Wellington.

Apart from medicaments the chemist shops also sell a wide range of products from cosmetic articles to photo accessories.

CLIMATE

New Zealand has a mild climate with temperatures at their warmest between October and April. The months June to August are cooler, especially in the south of the South Island, but in Northland the temperatures can still be quite pleasant.

As the European winter falls in the New Zealand summer, this is the time when most people decide to visit New Zealand. However it is probably better to avoid the months December to January as this is when most of New Zealand is on holiday too. Early and late summer are pleasant times to travel in New Zealand, as is autumn. If you are in New Zealand in autumn make sure you visit the area of Queenstown. The light and the colours at this time of the year are simply fantastic!

If you visit New Zealand in winter you are probably headed for the excellent ski fields of the South Island. But even if this is not the case there are still many things to see and do and accommodation will be quite a bit cheaper — at least outside the main ski areas.

It is possible to whizz around New Zealand in two weeks but most people find this far too short. Four weeks or more is much better. If you do have only limited time then it is best to stick to the main attractions and to fly as often as possible — check the airline discounts!. It might even be worth considering taking one of the many tours around the country that are offered.

CRIME

New Zealand is a relatively safe country and visitors need take no extra precautions against such things as violent crime or theft. However one problem that has got worse over the years is theft from cars. This is mainly a problem in major areas or car parks near attractions that are frequented by tourists. Leave no valuables in your car or at least make sure that they are hidden from view. In most cases, common-sense is all you will need to avoid problems.

CURRENCY AND CREDIT CARDS

New Zealand has a decimal system based on dollar and cent denominations. Dollars come in notes to the value of $5, $10, $50 and $100. There are 5c, 10c, 20c, 50c, $1 and $2 coins.

There is no limit on the amount of money that you can bring in or take out of New Zealand. New Zealand dollars can be exchanged for any foreign currency at the going rate.

All major credit cards (American Express, Bankcard, Mastercard, Visa and Diners Club) are widely accepted. The same applies to Travellers' Cheques. Banks will give a cash advance on Mastercard/Eurocard and Visa. Those with American Express credit cards should go to an American Express office.

ELECTRICITY

The mains electricity supply operates at 230 volts (AC), 50 hertz; three pronged plugs are used.

EMBASSIES

Main foreign Embassies in New Zealand:

Australia

Australian High Commission
72-78 Hobson Street
Thorndon, Wellington
☎ (04) 473 6411

Canada

Canadian High Commission
61 Molesworth Street
Wellington
☎ (04) 473 9577

UK

UK High Commission
44 Hill Street
Wellington
☎ (04) 472 6049

USA

29 Fitzherbert Terrace
Wellington
☎ (04) 472 2068

For a complete list of embassies and consulates, refer to 'Diplomat & Consular Representatives' in the Yellow Pages.

Main New Zealand Embassies Overseas:

Australia

New Zealand High Commission
Commonwealth Avenue
Canberra, ACT 2600
☎ (6) 270 4211

Canada

New Zealand High Commission
Suite 801
Metropolitan House
99 bank Street
Ottawa, Ont. K1P 6G3
☎ (613) 238 5991

UK

New Zealand High Commission
New Zealand House
The Haymarket
London SW1Y 4TQ
☎ (71) 973 0366/63

USA

New Zealand Embassy
37 Observatory Circle NW
Washington DC
☎ (202) 328 4848

EMERGENCIES

For police, fire and ambulance ☎ 111 and tell the operator which service you require.

FACILITIES FOR THE DISABLED

Facilities for disabled persons are available at airports and many other public buildings such as theatres, museums, shopping malls and public toilets. Some of the more modern hotels and motels also have facilities for the disabled and this is sometimes indicated in the *Where to Stay Guide* published by the NZTB and available from overseas tourist offices. Some short walks in the national parks are suitable for people in wheelchairs and the Park Visitor Centres can provide the necessary information. For information, contact the New Zealand Tourist Office in your country of origin or: **Disability Resource Centre,** PO Box 24-042, Royal Oak, Auckland ☎ (09) 625 8069, Fax (09) 624 1633.

FESTIVALS

Listed here are only some of the more important or interesting festivals and local events. Local Information Centres will have more details.

Year 2000 'Millennium' Celebrations

Because New Zealand is directly west of the International Dateline it will be one of the first countries in the world to experience the dawn not only of a new day but of a new millennium.

From 31 December 1999 to 1 January 2000 celebrations will take place in many places in New Zealand but some of the largest will be in Auckland and Gisborne. Gisborne City actually claims it will be the first city in the world to see the sun rise in the year 2000; 12 hours ahead of London, 18 hours ahead of New York and 21 hours ahead of Los Angeles. Those who travel to the Chatham Islands will see it even earlier though. On the first day of the year 2000 the sun will rise over Pitt Island at exactly 16.05 Greenwich Mean Time, making it the first inhabited place on Earth to see the Millennium.

Auckland

Fiesta Week: mid-March

Blenheim

Marlborough Food & Wine Festival: 2nd weekend in February.

Hamilton

Ngauruawahia Regatta for Maori Canoes: March

New Zealand Agricultural Field Days: June

Hastings

Highland Games: April

Hokitika

Wildfoods Festival: 14 March, food and entertainment.

Masterton

Golden Shears Sheep Shearing Contest: March

Taihape

Gumboot Day: Easter Tuesday

Wellington

International Festival of the Arts: February to March in even numbered years only.

Summer City Programme: January to February

FURTHER READING

Local bookshops will have at least some of the following titles. Also try one of the many second-hand bookshops scattered throughout the country — Auckland and Wellington are especially good in this respect. New Zealand's excellent public libraries are another good place to search for information.

Among the publications dealing with New Zealand history, the following can be recommended: *A History of New Zealand* by Keith Sinclair, (Penguin, 1991) is regarded as an authoritative study; *Struggle Without End* by Ranginui Walker (Penguin, 1990) looks at New Zealand history from the Maori perspective and Anne Salmond's award winning *Two World's* (Viking, 1993) examines the first meetings between Maori and Europeans in the period 1642-1772. The pre-European phase of Maori history is dealt with in Roger Duff's *The Moa-Hunter Period of Maori Culture* (Government Printer, 1977) and Janet Davidson's *The Prehistory of New Zealand* (Longman Paul, 1984). Andrew Sharp's provocative book *Ancient Voyagers in the Pacific* (Polynesian Society, Avery Press, 1956) questions the idea of organised voyages of discovery across the Pacific. A counter argument is presented by David Lewis in *We The Navigators* (A.H. & A.W. Reed, 1972).

There are numerous publications dealing with the country's flora and fauna but useful guides for the visitor are various titles in the series *Viking Sevenseas Pocket Guides* (Viking Sevenseas Ltd), along with Geoff Moon's *Common Birds in New Zealand* (Reed, 1995).

HEALTH

New Zealand is a clean and safe country and visitors need take no special precautions prior to arrival. The medical system is of a high standard with modern hospitals in all the larger towns and cities. There are no vaccination requirements for entering the country.

Because of the dramatic thinning of the earth's ozone layer over New Zealand the sun's harmful UV rays are more dangerous here than elsewhere. Make sure that you use a strong sunscreen and wear a hat if spending more time outdoors. Parents travelling with infants should take especial care that they are properly protected. The amount of time that you can spend outdoors without risking sunburn (the 'burn-time') is broadcast on local radio and television over the summer months. Note you can get sunburned even on cloudy days.

People walking in New Zealand's national parks should be aware that the intestinal parasite giardia lamblia has been found in some lakes and rivers. It causes severe diarrhoea in those unfortunate enough to drink infected water and the symptoms can last up to three weeks. The best preventative measures are to boil water for 5 minutes or to use suitable filters or water purifying compounds that are available from outdoor sports shops.

HEALTH AND TRAVEL INSURANCE

Visitors to New Zealand are still covered under the Accident Compensation Scheme for personal injury through an accident. Benefits include some medical and hospital expenses but the scheme does not provide for loss of earnings outside New Zealand. Therefore visitors are nevertheless advised to get a travel insurance policy that adequately covers them against accidents, theft or loss of possessions and in the event of falling ill in New Zealand.

Consult your local travel agent travel agent as to the various options available.

LANGUAGE

The two official languages are English and Maori, though English is the language that is most widely spoken. In spite of the fact that visitors are rarely required to speak Maori, it can nevertheless help to know a few words as many of New Zealand's towns and geographical features have Maori names. Maori place-names are either descriptive or refer to an event, real or legendary, that may have occurred at that particular spot.

Space precludes a detailed description of Maori pronunciation but it helps to know that, in Maori, 'wh' is normally pronounced like the English 'f' and that 'ng' is pronounced like the 'ng' in singer.

A few common greetings:

Haere mai	welcome
Haere ra	goodbye (spoken by the person staying, to the person going)
Ka pai	thank you
Kia ora	hello

Words commonly encountered in Maori place-names:

ao	cloud	*one*	sand, beach
awa	river or valley	*papa*	flat rock
ika	ish	*puke*	hill
iti	small	*rangi*	sky
kai	food	*roa*	long
manga	stream or tributary	*roto*	lake
		rua	two, cave
maunga	mountain	*tapu*	sacred
moana	sea or lake	*te*	the
motu	island	*wai*	water
nui	big	*whanga*	bay, body of water
pa	fortified settlement	*whenua*	land or country

Taumatawhakatangihangakoauauotamateapokaiwhenuaakitanatahu — or Taumata for short. A hill 5 miles (8km) south of Porangahau in Hawke's Bay. This is not even the longest version of the name which would then, beyond any doubt, be the longest place-name in the world. It roughly translates as 'after Tamatea's brother was killed in battle near here, Tamatea climbed this ridge and played a lament on his flute'.

MAORI CULTURAL TOURS

The Maori people have a unique cultural heritage, and those visitors who wish to learn more about this Polynesian people can do so on one of several cultural tours. Other tours are listed in the NZTB brochure *Maori Cultural Heritage Guide*.

Tall Tale Travel 'N Tours Ltd
PO Box 403
Kaitaia
☎ (09) 408 0870
Fax (09) 408 1100
A guided visit to Pukepoto Marae, Kaitaia

Tamaki Tours
PO Box 1492
Rotorua
☎/Fax (07) 346 2823
Overnight stay on marae, hangi and concert.

Te Rehuwai Safaris
Ruatahuna
☎/Fax (07) 362 7641
Learn about the Maori people
(Tuhoe) of Te Urewera National
Park. Horse treks and marae
visit included.

Tuwharetoa Tourism
145 Tongariro Street
Taupo
☎ (07) 378 0254
Fax (07) 378 3714
Marae stays with full
traditional welcome.

MAPS

Good road atlases and maps can be bought from any bookshop. Pathfinders maps are quite good for travelling around as are Wises maps. Particularly good are the AA road maps. These maps are free to AA members and to members of motor clubs overseas that are associated with the New Zealand AA. AA maps are available at any AA office.

MEASUREMENTS

The metric system is used in New Zealand:
    1 kilogram (1,000 grams) = 2.2lb
    1 litre = $1^{3}/_{4}$ pints
    4.5 litres = 1 gallon
    1 kilometre = 0.62 miles (10km = approximately 6 miles)

NATURE TOURS

Nature tours in New Zealand cover everything from bird-watching to whale watching. Some nature tours (or ecotours as they are fashionably known) are listed in the Additional Information sections at the end of each chapter. A useful booklet published by the NZTB is the *Natural Heritage Guide*. It lists a wide variety of nature tours throughout New Zealand. Nationwide operators that have been recommended include:

New Zealand Nature Safaris
PO Box 5035
Port Nelson
☎ (03) 542 3159
Fax (03) 542 3190

Nature Quest New Zealand
PO Box 6314
Dunedin
☎/Fax (03) 489 8444

NATIONAL PARK VISITOR CENTRES

Park Visitor Centres are located near the main entrances of all national parks. They not only offer all the necessary practical information about walking and other activities in the parks but also function as 'mini' natural history museums specialising in the local flora and fauna. Maps, brochures and books concerning the park in question can be bought here. These park books are excellent value and, because they are superbly illustrated with colour photos, they also make excellent souvenirs of your visit.

Another source of information about both national and forest parks are the Department of Conservation (DOC) offices. These offices are found in many towns and cities and can also provide you with maps, brochures etc.

The DOC runs summer visitor schemes for three months from Christmas at many of the national parks. These highly informative schemes include half day and full day field trips as well as evening talks on natural history.

The addresses of National Park Visitor Centres are listed at the end of the relevant chapters.

DOC Information Centre, Central Office, 59 Boulcott St, PO Box 10420, Wellington ☎ (04) 471 0726, Fax (04) 471 1082.

POST OFFICES

Are open Monday to Friday 9am-5pm. Mail can be sent poste restante to post offices all over the country. In cities, address poste restante to the chief post office (CPO). Mail is held for 30 days.

PUBLIC HOLIDAYS

1st & 2nd January	**New Years Day** and day after New Year
6th February	**Waitangi Day** (New Zealand Day)
March/April	**Good Friday** and **Easter Monday**
25 April	**Anzac Day**
1st Monday in June	**Queen's Birthday**
4th Monday in October	**Labour Day**
25 December	**Christmas Day**
26 December	**Boxing Day**

The main school holidays are from mid-December until January. There are also school holidays in May and August. The provinces (Northland, Otago, etc) also have their own anniversary day holidays.

RESTAURANTS AND TEAROOMS

Restaurants in New Zealand are divided into **BYO** (Bring Your Own) or **licensed** establishments, though some licensed places also allow BYO. Only licensed restaurants may serve alcohol but the BYOs, which are often cheaper, allow you to bring your own bottle of wine, etc. A corkage fee is charged for opening the wine bottle and providing glasses. Pubs often have restaurants attached which offer simple but reasonably priced food. Vegetarian restaurants are most likely to be found in the cities. Many Indian restaurants have at least a few vegetarian dishes.

The small tearooms which are found all over the country are the traditional New Zealand equivalent of the café. Though some are rather low on atmosphere they are usually very reasonably priced. The better ones offer excellent home-made cakes (the carrot cakes are especially good) along with piping hot tea or coffee. Devonshire teas, which are served in the mornings and afternoons, consist of a pot of tea with a hot water refill and a couple of scones or muffins with cream and jam. Many tearooms along the main tourist routes are combined with a handicrafts shop.

A cheap meal in an inexpensive 'no frills' cafe or restaurant might be around $10 (not including dessert or drinks) while the moderately priced category serve mains from about $16 to $18. The categories used in

Additional Information at the end of each chapter are intended only as a rough guide. They are:

$ = *inexpensive* $$ = *moderate* $$$ = *expensive*

SOUVENIRS

With all those sheep it is not surprising that most souvenir shops make sure that they have a good stock of woollen jerseys or sheepskin rugs. Hand-knitted jerseys are usually of very high quality but they are not cheap. More affordable are woollen walking socks (Norsewear is a good brand), scarves and hats.

A woollen garment that is favoured by many Kiwi trampers because of its robust quality is the Swann-Dri or 'Swannie' for short. They are also fairly expensive but will probably last longer than any other piece of clothing you have ever bought.

Traditional Maori carvings in either bone, wood or greenstone (jade) are also popular souvenirs. The famous Maori tiki (a stylized human figure) is often carved from both greenstone and bone. Paua (abalone) shell is, like greenstone, used for various items of jewellery.

Generally speaking, New Zealand handicrafts are of a very high standard and it is worth browsing through the many local arts and crafts shops for original souvenirs. Especially good is the pottery, weaving and wood carving. Articles range from objects of everyday usage to those that may be described (without any exaggeration) as works of art.

New Zealand-made outdoor equipment belongs to the world's best and if you need a new backpack, sleeping bag or tent it might pay to investigate one of the many sports shops throughout the country. Towards the end of summer it is often possible to get some good deals — try bargaining.

Other souvenirs might include a glossy picture book about New Zealand, a cassette of traditional Maori music or perhaps a t-shirt decorated with a kiwi-bird motif.

SPORTS AND PASTIMES

The scope for outdoor activities and sports in New Zealand is virtually unlimited. Not all the sports and pastimes available are listed below but more information is available from NZTB offices overseas and of course the local Tourist Information Centres. A very useful booklet published by the NZTB is *Adventure New Zealand*, listing a wide range of adventure activities ranging from dolphin swimming to tandem sky diving. Background information about some of the most exciting (and unusual) outdoor adventures is contained in the excellent book *Classic New Zealand Adventures* by J. Kennett, J. Mulheron, G. Carlyon & M. O'Neill (GP Publications, Wellington).

Angling

Some people come to New Zealand just for the fishing, it is that good! Trout, salmon, perch and a few other fresh water species have all been introduced to New Zealand and seem to thrive in the country's rivers and lakes, often reaching record sizes. For trout the best places to go are Lake Taupo and the Tongariro River near Turangi, but Gore and the Waitaki Valley in the South Island are also renowned for the excellent trout fishing. Salmon fishing is also good in many parts of New Zealand, though Southland and Otago are the regions where the fishing is meant to be at its best.

The main areas for big game fishing in New Zealand are Paihia and Russell in the Bay of Islands, Whitianga on the Coromandel and Tauranga and Whakatane in the Bay of Plenty. Launches can be chartered in these places and the sort of fish one is likely to catch include hammerhead shark, blue marlin, striped marlin, tuna and broadbill. The season for marlin and tuna is January-May, whereas sharks may be fished throughout the year.

For angling in lakes and rivers it is necessary to obtain a permit. Permits are usually issued for a particular area and may be valid for a day, week, month or an entire season. Special tourist fishing permits that are valid throughout New Zealand for a month are available from the larger sport shops or from Tourism Rotorua. For more information about permits and regulations contact the appropriate tourist information.

Guided fishing trips are available in Turangi, Taupo, Rotorua and a number of other places as well.

Bungy Jumping

(See also Queenstown in main text)
Throwing oneself off a bridge with a rubber cord tied around the ankles might not be everybody's cup of tea but there are still plenty of people only too happy to pay for the experience. The main area for bungy jumping is Queenstown but it is also offered at Hanmer Springs in the South Island and Taupo, Mangaweka, Masterton and Auckland in the North Island. Safety standards are very high — but the rush of adrenalin through your body is probably even higher.

Canoeing & Kayaking

With so many rivers and lakes and so much coastline it almost goes without saying that New Zealand is a great place to go canoeing or kayaking. If you have never tried it before, you can learn here and you will love every moment!

Canoes and kayaks can be hired at a number of places around the country and many of the companies that rent them out also offer guided tours. Tourist Information Centres can supply the necessary details.

One of the best rivers in the country for canoe/kayak trips is the Whanganui in the North Island. If you only have the time to canoe one river, then do this one. It is suitable for beginners and the stretch between Taumarunui and Pipiriki offers some superb scenery.

Sea kayaking is something that the authors cannot recommend highly enough. Explore New Zealand's fascinating coastline and discover lonely bays and beaches accessible only by water! Great places for sea kayaking include the Bay of Islands, Coromandel, the Marlborough Sounds and along the coast of Abel Tasman National Park. Sea kayaks can be hired and guided trips are offered in all these areas.

Cycling

In spite of all the hills, New Zealand is getting more and more popular among cyclists. Even on the main roads there is not too much traffic, the landscape is beautiful and varied and there are plenty of camping grounds along the way.

Mountain bikes can be hired in many towns and it is also possible to book guided mountain bike tours, with all equipment provided if you so wish. Bikes are hired by the day, week or even on a monthly basis. It is often possible to hire equipment for touring as well. The local Tourist Information Centres can provide the necessary addresses.

Trains and the main long-distance bus companies will transport bicycles but only if there is enough room in their luggage compartments. The Kiwi Experience bus (☎ (09) 366 1665) and other so-called 'alternative bus companies' are rather more generous in this respect and endeavour to make sure that there is always room for cyclists and their bikes.

In New Zealand it is compulsory to wear a helmet and it is forbidden to cycle along the tracks in the national parks.

Pedaltours, 164 Parnell Road ☎ (09) 302 0968, Fax (09) 302 0967, organise bike tours throughout New Zealand.

Golf

Golf is a very popular sport in New Zealand and just about every town seems to have at least one golf course. There are in fact over 400 golf courses to be found spread throughout the country — more per head of population than in the USA!

Most clubs welcome visitors and a few will also hire out the necessary equipment. Green fees range from about $10 at the smaller rural golf courses to about $50 at the top city clubs.

Not only are many of the country's golf courses of a very high standard but some can be counted among the most beautiful in the world. The American Golf Digest has included Wairakei International near Taupo in its list of the 25 top courses outside the USA.

Other top golf courses include Titirangi Golf Club (Auckland), Waitangi Golf Club (Bay of Islands), Paraparaumu Beach Golf Club (near Wellington) and Queenstown Golf Club, Kelvin Heights.

The Rotorua Golf Club's Arikikapakapa Course is worth a visit if you like a bit of volcanic activity to accompany your game. However those golfers who misjudge the 15 hole may will find that their ball has been irretrievably lost in a boiling hot pool.

Horse Trekking

An interesting way to explore New Zealand is on horse-back, and horse treks to suit all levels of experience are offered at many places throughout the country. Some of the longer treks may last well over a week but there are also plenty of half day and full day trips being offered. A few addresses are on the next page.

NORTH ISLAND

Rangihau Ranch
Rangihau Rd, Coroglen,
Whitianga
☎ (07) 866 3875
Book at Whitianga Information
Centre 1 hour and overnight treks
into the Coromandel Ranges.

Waitomo Horse Trekking
Juno Hall
Waitomo Caves
☎ (07) 878 7649
1 hour rides and overnight treks.

Whananaki Trail Rides
Hales Rd, RD1
Hikurangi, Northland
☎ (09) 433 8299
2 hour and overnight treks.

Windyglen Farm
Peter & Lynda Wilson
Bertrand Rd, RD43
Waitara, Taranaki
☎ (06) 752 0603
1 hour and full day treks.

SOUTH ISLAND

Ardachy Trail Rides
Leila Graham
Private Bag
Hindon, Dunedin
☎ (03) 489 1499
1 hour, $\frac{1}{2}$ day and full day treks
in Otago hill country.

Cape Farewell Horse Treks
Golden Bay
Book at Farewell
Spit Visitor Centre
☎ (03) 524 8454 or 524 8031
1 hour rides to 6 day treks
on West Coast.

Clarence Alpine Rides
David King
Clarence Bridge
Kaikoura RD1
☎/Fax (03) 319 4339
1-4 day treks through river
valleys and alpine regions.

Mount Vernon Stables
Rue Balguerie
Akaroa
☎ (03)304 7180
$\frac{1}{2}$ - $2\frac{1}{2}$ hour rides.

Jet Boating

Racing down a narrow river canyon at breakneck speed in a boat that can
execute a 360° spin just when a collision seems imminent is, in essence,
what jet boating is all about.

Jet boating is offered just about everywhere in New Zealand where there
is a river or lake. Popular jet boating rivers in the North Island are the Motu
River near Opotiki and the Whanganui River. In the South Island the rivers
around Queenstown are the location of some of New Zealand's most
exciting jet boat trips.

Mountaineering

The best area for mountaineering is of course the Southern Alps.
Mountaineering Centres within this region are Mount Cook National Park,
Mount Aspiring National Park and Arthur's Pass National Park. All these
parks offer climbs suited to all levels of experience. Mountain huts are
provided as are mountaineering guides. For those who wish to learn
mountaineering skills there are climbing schools at both Mount Cook and
Mount Aspiring.

Scuba Diving

Popular diving areas in the North Island include Goat Island Marine Reserve north of Auckland, the Poor Knights Islands and the Bay of Islands. The fiords of the South Island attract divers because there is no other place in the world where black and red corals grow so close to the surface. Normally black coral is only found at depths of over 400ft (120m) but in the clear water of the fiords it may be seen at depths of just 20ft (6m).

Scuba divers also have plenty of historic shipwrecks to explore from the days when sailing ships plied the sometimes treacherous coastal waters. Of more recent vintage is the wreck of the *Rainbow Warrior*. Having been sunk by the French secret service in 1985 it was towed out to its final resting place near the Cavalli Islands off the Northland Coast. Regular diving tours to the Cavalli's are offered from the Bay of Islands and Matauri Bay.

Another wreck worth exploring is that of the Russian cruise ship *Mikhail Lermontov*. It sank in the Marlborough Sounds in 1986 and it is claimed that it is the largest easily accessible wreck in the world. Tours to this wreck can be booked at diving shops and travel agents throughout the country.

Diving equipment can be hired from the various diving or sports shops. At some of the more popular diving areas there are also diving schools. Divers should remember to bring their diving licence and logbook. For details about diving in New Zealand contact:

New Zealand Underwater Association, PO Box 875, Auckland 1 ☎ (09) 895 456, Fax (09) 897 051.

Skiing

New Zealand offers some of the best skiing in the Southern Hemisphere. The large ski fields have all the necessary facilities and ski equipment can be hired. The season varies from place to place but it is usually from June to October.

In the North Island the best fields are to be found within Tongariro National Park. Whakapapa and Turoa ski fields both lie on the slopes of Mt Ruapehu, an active volcano. Needless to say the slopes will be closed in case of an eruption!

In the South Island the best skiing is in the vicinity of the Southern Lakes, around Queenstown and Wanaka. The skiing is fantastic and the scenery even more so. The main ski areas are Coronet Peak and The Remarkables near Queenstown and Treble Cone and Cadrona near Wanaka. Treble Cone is more suited to experienced skiers whereas Cadrona has a number of runs suitable for beginners. Another excellent ski region is Mt Hutt, not too far from Christchurch. Mt Hutt has the longest ski season in the country. It lasts from the end of May to the start of November. Even closer to Christchurch is the Porter Heights ski area.

Apart from the commercial fields there are also a number of smaller club fields. Facilities here are generally simpler than at the commercial fields but they tend to be cheaper and the skiing can be just as good. Club fields close to Christchurch include Temple Basin, Craigieburn, Broken River, Cheeseman and Mount Olympus. Mt Robert is located inside Nelson Lakes National Park and Amuri is near Hanmer Springs.

Club fields in the North Island are Manganui on the slopes of Mt Egmont (Taranaki) and Tukino on Mt Ruapehu.

The Waiorau Nordic ski area is situated in the Pisa Range near Wanaka. This is New Zealand's only commercial cross-country ski area and offers around 15 miles (25km) of prepared trails.

Heliskiing is possible from Wanaka, Queenstown, Mt Cook, Fox Glacier and Methven. Companies offering heliskiing trips include Harris Mountains Heliskiing, Wanaka ☎ (03) 443 7930, Mt Hutt Helicopter, Methven ☎ (03) 302 8401 and Alpine Guides Westland, Fox Glacier ☎ (03) 751 0825.

Tramping (Trekking)

New Zealanders refer to trekking in their national and forest parks as *tramping*. The main tracks are usually very well marked and there is a good system of huts providing simple accommodation in both types of park. Some of the more popular tracks can get rather overcrowded during the summer but there are plenty of lesser known and often equally beautiful tracks that can be walked instead.

New Zealand's most popular walks are classified as 'Great Walks'. They are: **Lake Waikaremoana**, Te Urewera National Park (NP); **Tongariro Northern Circuit**, Tongariro NP; **Whanganui Journey**, Whanganui NP (actually a 5 day canoe trip); **Abel Tasman Coastal Track**, Abel Tasman NP; **Heaphy Track**, Kahurangi NP; **Routeburn Track**, Mt Aspiring/Fiordland NP; **Kepler Track**, Fiordland NP; **Rakiura Track**, Stewart Island. **The Milford Track** is certainly a 'Great Walk' but is in a class all of its own — see Chapter 9.

The huts in New Zealand's national, maritime and forest parks are divided into four categories. Category One is the best and these huts have stoves, bunks with mattresses, toilet and washing facilities and maybe even lighting and other 'luxuries'. Categories two and three have at least toilets, bunks and a water supply but category four is not much more than a (at least free) roof over the head.

In the national parks, wardens collect hut fees from November to April. However huts can be paid for in advance at any Park Visitor Centre or DOC office. Hut fees should always be paid whether a warden is present or not. The back country hut tickets (what you get if you pay for huts in advance) that can be used on most walks are not valid on the Great Walks. These require a special Great Walks Pass for the walk in question. Such passes are available at DOC offices or Park Visitor Centres near each walk. The use of huts is on a first come first served basis, therefore it is a good idea to bring a tent during the peak season. Camping, however, is only allowed at designated camping sites — contact local DOC offices.

To go tramping in New Zealand you need to have the right equipment. A pair of good quality walking books, a backpack that is comfortable to wear even when it is fully loaded, wet weather gear and warm clothing (even in summer) are all essential equipment for longer walks in the national parks. As the huts on some walks are quite far apart it is wise to carry a tent or at least a fly in case you do not make it to the hut in daylight. Also important to carry is a torch, eating utensils, candles, a first aid kit and a portable stove — the firewood provided in the huts should only be used when really necessary. Enough food should be carried to last for the duration of the walk as you cannot buy food at the huts. The food should be high in energy and as light as possible. Bring extra rations in case of unforeseen delays.

Safety tips

- Giardia parasites have been found in many of New Zealand's rivers and lakes so it is important to treat the water before you drink it.
- Always fill out the intentions form at a DOC office or Park Visitor Centre before setting out on a walk.
- Check the difficulty of a track before you set out. If you have doubts about a certain track get advice from the local DOC or Park Visitor Centre.
- Do not tramp alone.

Before setting out on a walk it is important to have a good topographical map showing the track in question. These maps are available from DOC offices, local bookshops and Park Visitor Centres. There are walking maps for each national park. This book cannot and does not attempt to replace a good tramping guide.

Inexperienced trampers are strongly advised to buy one of the tramping manuals or guides that are available in bookshops all over New Zealand. They have detailed descriptions of many of the country's most interesting tracks as well as tips on safety, what to take, etc.

White Water Rafting

For those who like to get wet while having their thrills, then white water rafting is ideal. It is offered on many of the country's rivers, both in the North and South Islands. Some of the most exciting rivers to raft include the Motu River near Opotiki in the North Island and the Karamea River in the South Island. The rivers are graded from 1 to 6, though grade 6 is only of theoretical interest as rivers of this grade are considered unraftable.

TELEPHONES

In New Zealand there is no longer a government monopoly on the phone system. For long-distance calls local subscibers can choose between Telecom and Clear. Public phones and local calls are, however, still controlled by Telecom. Most new public telephones are operated with phone cards and in the larger towns and cities it is sometimes possible to use credit cards. Phone cards are available from many Visitor Information Centres, hostels, hotels or those shops that advertise the fact. In some rural areas where only coin-operated phones are available it is useful to have a pocketful of 20c coins. A local call made from a public booth costs 20c a minute. Local calls from private telephones cost either nothing or only a nominal fee.

In New Zealand, area codes are known as STD codes. The STD codes in the North Island are:
Auckland and Northland (09),
Coromandel Peninsula, Bay of Plenty and Central North Island (07),
East Coast (East Cape), lower central North Island and Taranaki (06) and for the Wellington region (04).
For all the South Island and Stewart Island the STD code is (03).

STD codes are used when calling long distance within the country and even within a region if the town you are calling is some distance from you. 0800 numbers are toll free numbers. Remember that, when using a cardphone it is still necessary to insert the card even with an 0800 number.

International

Public phones are expensive to use for international calls, if possible it is better to use a private phone. Many hotels and hostels have cardphones for their guests which is a convenient way of avoiding extra costs. Those places without their own cardphones will often allow guests to use their phones if they make a price required call — see below.

When making an international call, dial the international code you require and drop the first zero of the number you are ringing. Instructions for direct dialling are also in the phone directories.

There are reduced telephone call rates to a number of countries outside New Zealand. Details of rates and the times to which they apply are listed in local telephone directories.

Main international direct dialling codes are:

Australia	0061
Britain	0044
Irish Republic	00353
New Zealand	0064
USA and Canada	001

Other services:

National Directory	018
International Directory	0172
National Tolls	010
International Tolls	0170

Price-required calls are useful when telephoning long-distance or internationally. After making a price required call the operator will ring back and tell you what it cost. When dialling internationally drop the 00 of your country code and replace it with 016 (eg. to Britain: 016-44). For long-distance calls within New Zealand dial 013 and drop the zero of the area code (eg. to Auckland: 013-9).

TIME

New Zealand is 12 hours ahead of Greenwich Mean Time, however daylight saving during the summer in New Zealand and in other countries means that this can vary.

Daylight Saving Time in New Zealand starts on the last Sunday in October and finishes on the first Sunday of March. The clocks are put ahead 1 hour.

During Daylight Saving Time (New Zealand), when it is 12 noon in New Zealand it is:

11pm in London	6pm In New York
10am in Sydney	5pm in Chicago
3pm in San Francisco	6pm in Montreal

TIPPING

Is not customary in hotels or restaurants but it is becoming more common to tip for excellent service.

TOURIST OFFICES

Local Offices

Opening times have only been given for the more important Visitor Centres. As a rule of thumb one can expect that they (and National Park Visitor Centres) will usually be open between 8.30am and 5pm, Monday to Friday. In summer many are often open at weekends, especially in the larger parks.

Many of the tours mentioned in this guide can be booked through one of the various Visitor Information Centres. All the larger offices will also assist visitors with hotel bookings and travel reservations. On arrival in Auckland it is certainly worthwhile visiting the main Visitor Information Centre as they can provide you with many useful tips for your stay.

The head office of the New Zealand Tourism Board Offices (NZTB) is in Wellington ☎ (04) 472 8860, Fax (04)478 1736. They have a very useful site on the Internet. From their web site it is even possible to send electronic postcards back home. All you need to do is find an internet cafe in one of the main towns or cities; for instance at Downtown Queen Street Backpackers in Auckland. Their web address is: http://www.nztb.govt.nz/index.html

New Zealand Tourism Board Offices Overseas

Australia

Ground Floor
288 Edward Street
Brisbane
Qld 4000
☎ (7) 221 3176
Fax (7) 221 3178

Level 19
Como Office Tower
644 Chapel Street
South Yarra
Melbourne, Victoria 3141
☎ (3) 823 6283
Fax (3) 823 6276

Prudential Finance House
84 Pitt Street
Sydney
New South Wales 2000
☎ (2) 221 7333
Fax (2) 235 0737

Canada

Suite 1200-888, Dunsmuir Street
Vancouver, BC, V6C 3K4
☎ (604) 684 2117
Fax (604) 684 1265

UK

New Zealand House
Haymarket, London SW1Y 4TQ
☎ (071) 973 0363
Fax (071) 839 8929

USA

1825 North Lincoln Plaza
Suite 603, Chicago IL 60614
☎ (312) 587 1190
Fax (312) 587 1192

501 Santa Monica Blvd #300
Santa Monica, CA 90401
Freephone 1 800 388 5494
(this number may be called from anywhere in the USA for information about New Zealand)
Fax (310) 295 5453

TRAVELLING TO NEW ZEALAND

Most people arrive in New Zealand by air. The main entry point is Auckland International Airport but there are also international airports at Wellington in the North Island and Christchurch in the South Island.

The flight from Britain via the USA/Canada or South-east Asia takes about 30 hours. Because it is such a long, tiring flight it is a good idea to plan a stop-over en route. Air New Zealand offers stop-overs in Fiji, West Samoa, Tonga and a number of other destinations as well. Other interesting stop-overs can be made with Cathay Pacific in Hong Kong; Singapore Airlines in Singapore; Thai Airways in Bangkok; Malaysian Airlines in Kuala Lumpur; United Airlines in San Francisco, Los Angeles or Hawaii; Qantas in Sydney or Melbourne and Canadian Airlines in Toronto or Hawaii. All these options and others are best discussed with your local travel agent.

Another very interesting possibility is a 'Round the World' ticket. They do not cost much more than a normal return ticket and give you have an even greater choice of stop-over destinations. Most importantly, take the time and shop around for the best deals. Prices can vary substantially. The so-called bucket shops are often quite a bit cheaper than the regular travel agents.

Note that baggage allowance is much more generous on flights that go via the United States than those via Asia.

Visitors from the USA and Canada will find the 'Circle Pacific Tickets' good value. These tickets link the American west coast with destinations in Australia, New Zealand, the Pacific Islands and Asia; in other words you circle the Pacific region. Your local travel agent will have all the details about these tickets and the restrictions that apply.

Departure Tax: For international flights is NZ$20.

TRAVELLING WITHIN NEW ZEALAND

Air Services

The main domestic airlines are Air New Zealand and Ansett New Zealand. Mt Cook Airline is partly owned by Air New Zealand. There are regular flight connections between Auckland, Wellington, Hamilton, Palmerston North, Christchurch, Dunedin and Invercargill. Ansett and Mt Cook airlines also fly the popular tourist route Rotorua — Christchurch — Mount Cook — Queenstown. This is obviously a good alternative to travelling overland if you have limited time.

There are a number of discounts available on inland flights which can make flying within New Zealand reasonably economical. The Air New Zealand 'Explore New Zealand Airpass' can only be bought outside the country and is valid on all inland flights with Air New Zealand or airlines belonging to 'Air New Zealand Link' (Mt Cook Airline, Air Nelson & Eagle Air). Though the route and number of flights have to be fixed before departure the times for the flights can be decided on arrival. Ansett's 'New Zealand Airpass' can be bought overseas or in New Zealand. Those who buy it overseas save $12^{1}/_{2}$ per cent GST (Government Service Tax). The advantage of Ansett's airpass is that it is possible to change your itinerary within New Zealand at any time. All you are required to do is to pay a (not too expensive) surcharge. With Air New Zealand you can only alter your flight route up to the point where you take your first flight. After that you have to stick to the routes you have chosen. As details of the above can change, please check with your travel agent.

Both Air New Zealand and Ansett Airlines offer substantial discounts (50 per cent) to holders of International Student Identity Cards, YHA cards and VIP Backpackers cards. These discounts only apply to standby flights but you usually have a good chance of getting on. Even if you do not intend staying at YHA hostels or backpackers hostels it could be well worth your while getting one of these cards.

If you can at all afford it, take one of the spectacular scenic flights that are offered in New Zealand. 'Flightseeing' trips over the volcanoes of Tongariro National Park and the Southern Alps are especially rewarding. The Additional Information sections at the end of each chapter in this book have details about especially interesting flights.

Air New Zealand
Head Office
29 Customs Street West
Auckland
☎ (09) 379 755
Fax (09) 388 075

Ansett New Zealand
PO Box 4168, Auckland
☎ (09) 309 6235
Fax (09) 309 6434

Mount Cook Airline
PO Box 4644, Christchurch
Freephone 0800 800 737

Bus Services

The main bus companies in New Zealand are InterCity, Newmans and Mount Cook Landline. Of these it is InterCity that offers the most extensive service. Virtually all of the country's larger towns can be reached by bus. In addition to the main bus companies there are a number of smaller operators who offer services within a particular region. See Additional Information at the end of each chapter for details of local operators.

Off the main routes, travel by bus can be rather slow as one often has to change buses which can result in lengthy waits.

All the main bus companies publish free timetables which also have details of the many discounts available. It pays to be aware of these discounts as travel by bus can be rather expensive. **Holders of YHA and VIP Backpackers cards are entitled to 30 per cent discounts on the main bus lines. Discounts of 30 per cent are also available to persons over 60 years of age and for the disabled**. If you travel overnight between Auckland and Wellington with an InterCity or Newmans bus you can also save money.

An interesting option for those who want to do a lot of travelling within a short time is Travelpass New Zealand. The 3 in 1 Travelpass allows unlimited travel on Tranz Scenic's long-distance trains, InterCity Coachlines bus network and also on the Interislander ferries. Travelpass lets you choose your itinerary and may be used for 5 days travel over 10 days or up to 22 days travel over 8 weeks. There is also a 4 in 1 Travelpass that includes an Air New Zealand National and Link flight. Travel agents will have more details on this and other options.

'Backpacker' or 'alternative' buses provide a tour rather than just a simple bus connection along the routes they follow.

Budget accommodation along each route is pre-booked and there are plenty of stops for the sights and activities along the way. The atmosphere on these buses is very relaxed and they are definitely bettered tailored to the needs of independent or budget visitors than are the normal buses.

Backpacker buses in New Zealand include the 'Kiwi Experience', 'Magic Bus' and 'West Coast Express'. The first two operate in both the North and South Islands, whereas the latter only operates between Nelson and Queenstown along the West Coast. For more information and bookings, contact the Visitor Information Centres or the various YHA and backpacker hostels in New Zealand.

'Backpacker'/'Alternative' Buses (a selection):

Green Beetle Bus Co
PO Box 31-228
Auckland 1330
☎ (09) 358 4874
Fax (09) 354 4871
5-6 day tours around Northland

Kiwi Experience
36 Customs Street East
PO Box 1553
Auckland
☎ (09) 366 1665

Magic Bus
☎ (09) 358 5600

West Coast Express
YHA Nelson
☎ (03) 548 8817

Main Bus Companies:

InterCity
InterCity Travel Centre
Sky City Coach Terminal
Sky City
102 Hobson St
Auckland
☎ (09) 357 8400
Fax (09) 270 5383

Mount Cook Landline
PO Box 4644
Christchurch
☎ (03) 319 5012
Freephone 0800 800 737

Newmans Coachlines
PO Box 90 821
Auckland
☎ (09) 309 9738
Freephone 0800 777 707

Car and Campervan

Campervans

Travelling by campervan is a very popular way of getting around New Zealand. Costs for a smaller (2 beds) campervan with one of the main hire firms start at around NZ$100-$150 per day but prices vary greatly according to the season. Some local operators may offer 'no frills' two berth campers for NZ$70 or less but, as with cars, it pays to check conditions. Auckland is the best place to start looking for local bargains but those who prefer to have transport prearranged will find that travel agents in their home country can get reasonable discounts with the main companies. Note that it can be cheaper to travel by car and to stay at camping grounds or hostels. Reservations for campervans are necessary in the high season (December to March).

Fact File

Brits
Auckland
☎ (09) 275 9090
Fax (09) 275 1834

Maui
Auckland
☎ (09) 275 3013
Fax (09) 275 9690

Horizon
Auckland
☎ (09) 307 8226

Newmans
Auckland
☎ (09) 303 1149

Car Rental

A car is a good way to get around New Zealand if you plan to do a lot of travelling. The main roads are generally very good though minor roads may be unsealed. These unsurfaced roads are only covered by gravel and are much slower to drive.

The distances between gas/petrol stations (especially in the South Island) can be considerable. It is best to fill up the tank before it gets too low.

To rent a car you must be at least 21 years of age and you need to have held your driving licence for at least one year. Car insurance is obligatory for rental cars. Remember: it always pays to read the small print before signing the contract.

The main international car rental firms are **Avis**, **Budget** and **Hertz**. These companies have offices in all New Zealand's main cities, towns and airports. Apart from them there are also many local firms which are often cheaper.

Because of the stiff competition, Auckland is the best place to start looking around for a good deal. The average price for a medium sized car with unlimited mileage is around NZ$60-$100 per day but this depends on the season, duration of rental and so forth. Prices can vary greatly from dealer to dealer so shop around and haggle, it can help!

If you wish to drive on both main islands it pays to find out whether or not you have to take your car on the ferry or whether you can leave it in Wellington and pick up another one in Picton. One-way rentals can be very practical when possible. For instance you could rent your car in Auckland and then hand it over in Christchurch or Queenstown and fly back north. This saves all the driving and you do not have the expense of the Cook Strait Ferry. Often it is only the larger companies that offer such one-way rentals.

Avis
Building 4
Central Park
666 Great South Road
Auckland
☎ (09) 525 1982
Fax (09) 373 5830

Budget
83 Beach Road
Auckland
☎ (09) 379 6768 or
Freephone 0800 652 227
Fax (09) 366 0210

Hertz
Auckland
154 Victoria St
Auckland
☎ (09) 309 0989
Fax (09) 373 5923

Ace Tourist Rentals Ltd
39 The Strand
Parnell
Auckland
☎ (09) 303 3112
Fax (09) 309 2258
This local company offers second-hand cars at very reasonable rates

Carshare

Sharing not only the ride but also the fuel costs with private motorists is an interesting alternative to hitch-hiking. Travelpool-Travelshare in Auckland and Wellington organise carshares to destinations anywhere in New Zealand. The carshare office basically puts motorists offering a lift in contact with people wanting a lift. On top of the cost of fuel for the trip (worked out between passenger and motorist) there is also a modest commission fee to be paid. However it still works out cheaper than either bus or train. ☎ Auckland (09) 307 0001 or Wellington (04) 473 5558. Calls are taken daily 8am-9pm.

Breakdown Services

The AA (Automobile Association) have emergency breakdown services available to their members or members of affiliated motor clubs overseas. Short-term membership (6 months) is available for foreigners. AA offices are found throughout New Zealand. Some local garages also have their own tow-trucks.

If you do breakdown and are a long way from any phone then do not despair. Eventually some passing motorist is bound to stop and offer you help. New Zealanders are renowned for their friendliness and what is (in this case) more important, their practical ways. Many foreign visitors come away with the impression that every second Kiwi is a mechanic!

Automobile Association (AA), 33 Wyndham Street, Auckland
☎ (09) 377 4660

Driving Regulations

Australian, UK, American and Canadian drivers only require their valid national driving licences. This enables the motorist to drive for a period of up to one year in New Zealand.

New Zealanders drive on the left-hand side of the road. At intersections you must give way to all traffic crossing or approaching from your right. If you yourself are turning you must give way to all traffic not turning. The New Zealand road code is readily available from most bookshops or AA offices.

The speed limit on the open road is 100kph (62mph), in urban areas it is 50kph (31mph). The sign LSZ stands for 'Limited Speed Zone'. This is an area where the speed limit is usually 100kph but when visibility, etc, is low a 50kph speed limit applies. Road signs in New Zealand generally keep to the international standards and should present no problem for overseas motorists.

Seat belts are compulsory. The legal limit for alcohol while driving is .08. The penalties for drinking and driving are very high.

Inter-Island Ferries

The Interislander ferry operates between Wellington on the North Island and Picton on the South Island. The ferry takes cars as well as passengers. From Wellington there are three to four sailings daily and the crossing takes about three hours. In the high season (December to January) and holiday periods it is necessary to book well ahead if you are taking a car.

As the trip with the ferry takes you through the picturesque Marlborough Sounds it is best to do the crossing in daylight. Bear in mind that the crossing can be quite rough.

There is a free bus service between the Wellington Interislander terminal and Wellington Railway Station. Buses leave Platform 9 at the railway station 35 minutes before scheduled sailings between 8am and 6.40pm. In Picton a free bus service is provided for passengers connecting with Coastal Pacific Express to Christchurch. However this service only applies to the 10am sailing from Wellington.

The Lynx catamaran is a new service between Wellington and Picton. It is promoted as one of the fastest passenger and car carriers in the world. Time required for the journey is $1^3/_4$ hours. Like the Interislander it connects at either end of its journey with the major train routes.

For bookings and enquiries see under Train below.

Train

Tranz Scenic's long-distance trains link the main cities and are quite modern and comfortable. They often travel along particularly scenic routes and snacks are served on board. Most rail services also have a buffet car. Smoking is not allowed on any of the trains.

North Island

The Overlander is the daytime daily rail service between Auckland and Wellington.

The Northerner does the overnight run between Auckland and Wellington. Sunday to Friday.

The Kaimai Express runs daily between Tauranga and Auckland.

The Geyserland runs twice daily between Auckland and Rotorua. The Bay Express runs daily between Wellington and Napier.

South Island

The Coastal Pacific runs daily between Christchurch and Picton. The 10am Interislander Ferry from Wellington connects with Coastal Pacific. The Coastal Pacific departs Christchurch at 8.15am to connect with ferry departing Picton at 2.20pm.

The TranzAlpine runs daily between Christchurch and Greymouth. This is a spectacular trip across the Southern Alps.

The Southerner runs between Christchurch and Invercargill, Monday to Friday.

For more information and bookings concerning both rail and inter-island ferry links contact:

Tranz Scenic
Tranz Rail Ltd
Private Bag
Railway Station
Wellington
(Correspondence)

Tranz Scenic Reservations
(also for Inter-Island Ferries)
☎ 0800 802 802 (toll free
within New Zealand)
7am-9pm daily
Fax 0800 101 525 (toll free)

From other countries: ☎ 0064 4 498 3301
Fax 0064 4 498 3089

LANDMARK
Publishing Ltd ● ● ● ●

VISITORS GUIDES

* Practical guides for the independent visitor
* Written in the form of touring itineraries
* Full colour illustrations and maps
* Detailed Landmark FactFile of practical information
* Landmark Visitors Guides highlight all the interesting places you
  will want to see, so ensuring that you make the most of your visit

1. *Britain*
Cornwall	Jersey
Cotswolds &	Kent
Shakespeare Country*	Lake District*
Devon	Peak District
Dorset	Scotland*
East Anglia	Somerset
Guernsey	Yorkshire Dales & York
Hampshire	

2. *Europe*
Bruges	Provence*
Cracow	Riga
Italian Lakes*	Tallinn
Madeira	

3. *Other*
Dominican Republic	Florida Keys*
India: Goa	Florida: Gulf Coast*
India: Kerala & The South	Orlando & Central Florida*
The Gambia	New Zealand*
St Lucia*	

Landmark Publishing
Waterloo House, 12 Compton,
Ashbourne, Derbyshire
DE6 IDA England
Tel: 01335 347349
Fax: 01335 347303
e-mail: landmark@clara.net
Catalogue sent on request

*In the USA order from:
Hunter Publishing Inc,
130 Campus Drive,
Edison NJ 08818
Tel: (732) 225 1900
or (800) 255 0343
Fax: (732) 417 0482
www.hunterpublishing.com

Index

Index

Published by
Landmark Publishing Ltd,
Waterloo House, 12 Compton, Ashbourne, Derbyshire DE6 1DA England
Tel: 01335 347349 Fax: 01335 347303 e-mail: landmark@clara.net

Published in the USA by
Hunter Publishing Inc,
130 Campus Drive, Edison NJ 08818
Tel: (732) 225 1900, (800) 255 0343 Fax: (732) 417 0482
Web site: www.hunterpublishing.com

2nd Edition
ISBN 1 901 522 36 9

© **Grant Bourne & Sabine Körner-Bourne 1999**

British Library Cataloguing in Publication Data: a catalogue record for this book is available from the British Library.

Print: Editoriale Libraria, Trieste, Italy
Cartography: James Allsopp
Design: Samantha Witham

Cover Pictures
Front: Abel Tasman NP
Back top: Mt Ruapehu, Tongariro NP
Back bottom: Auckland Harbour

Picture Credits
Authors: all cover photos, 3, 6/7,10,11 both, 14/15, 18,23 all, 26B, 30, 32 all, 35, 39T, 42, 47, 55T&M, 63, 67, 79, 82, 83, 87 both, 91, 114 both, 122T, 122L, 131B, 134M, 138B, 143, 154 both, 158 all, 166, 175M&B, 182T&M, 183, 191, 195k 198, 199, 206 both, 214M, 218T&M, 222 both, 234, 238, 239, 242M, 247, 251 all, 254 both, 258, 267B, 270M&B, 271B

New Zealand Tourism: 22, 26M, 39B, 42 insert, 51, 55B, 62, 74T, 90 both, 98, 107 all, 115, 122R, 126, 131T, 134T&B, 135, 138T, 150 all, 163 both, 175T, 182B, 190, 203both, 207, 210, 211, 214T&B, 218B, 227, 242T&B, 246, 262, 266, 267T, 270T, 271T

Destination Northland Ltd: 19 both, 26T, 59, 70 all, 71, 74M, 74B both, 75, 111 both

Whaleway Station Kaikoura: 178 both

The Publishers would like to thank the London office of New Zealand Tourism for permission to reproduce their pictures.